THE

THEORY OF STRAINS.

A COMPENDIUM FOR THE

CALCULATION AND CONSTRUCTION OF BRIDGES, ROOFS AND CRANES,

WITH THE APPLICATION OF

TRIGONOMETRICAL NOTES.

CONTAINING

THE MOST COMPREHENSIVE INFORMATION IN REGARD TO THE RESULTING STRAINS FOR A PERMANENT LOAD, AS ALSO FOR A COMBINED (PERMANENT AND ROLLING) LOAD.

IN TWO SECTIONS.

ADAPTED TO THE REQUIREMENTS OF THE PRESENT TIME.

BY

JOHN H. DIEDRICHS,
CIVIL AND MECHANICAL ENGINEER.

ILLUSTRATED BY NUMEROUS PLATES AND DIAGRAMS.

BALTIMORE:
SCHMIDT & TROWE.
1871.

Entered according to Act of Congress, in the year 1871, by
JOHN H. DIEDRICHS,
In the Office of the Librarian of Congress, at Washington.

WESTCOTT & THOMSON,
Stereotypers, Philada.

INSCRIBED TO

WENDEL BOLLMAN, Esq.,

IN TESTIMONY OF HIS INTEREST IN SCIENCE AND ART.

CONTENTS.

	PAGE
PREFACE	7
EXPLANATION OF CHARACTERS USED IN THE CALCULATIONS	11

SECTION I.

A. INTRODUCTION 13
    I. THE LEVER 15
    II. SUSPENDED WEIGHTS AND THE RESULTING STRAINS 18
    III. TRUSSES WITH SINGLE AND EQUALLY-DISTRIBUTED LOAD 21
        Suspension Truss Bridge 23
        Suspension Bridge 27

B. ROOF CONSTRUCTION 31

C. SEMI-GIRDERS 43
    I. SEMI-GIRDERS LOADED AT THE EXTREMITY 43
        Cranes 44
    II. SEMI-GIRDERS LOADED AT EACH APEX 45

D. GIRDERS WITH PARALLEL TOP AND BOTTOM FLANGES 48
    I. STRAIN IN DIAGONALS AND VERTICALS 48
    II. STRAIN IN FLANGES 51
    III. TRANSFORMATIONS 53
    IV. GENERAL REMARKS 53
        Directions for the Calculation of Complex Systems 54

E. COMPARATIVE TABLES OF RESULTING STRAINS FOR A PERMANENT LOAD 56
    I. SYSTEM OF RIGHT-ANGLED TRIANGLES 56
    II. SYSTEM OF ISOSCELES BRACING 58

SECTION II.

GIRDERS CALCULATED FOR COMBINED (PERMANENT AND ROLLING) LOAD.

	PAGE
A. GIRDERS WITH PARALLEL TOP AND BOTTOM FLANGES	59
I. THE RIGHT-ANGLED SYSTEM	59
II. ISOSCELES BRACING	66
1. Triangular Truss	66
Calculation of Strains y and u in Diagonals	67
2. Isometrical Truss	69
a. Calculation of Diagonals	70
b. Calculation of Top and Bottom Chords (Flanges)	72
B. CAMBER IN TRUSSES, WITH PARALLEL TOP AND BOTTOM CHORDS	73
TABLES CONTAINING THE LENGTH OF ARCHES FOR DEGREES, MINUTES AND SECONDS, FOR A RADIUS AS UNIT	77
C. PARABOLIC GIRDER OF 48 FEET, OR 16 METRES, SPAN	80
D. THE ARCHED TRUSS	86
Calculation of Strain y in the Diagonals	88
Calculation of Strain in the Verticals V	90
Transformations	93
E. THRUST CONSTRUCTION	94
I. GIRDER 20 FEET IN LENGTH (WITH A SINGLE WEIGHT AT THE CENTRE).	
II. GIRDER 72 FEET IN LENGTH (CALCULATED FOR PERMANENT AND ROLLING LOAD).	
Definition of Strain x in the Horizontal Flanges	97
Definition of Strain y in the Diagonals	98
Calculation of the Tensile Strains z in the Lower Flanges	99
Calculation of the Verticals u	101
III. CALCULATION OF A TRUSS SUSTAINING A DOME	102
Calculation of Strains x of the Outside Arch	104
Calculation of Strains z of the Inside Arch	105
Calculation of the Diagonals y	106

PREFACE.

THE want of a compact, universal and popular treatise on the construction of Roofs and Bridges—especially one treating of the influence of a variable load—and the unsatisfactory essays of different authors on the subject, induced me to prepare the following work.

Bridge-building has been and always will be an important branch of industry, not only to engineers, but also to the masses for the purposes of travel and trade, and, as Colonel Merrill in his recent essay on Bridge-building remarks, "important to railroad companies on account of the large amount of capital invested in their construction."

Bridge literature has often been used by rival parties for the purpose of advancing their own private interests, their motive being competition. Imposing upon the faith and credulity of those whom they pretend to serve, there is no guarantee that worthless structures will not be erected.

Thoroughly independent of any such motive, my aim is to give, especially to bridge-builders and to engineers and architects, the results of my investigation on the subject of calculating strains, in order that capitalists and the public may be benefited and protected.

These calculations will also enable those who have but a limited knowledge of mathematics to acquire the necessary information. For this reason special attention is paid to the arrangement of the work, the whole being made as plain and simple as possible, in order to meet the wants of the common mechanic as well as the experienced engineer.

Though there are many valuable treatises of this kind, there has as yet been no work published serviceable to the degree desired by the practical builder or mechanic—most of the dissertations being too theoretical and hard to comprehend by one not versed in the higher mathematics; and some are so arranged that a clear understanding of the calculations is very difficult.*

The most valuable work in the language is doubtless Mr. Stoney's "Theory of Strains," though the Method of Moments is not developed to that degree which I think necessary for the practical man.

We owe to the renowned German engineers Ritter and Von Kaven the universal application of this *Method* in the work entitled "Dach und Brücken Constructionen," in which it is fully explained by examples and illustrated by diagrams, these being often carelessly neglected in other works.

The above-mentioned work served me very much in the arrangement of this, which I hope will be kindly received.

The work being expressly prepared, as aforesaid, for the use of beginners in the study of mathematics, as well as for the

---

* As an exception, may be named Mr. Shreve's brief but popular treatise in Van Nostrand's "Engineering Magazine," No. xx., August, 1870; Vol. III.

more advanced practical engineer, it will enable them, after a short perusal, to acquire all the necessary information, for which even the trigonometrical notes accompanying the general results are not really required.

The higher classes of colleges and other institutions of learning will find the work very valuable.

On account of the expense, an intended Appendix, containing a rational and concise investigation on "The Strength of Materials," had to be dispensed with; yet I hope with this volume to gratify not only the desire of friends, but to be able with great satisfaction to assist engineers in the pursuit of their high and noble calling.

OCTOBER, 1870.

THE AUTHOR.

EXPLANATION OF CHARACTERS USED IN THE CALCULATIONS.

$=$ Equal, or the sign of equality.
$+$ Plus, or the sign of addition; also, the symbol of positive (tensile) strain.
$-$ Minus, or the sign of subtraction; also, the symbol of negative (compressive) strain.
$\times$ *or* . Sign of multiplication.
: *or* $\div$ Sign of division.
, Sign of decimals; also, of thousands.
∞ Sign of infinite.
$<$ Sign of angle, signified by the Grecian cyphers $\alpha, \beta, \gamma, \delta, \varepsilon$.
^{2} Sign of square of a number.
$\sqrt{\ }$ Sign of square root of a number.
$°$ Sign of degrees.
$'$ Sign of minutes; also, of feet.
$''$ Sign of seconds; also, of inches.
( ) *or* [ ] Brackets, to enclose the mathematical expression bound to the same operation.
π The number 3, 14, or periphery for a unit of the diameter.
R Right angle, or 90°.
$\perp$ Vertical.

THE THEORY OF STRAINS.

SECTION I.

A. INTRODUCTION.

To enable the student to comprehend the work, and have a thorough knowledge of certain conditions and examples without studying the whole, it is necessary for him to understand the arrangement of the following pages.

On the first few pages and the appertaining figures at the close of the chapter is found a short description of the lever in its different appliances, the application being only a key to the calculations of strains which follow.

The trigonometrical notes are in many cases almost superfluous. Still, it may be advantageous in this way to accustom the reader to their use. The "Suspended Weights and Resulting Strains" are developed by the parallelogram of forces, and for a plain illustration the results are appended to the figures, which will also be observed on figures of "Trusses with Single and Distributed Load."

In the "Suspended Weights and Resulting Strains" a more elaborate calculation was thought necessary, and therefore an Introduction to the calculation by the "Method of Moments" may be found in its proper place.

This Introduction presents the beginner with a clear and comprehensive knowledge of the formation of Moments; and the equations for Figs. 20, 21, etc., explain the equilibrium of force and leverage.

At the close of this chapter is found the explanation of maximum compressive and tensile strain in the top and bottom chords of a parallel-flanged truss or girder.

On "Roof Construction" (B), Plates 6 to 11, remarks are unnecessary. The builder can with ease find from the figures a system to suit his purpose. (See also "Arched Trusses," D, Section II.)

On "Semi-Girders" (C) the calculation of strains is treated in the way heretofore generally known (determining from the centre toward the abutment), after which the "Method of Moments" is applied to the same example, followed by a more elaborate explanation of the principles of Moments on the crane skeleton (Plate 14), whose single members are altogether divergent.

The thorough calculation of a truss with horizontal top and bottom flanges (right-angled system D, Sect. I.), with the resulting strains for a system of braces, all of which are inclined in the same direction, shows how easily by transformation of the strains a system of bracing just reversed can be formed. (Comp. D, Sect. II.)

From the comparative tables, E, I., II. (Plate 18, 19) those who are not mathematicians can find, by a little study (for an assumed load "W"—a variable load not considered), the strains in flanges, braces and ties. (See D, IV., Sect. I.)

The progress of panels, and by this the increase of stress in the different members, are *ad libitum* to be extended (are optional).

Where no composite strains appear, in the skeletons double lines make the compressive (—) strains more obvious, the tensile (+) strains being always represented by single lines. The assumed load in the calculations is equally divided on the apexes; but in general some attention may be paid to a peculiar load—say from a single locomotive—at a certain apex, this being observed in examples on "Suspension Truss" (III., Sect. I.).

The calculations in Sect. II. with regard to the influence of a variable load are more difficult to understand. Still, by the results of strains in the skeletons it is easy enough to form an idea about this matter, and to see the importance of counter-bracing or tying at centre of railroad-bridge trusses.

What experience and observation have already taught to the practical railroad man is here *fully* shown by figures.

Information is given on parallel-flanged trusses for the so-called "Camber in Bridges" at B, Sect. II., which to many builders has heretofore been only a matter of experiment.

Yet it is to be remarked that for the calculations E, Sect. II., Plates

THE LEVER.

29 to 34, a variation in the determination of the principal force will be perceived, the base of calculating "Thrust Construction" being the horizontal strain H and the vertical strain V at the vertex (centre), and not, as before, the reactive force, D, of abutments.

Farther explanation will be found in the examples and figures referred to.

The calculations of strains involve the supposition that the connections at the joints (apexes) are effected by link-bolts, thus relieving the single members (struts and ties) from all transverse strain. The equally-distributed load and even the weight of structure are supposed to be transmitted to the adjacent joints.

I. *THE LEVER.*

Plate 1, Fig. 1ª, " 1ᵇ, " 1ᶜ. When for a double-armed and compound lever (Figs. 1ª, 1ᵇ, 1ᶜ) by P, a force represented, whose direction right-angled to its arm or lever a, and when Q, a force, acting at the leverage b, so are $P.a$ and $Q.b$ the "moments," and for the equilibrium,

$$P.a = Q.b \text{ (fulcrum } f\text{)}.$$

2.] For the single lever from Fig. 2,

$$\text{Mom.} = p.l = W.\frac{1}{n}.l,$$

$$p = \frac{W}{n}.$$

Example.—When $W = 100$ lbs., $l = 20$ feet,

and $$n = \frac{l}{4} = 5 \text{ feet};$$

so $$p \times 20 = 100 \times 5, \text{ or } p = \frac{100}{4} = 25 \text{ lbs.}$$

3.] In the same way in Fig. 3,

$$p.l = W.\frac{1}{n}l + W.\frac{2}{n}l,$$

or $$p = W\left(\frac{1}{n} + \frac{2}{n}\right) \text{ and for } n = 4;$$

THE THEORY OF STRAINS.

i.e., the weights suspended at a distance from the fulcrum equal $\frac{1}{4}l$ and $\frac{2}{4}l$.

$$p = W\left(\frac{1}{4} + \frac{2}{4}\right)$$

or
$$p = \frac{3}{4}W.$$

4.] Similar to this in Fig. 4, when the length, l, is divided in eight equal parts.

$$pl = W.l\left(\frac{1}{8} + \frac{2}{8} + \frac{3}{8} + \frac{5}{8}\right)$$

or
$$p = \frac{W}{8}(1 + 2 + 3 + 5);$$

i.e.,
$$p = \frac{11}{8}W.*$$

5.] For a combined weight, W, and an equally-distributed load, q, from Fig. 5,

$$p.l = W.\frac{l}{4} + q.\frac{l}{2},$$

or
$$p = \frac{1}{4}W + \frac{1}{2}q \quad \text{(fulcrum } f\text{)},$$

and
$$p_1 = \frac{3}{4}W + \frac{1}{2}q \quad \text{(fulcrum } p\text{)}.$$

---

* For the summation, S, of figures from 1 to n,

$$S = \frac{n(n+1)}{2}.$$

So for the sum of figures from 1 to 12,

$$\frac{12 \times 13}{2} = 78,$$

and from 1 to 15,

$$\frac{15 \times 16}{2} = 120.$$

Further, the sum S, from 1 to n, for $n = \infty$.

$$S = \frac{n^2}{2}$$

The sum of the square from 1 to n, or $1^2 + 2^2 + 3^2 + \ldots + n^2$.

$$S = \frac{n^3}{3}, \text{ for } n = \infty.$$

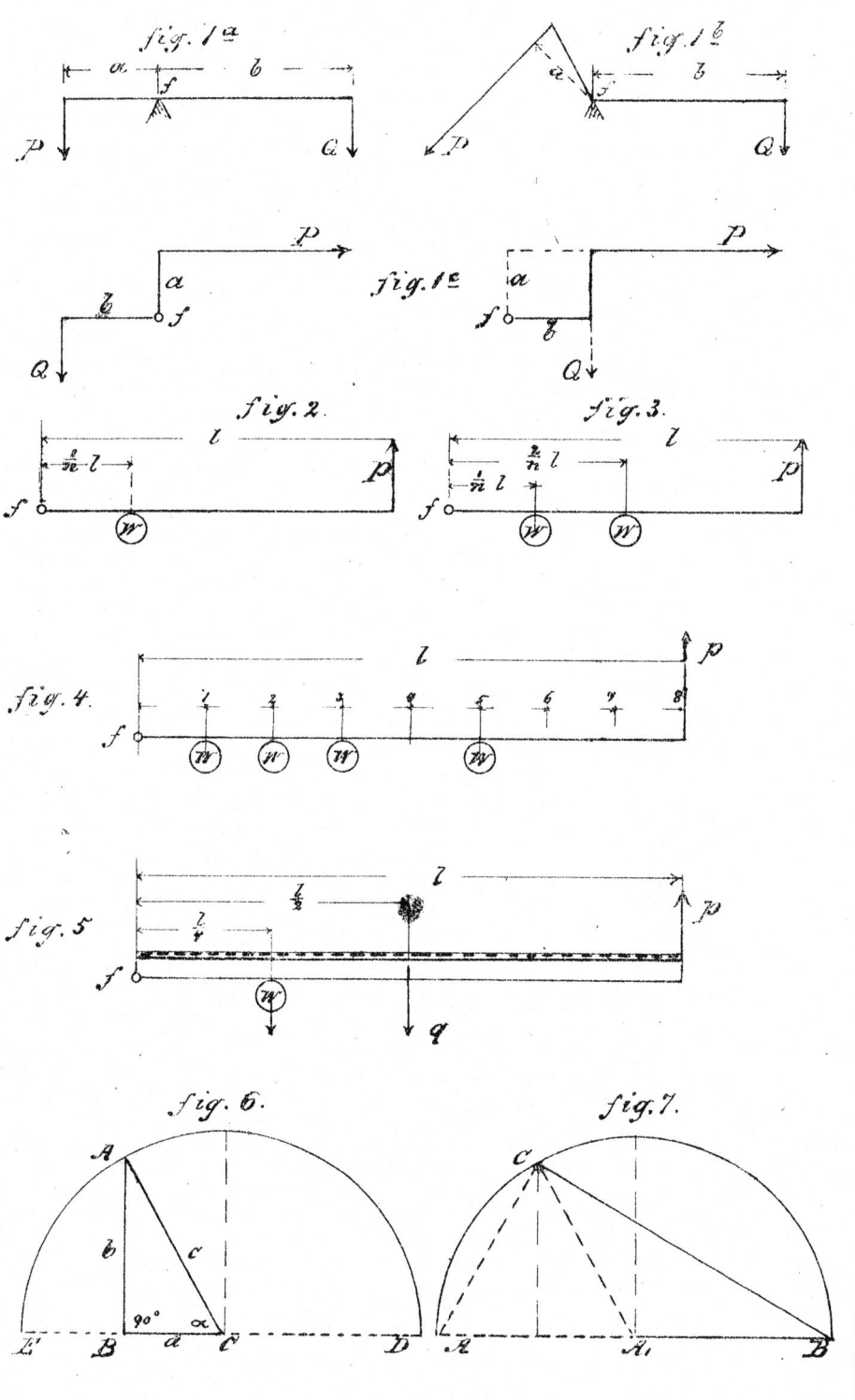

THE LEVER.

In every triangle the sum of enclosed angles,

$$2R = 2 \times 90°,$$

6.] so in the right-angled triangle ABC, Fig. 6, the angles A and C together $= 90° = R$, because angle $B = 90°$.

In Trigonometry we say—

$\frac{b}{c} = $ sine α; $\frac{b}{a} = $ tangent α; $\frac{c}{a} = $ secant α.

$\frac{a}{c} = $ cosine α; $\frac{a}{b} = $ cotangent α; $\frac{c}{b} = $ cosecant α; or, contracted,

sin., cos., tang. or tg., cotang. or cotg., sec. and cosec.

For a radius, AC, as a unit, the line AB simply is called sine; the central distance, BC, cosine; and BE the versed sine of the angle α.

For certain angles α the relation $\frac{b}{c}, \frac{b}{a}, \frac{c}{a}$, etc., have certain and distinct numerical values. (See Haslett's or Haswell's "Tables of natural sines, cosines, tangents and cotangents from 1 to 90 degrees.")

Each triangle, ABC, A_1BC (Fig. 7), consists of six members—*i. e.*, three sides and three angles, from which always three are dependent on the rest; therefore, when three out of these six members are known, we can construct, or with more exactness we can calculate, the others, provided one at least of the given parts is a side.

For the transformation of trigonometrical functions, short notices in the form of a table, also the numerical values (natural sin, cos, etc.) of the principal angles, may be serviceable, viz.:

$$\sin x = \frac{1}{\operatorname{cosec} x} = \frac{\operatorname{tang} x}{\sec x} = \sqrt{1 - \cos^2 x}.$$

$$\cos x = \frac{1}{\sec x} = \frac{\operatorname{cotang} x}{\operatorname{cosec} x} = \sqrt{1 - \sin^2 x}.$$

$$\operatorname{tang} x = \frac{1}{\operatorname{cotang} x} = \frac{\sin x}{\cos x} = \sqrt{\sec^2 - 1}.$$

$$\operatorname{cotang} x = \frac{1}{\operatorname{tang} x} = \frac{\cos x}{\sin x} = \sqrt{\operatorname{cosec}^2 x - 1}.$$

$$\sec x = \frac{1}{\cos x} = \frac{\csc x}{\cotang x} = \sqrt{1 + \tang^2 x}.$$

$$\csc x = \frac{1}{\sin x} = \frac{\sec x}{\tang x} = \sqrt{1 + \cotang^2 x}.$$

Degrees.	Sin.	Cos.	Tang.	Cotang.
0	0	1	0	∞
15	0,258	0,965	0,267	3,732
20	0,342	0,939	0,363	2,747
25	0,422	0,906	0,466	2,144
30	$\frac{1}{2} = 0{,}5$	$\frac{1}{2}\sqrt{3} = 0{,}866$	$\frac{1}{3}\sqrt{3} = 0{,}577$	$\sqrt{3} = 1{,}732$
40	0,642	0,766	0,839	1,191
45	$\frac{1}{2}\sqrt{2} = 0{,}707$	$\frac{1}{2}\sqrt{2} = 0{,}707$	1,00	1,00
50	0,766	0,642	1,191	0,839
60	$\frac{1}{2}\sqrt{3} = 0{,}866$	$\frac{1}{2} = 0{,}5$	$\sqrt{3} = 1{,}732$	$\frac{1}{3}\sqrt{3} = 0{,}577$
65	0,906	0,422	2,144	0,466
75	0,965	0,258	3,732	0,267
$R = 90$	$+1$	0	$+\infty$	0
$2R = 180$	0	-1	0	$-\infty$
$3R = 270$	-1	0	$-\infty$	0
$4R = 360$	0	$+1$	0	$+\infty$

$\sin(R - x) = {}^+\cos x$, and $\cos(R - x) = {}^+\sin x$.
$\sin(R + x) = {}^+\cos x$, and $\cos(R + x) = {}^-\sin x$.

II. SUSPENDED WEIGHTS AND THE RESULTING STRAINS.

Plate 2, Fig. 8ª, " 8ᵇ.] In Fig. 8ᵇ, when $W = 5000$ lbs, $ab = be = 10$, $bc = 8$, and $ac = ce = 12{,}8$ feet; the vertical strain at c on each string $= \dfrac{W}{2} = \dfrac{5000}{2}$.

And, further, the actual strain in the direction of the string,

$$p = q = \frac{W}{2} \cdot \frac{ac}{bc},$$

or $\qquad p = q = \dfrac{5000}{2} \times \dfrac{12{,}8}{8} = 4000$ lbs.

All other information is given in Fig. 8ᵇ.

8°.] When a heavy body, $ABCD$ (Fig. 8ᶜ), is suspended by two oblique strings, DH and CH, in a vertical plane, a straight line drawn through the intersection will pass through the **centre** of gravity, G, of the body.

SUSPENDED WEIGHTS AND RESULTING STRAINS.

9.] For the force in the direction ad, represented by q, we find from Fig. 9,

$$gh = ab \cdot \frac{bd}{L} = ab \cdot \frac{W}{L};$$

$$W = gh + id = gh + q \cdot \cos \alpha;$$

$$W = ab \cdot \frac{W}{L} + q \cdot \frac{bd}{ad};$$

or

$$q = W \cdot \left(1 - \frac{ab}{L}\right) \cdot \frac{ad}{bd} = W \cdot \frac{L - ab}{L} \cdot \frac{ad}{bd};$$

i. e.,

$$q = W \cdot \frac{bc}{L} \cdot \frac{ad}{bd};$$

and in the same manner from similarity of triangles,

$$p = W \cdot \frac{ab}{L} \cdot \frac{cd}{bd}.$$

In the equation for q is $W \cdot \frac{bc}{L}$, the vertical strain at d for the string ad; in the second equation is $W \cdot \frac{ab}{L}$, the vertical strain at d for the string cd,—equal to the shearing strains V and V_1 on the supports.

Example.—When, again,

$W = 5000$ lbs., $L = 100$ feet,
$ab = 10'$, $bc = 90'$, and $bd = 8'$,
$ad = 12,84'$, and $cd = 90,35'$,

so

$$p = 5000 \times \frac{10}{100} \times \frac{90,35}{8} = 5646 \text{ lbs.},$$

and

$$q = 5000 \times \frac{90}{100} \times \frac{12,84}{8} = 7020 \text{ lbs.};$$

then the results for the horizontal strain x and the vertical strain V at the right support are—

$$x = p \cdot \frac{cb}{cd} = p \cdot \sin \beta, \text{ or } x = W \cdot \frac{ab}{L} \cdot \frac{bc}{bd},$$

and

$$V = p \cdot \frac{bd}{cd} = p \cdot \cos \beta, \text{ or } V = W \cdot \frac{ab}{L};$$

thus

$$x = 5000 \times \frac{10}{100} \times \frac{90}{8} = 5625 \text{ lbs.};$$

$$V = 5000 \times \frac{10}{100} = 500 \text{ lbs.}$$

The results for the horizontal strain x_1 and the vertical strain V_1 at the left support are—

$$x_1 = W . \frac{bc}{L} . \frac{ab}{bd},$$

and
$$V_1 = W . \frac{bc}{L};$$

thus
$$x_1 = 5000 \times \frac{90}{100} \times \frac{10}{8} = 5625 \text{ lbs.},$$

and
$$V_1 = 5000 . \frac{90}{100} = 4500 \text{ lbs.};$$

therefore, also, $x = x_1$,

for
$$W . \frac{ab}{L} . \frac{bc}{bd} = W . \frac{bc}{L} . \frac{ab}{bd}. \qquad \text{(Fig. 17.)}$$

10.] For Fig. 10, when $W = 5000$ lbs.; ab, ad and bd the same as before—

$$Y = W . \frac{ad}{bd} = 5000 \times \frac{12.84}{8} = 8025 \text{ lbs.},$$

and
$$Y_1 = W . \frac{ab}{bd} = 5000 \times \frac{10}{8} = 6250 \text{ lbs.}$$

11.] In Fig. 13,
$$P : Q : R = \sin . \, cdb : \sin . \, adb : \sin \, adc.$$

12.] In general, for every triangle,
$$y = x + z, \qquad \text{(Fig. 12.)}$$
and, as here,
$$x + y = z + m = R,$$
$$x + x + z = z + m,$$
or,
$$m = 2x.$$

Also, from similarity of triangles ABC, ADC and DBC,

$$\frac{c}{b} = \frac{b}{a}, \quad \text{or } c = \frac{b^2}{a};$$

and as $AB = c + a$, the diameter $= \frac{b^2}{a} + a$;

i.e., the diameter equals the square of one-half the chord divided by the height of the arc added to the height of the arc.

The height of the arc CB results from the chord CB in the same way.

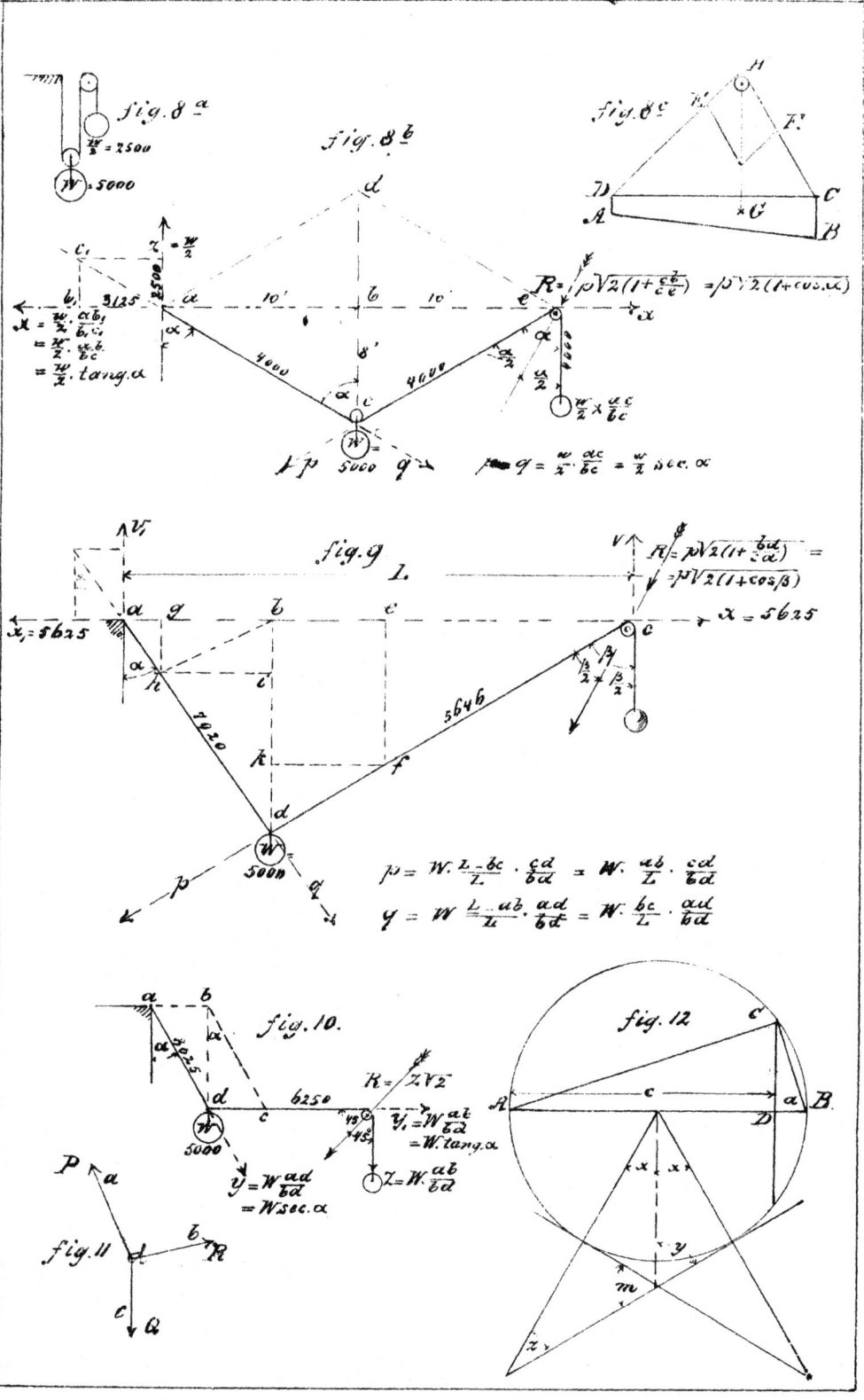

Application in "Camber in Bridges," B, Sect. II. There, also, the geometrical rule,

$$\frac{\text{arc}}{\text{circumference}} = \frac{\text{angle at centre}}{360°}$$

[Plate 2—Figs. 8 to 12.]

III. *TRUSSES WITH SINGLE AND EQUALLY-DISTRIBUTED LOAD.*

Plate 3, Fig. 13.] A most frequent structure is the trussed beam (Fig. 13).

The post at the centre is called the king-post.

14.] The whole is a combined system, in which the horizontal beam, according to its stiffness, relieves the tie-rods from an aliquot amount of strain.

For the greatest exertion to which the tie-rods in the most unfavorable case could be exposed, we may use the result from Fig. 8^b, under the supposition that the horizontal beam counteracts only the horizontal forces. (For instance, when butted at the centre.)

To compute the stress we have the following:

$$p = q = \frac{W}{2} \cdot \frac{ac}{bc} = \frac{W}{2} \cdot \sec \alpha,$$

for a single weight at centre.

Example.—The assumed weight = 20000 lbs.; between supports, 24 feet.

The length $bc = 5{,}59'$, and $ac = 13{,}24$ (which can be measured near enough for most purposes from a skeleton);

$$p = q = \frac{W}{2} \cdot \frac{ac}{bc} = 10{,}000 \times \frac{13{,}24}{5{,}59} = 23{,}700 \text{ (approx.)}.$$

The angle α being in this case 65°, for a calculation, using the preceding tables,

$$p = q = \frac{W}{2} \cdot \sec \alpha = \frac{20000}{2} \times \frac{1}{\cos \alpha} = 10000 \times \frac{1}{0{,}422} = 23700,$$

$$bc = ab \cdot \tang 25° = 12 \times 0{,}4663 = 5{,}595,$$

$$ac = ab \cdot \sec . 25° = ab \cdot \frac{1}{\cos . 25°} = 12 \times \frac{1}{0{,}906} = 13{,}24.$$

The vertical pressure in the king-post under the supposition before $= 20{,}000$ lbs.; at each support $= 10{,}000$ lbs.; and the compression in the horizontal beam,

$$H = \frac{W}{2} \cdot \frac{ab}{bc} = 10000 \times \frac{12}{5{,}59} = 21467 \text{ lbs.}$$

15ª.] When in Fig. 15ª the strains p or q and the angle γ are known, we find the resulting vertical strain, R, also by means of the parallelogram of forces, viz.,

$$R = \sqrt{p^2 + q^2 + 2\,p \cdot q \cdot \cos \gamma};$$

or, because in this case $\alpha = \beta$, therefore, $p = q$;

also, $\gamma = 2.65° = 130°$, or $= R + 40$,

and $\cos (R + 40) = -\sin 40$ (see preceding table),

so $R = \sqrt{2 p^2 + 2 p^2 (-\sin 40)} = \sqrt{2 p^2 (1 - \sin 40)}$,

15ᵇ.] $R = \sqrt{2 \times 23700^2 (1 - 0{,}642)} = 20000$ lbs.*

For a structure, Fig. 15ᵇ, reserved to the preceding one (15ª), the numerical value of strains is quite the same, but of opposite character, provided the enclosed angles are the same.

If, as in Fig. 16, the load $= 40000$ lbs., equally distributed on the beam, then each support will sustain again one-half of the load;

16.] but the reaction, D, of each support will be only one-quarter of the load $= 10000$ lbs.; and for the same exertion a truss or beam, charged with an equally-distributed load, will sustain twice as much as when loaded with a single weight at the centre. (Comp. Fig. 14.)

The distribution of forces on supports and at the centre is explained by Fig. 16.

For an angle, $\alpha = 63° 26'$, or, also, $\beta = 26° 34'$,

the depth of the truss being always equal to one-fourth of its length,

for $\tang . 26° 34' = 0{,}5$.

Now, $\dfrac{bc}{ab} = \tang . \beta,$ · or, $bc = db \cdot 0{,}5 = 12 \times 0{,}5 = 6$,

---

* For the angle $acd = \delta$ in Fig. 15ᵇ,

$R = \sqrt{p^2 + q^2 + 2 pq \cos \delta}$, and for the angle $edS = \varepsilon$,

$R = \sqrt{p_1^2 + p^2 - 2 p_1 \cdot p \cdot \cos \varepsilon}.$ (See Fig. 8ᵇ and Fig. 9.)

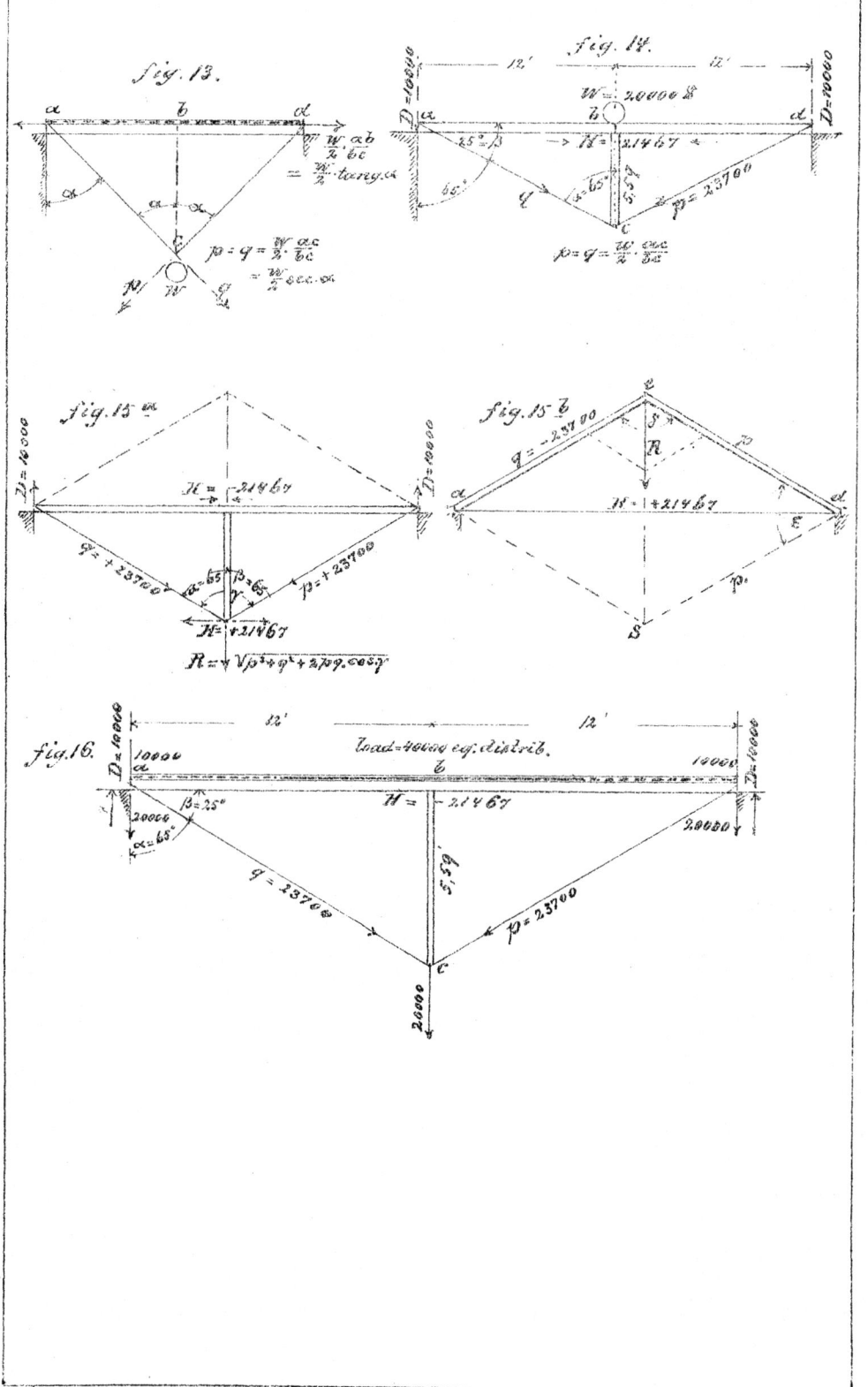

and (Fig. 14), the horizontal strain,

$$H = \frac{W}{2} \cdot \frac{12}{6} = \frac{20000}{2} \times \frac{12}{6}, \quad \text{or } H = 20000,$$

thus being in this case the same as the weight, W, at the centre.

The horizontal strain (thrust) and the strain on the oblique rods increase with the angle α, thus being ∞ for an angle $\alpha = 90°$.

Suspension Truss Bridge.

We find a combination of trussing in the well-known "Suspension Truss" bridges, the principles for calculation of the strains being contained in the preceding.

The *Bollmann truss* forms a continuous system of independent trusses, in number equal to the number of vertical posts combined to a common top chord (stretcher).

Plate 4,] By Fig. 17 the dimensions of such a truss may be
Fig. 17.] represented.

When for a single-track railroad-bridge the assumed load, including the weight of structure $= 1\frac{1}{2}$ tons $= 3360$ lbs. per lineal foot, or for one rib (single truss) $= 1680$ lbs. per lineal foot—*i. e.*, for the given dimensions $12 \times 1680 = 20160$ lbs. on each post, for which may be said in round figures 20000 lbs. $= W$, for calculation, then in Fig. 17, according to Fig. 9, the tension in the first rod nearest the abutment,

Strain No. 1, rod $= W \cdot \dfrac{bF}{AF} \cdot \dfrac{Ak}{bk} = 20000 \times \dfrac{7}{8} \times \dfrac{15,6}{10} = 27300$ lbs.,

the section of which for a value of iron $= 10000$ lbs. per square inch (five to six times security) $= 2,73$ square inches; thus, when two rods are applied, the size of each rod $= 1 \times 1\frac{3}{8}''$.

Strain No. 2, rod $= W \cdot \dfrac{cF}{AF} \cdot \dfrac{Al}{cl} = 20000 \times \dfrac{6}{8} \times \dfrac{26}{10} = 39000$ lbs.

Section $= 3,9$ sq. in., or 2 rods, each $1 \times 2''$.

Strain No. 3, rod $= W \cdot \dfrac{dF}{AF} \cdot \dfrac{Am}{dm} = 20000 \times \dfrac{5}{8} \times \dfrac{37,3}{10} = 46625$ lbs.

Sect. $= 4,66$, or 2 rods, each $1 \times 2\frac{3}{8}''$.

Strain No. 4, rod $= W \cdot \dfrac{EF}{AF} \cdot \dfrac{AN}{EN} = 20000 \times \dfrac{4}{8} \times \dfrac{49}{10} = 49000$ lbs.

Sect. $= 4,90$, or 2 rods, each $1 \times 2\frac{1}{2}''$.

Strain No. 5, rod $= W \cdot \dfrac{fF}{AF} \cdot \dfrac{Ao}{fo} = 20000 \times \dfrac{3}{8} \times \dfrac{60{,}8}{10} = 45600$ lbs.

Sect. $= 4{,}56$, or 2 rods, each $1 \times 2\frac{1}{4}''$.

Strain No. 6, rod $= W \cdot \dfrac{gF}{AF} \cdot \dfrac{Ap}{gp} = 20000 \times \dfrac{2}{8} \times \dfrac{72{,}6}{10} = 36300$ lbs.

Sect. $= 3{,}63$, or 2 rods, each $1 \times 1\frac{7}{8}''$.

Strain No. 7, rod $= W \cdot \dfrac{hF}{AF} \cdot \dfrac{Aq}{hq} = 20000 \times \dfrac{1}{8} \times \dfrac{84{,}6}{10} = 21150$ lbs.

Sect. $= 2{,}11$, or 2 rods, each $\frac{7}{8} \times 1\frac{1}{4}''$.

When for a partial load at a certain panel the exertion of a pair of suspenders is greater than for a distributed load in calculation, those rods would be strained more than to one-fifth or one-sixth of their ultimate strength. So, when a locomotive of 84000 lbs. weight rests at a certain panel on a wheel-base of 12 feet, to each of the four supporting posts would be transmitted one-fourth of its weight $= 21000$ lbs.—this differing very little from the calculation in the example. Additional rods (panel-rods) are applied, sustaining the main suspenders and at the same time the top chord, transmitting and distributing the weight on the posts, these being always in a state of compression equal to the weight on the post.

Without the panel-rods for an over-grade bridge (through bridge) there would be in the post no further compression than that produced by the weight of the top chord and appendages, leaving for a strong cambered truss (B, Sect. II.), in case of a partial load, the possibility of raising.

The following is the strain in panel-rods according to Fig. 8[b]:

Strain $= \dfrac{W}{2} \cdot \dfrac{Er}{fr} = \dfrac{20000}{2} \times \dfrac{16}{10{,}5} = 15238$ lbs.

Sect. $= 1{,}52$, or 1 rod $= 1 \times 1\frac{1}{2}''$.

The influence of temperature upon the single systems of main suspenders (their length being different) is regulated by a link connection.

For the compressive strain in the top chord the rule for a girder, sustained at both ends and charged with an equally-distributed load, may be applied (see at the close of this chapter), then,

SUSPENSION TRUSS BRIDGE.

$$\frac{20000 \times \frac{7}{2} \times \frac{9.6}{4}}{10} = 168000.*$$

The compression in the top chord is the same all over.

For the result we have as momentum one-half of the entire weight on posts at one-fourth the length of truss as leverage,

or
$$\text{Mom.} = \frac{Q}{2} \times \frac{L}{4},$$

which, when divided by the depth of truss, gives the compression = 168000 lbs. as before.

For a single load, P, at the centre would be

$$\text{Mom.} = \frac{P}{2} \times \frac{L}{2},$$

which, when divided by the depth of truss, gives for the compression twice as much, or 336000 lbs.; but for an addition of the results of each single truss with its single load, according to x and x_1 in Fig. 9, it would be

$$\text{Mom.} = \frac{P}{2} \times \frac{3L}{8},$$

this being one-half of the result for a single load, P, at the centre, added to one-half of the result for an equally-distributed load, Q.

18.] The *Fink truss* (Fig. 18) is different in principle.

Whilst in the Bollmann system there are as many independent trusses as there are posts, in the Fink all the trusses are dependent on each other and transfer the load toward the centre.

The centre post (king-post) has to sustain the compression of one-half of the entire load on the truss, including one-fourth of the weight of the rib, the main suspenders (tie-rods) depending again, as before, on the depth of the truss.

---

* For a simple compressive strain an area of section of stretcher = 9 square inches would be sufficient (18000 lbs.—safe load for cast iron)—the actual dimensions to be taken by Hodgkinson's formula on the strength of hollow cast-iron pillars:

$$W = \text{breaking weight in tons} = 44{,}3 \times \frac{D^{3.6} - d^{3.6}}{l^{1.7}};$$

therefore, when for a pillar, the external diameter, D, in inches, and the length, l, in feet, are known; and for six times security, with the weight, W, multiplied by 6, we can define the internal diameter, d, consequently the thickness of metal.

The calculation of an example in its simplicity will give the best explanation.

Taking the same dimensions and the same load as in the calculation for the preceding (Fig. 17), according to Fig. 8^b we have,

$$\text{Strain in } A \cdot N \text{ or } IN = \frac{W}{2} \times \frac{AN}{EN};$$

i.e., $\quad \dfrac{80000}{2} \times \dfrac{49}{10} = 196000$ lbs.,

the section of which for a value of iron = 10000 lbs. per square inch = 19,6 square inches. Thus, when two rods are applied, the size of each = 2×5 inches.

$$\text{Strain in } kc, Ak \text{ or } cm = \frac{20000}{2} \times \frac{13}{5} = 26000 \text{ lbs.}$$

Section of a single rod = $1 \times 2\frac{1}{2}$ in. (full).

$$\text{Strain in } Al \text{ or } lE = \frac{40000}{2} \cdot \frac{26}{10} = 52000 \text{ lbs.}$$

Section of a single rod = $2 \times 2\frac{1}{2}$ in., or 1×5 in.

For a single locomotive (weight 84000 lbs.), resting at cd on a wheel-base of 12 feet, the vertical force for one post at c or $d =$

$$\frac{42000}{2} = 21000 \text{ lbs.} = W;$$

then, $\quad \text{Strain in tie-rods} = \dfrac{21000}{2} \times \dfrac{13}{5} = 27300$ lbs.;

so the size of rod kc, Ak or cm should be corrected to $1 \times 2\frac{3}{4}$ in.

For the compressive strain on the top chord (stretcher), according to Fig. 14,

$$H = \frac{W}{2} \cdot \frac{AE}{EN},$$

and for a vertical strain $W = 80000$ lbs. in the centre post, as before mentioned,

$$H = \frac{80000}{2} \times \frac{48}{10} = 192000 \text{ lbs. (compr.).}$$

In this truss, as in the Bollmann, the compression in the top chord is the same all over.

For this truss, when applied for an over-grade railroad-bridge, a safe longitudinal connection (bracing or tying) will be essential on account of the variable load.

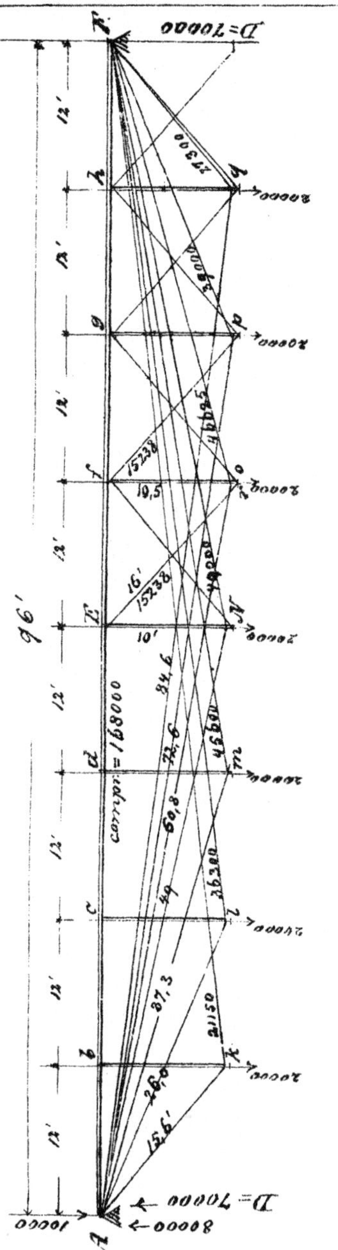

Fig. 17.

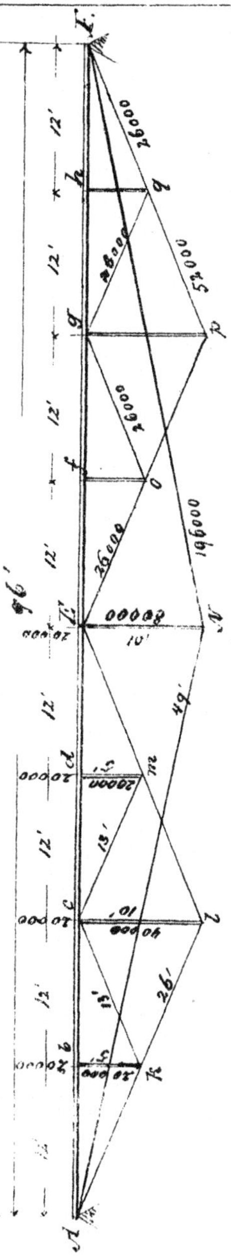

Fig. 18.

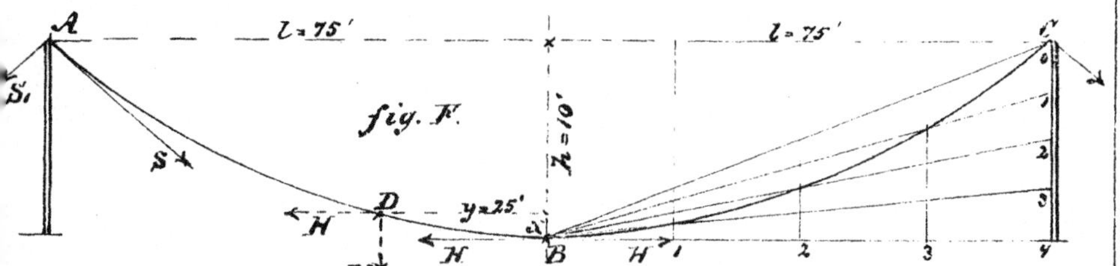

fig. F.

Suspension Bridge,

To the same category of bridges belongs the

Suspension Bridge,

though, in regard to mathematics, very different.

The curve formed by a chain or cable lies between the parabola and the catenary, and is very nearly an ellipse. The curve in a loaded state approaches the parabola; in an unloaded state, the catenary. (Weisbach, vol. II.)

In the following example the curve may be considered a parabola or the bridge in its loaded state.

The thesis is—

The vertical force at every point of the chain equals the weight on the chain from the point in consideration unto the vertex.

Plate 4,] So, when y in Fig. F = 25 feet and the length of
Fig. F.] bridge = 150 feet,

Width = 4 feet;

load, 50 lbs. per square foot, or 200 lbs. per lineal foot;

maximum load = 200 × 150 = 30000 lbs.;

the vertical force at D = 200 × 25 = 5000 lbs.

Further, *the horizontal force at every point of the chain is equal, and therefore equal to the horizontal strain in the vertex.*

Thus, when by p is represented the weight *pro unit* of horizontal projection = 200 lbs., for our example,

I. $H = \dfrac{pl^2}{2h}$, which is at the same time the horizontal force in A and C, to overturn the towers, and amounting here to $\dfrac{200 \times 75^2}{20} = 56250$ lbs.

II. $S = \dfrac{pl}{2h} \sqrt{l^2 + 4h^2} = \dfrac{15000}{20} \times 77{,}6 = 58500$ lbs.

III. $y^2 = \dfrac{l^2}{h} \cdot x.$

The length, L, of chain results by the formula,

$$L = 2l + \frac{4}{3} \times \frac{h^2}{l} = 151{,}75.*$$

---

* For more specifications I ought to refer to Weisbach and other authors.

THE THEORY OF STRAINS.

For a trussed system with two posts (queen-posts), between supports 36 feet, and an assumed load = 30000 lbs., equally distributed, the distribution of forces on the bearings is denoted in Fig. 19, and for the calculation of strain, when compared with Fig. 10, we find for

Plate 5,
Fig. 19.

$$Y = W \cdot \frac{ad}{bd};$$

$$Y = 10000 \times \frac{13,24}{5,59} = 23700 \text{ (approx.)}$$

and for

$$Y_1 = W \cdot \frac{ab}{bd};$$

$$Y_1 = 10000 \times \frac{12}{5,59} = 21467.$$

The compression on the vertical posts = 10000 lbs.; the vertical pressure on supports = 15000 lbs.; and, reduced by those 5000 lbs. directly sustained (comp. Fig. 16), the reactive force of supports, signified by D = 10000 lbs.

Upon this structure, the *Method of Moments* being applied (see Preface), we suppose a section separated from the original by a cut, *st*.

Considering the forces acting upon such a section, we form the equation of equilibrium for a suitable point of rotation, by solution of which we find the strain in the member in question; and observe the rule, that, *for a strain, Y, the point of rotation ought to be chosen in the intersection of x and z, making their lever = 0, when these are the members of the structure, separated by a cut, st, likewise as Y.*

20.] But when by *st* only one member, excepting Y, is separated, we lay the point of rotation on the next joint, as, per example, for Y in b, Fig. 20.

$$Y \cdot 5,07 = 10000 \times 12,$$

or, I., $\quad 0 = -Y \cdot 5,07 + 10000 \times 12$ (rotation round b);

$$Y = \frac{10000 \times 12}{5,07} = +23700;$$

and because in the following the form of equation always will be kept similar to I., the forces in their aim to turn to the left, like Y round b, will be signified by —, the same as a compressive strain; and the forces to the right, like the hands on a watch, or D round b, will be signified by +, the same as a tensile strain.

21.] According to this we have for Z, Fig. 21,

$$0 = Z \cdot 5{,}59 + D \cdot 12 \ (\text{rot. } r \cdot d),$$

$$Z = \frac{10000 \times 12}{5{,}59} = 21467,$$

and for Y_1, Fig. 22,

22.] $\qquad 0 = -Y_1 \cdot 5{,}59 + D \cdot 12 \ (\text{rot. } r \cdot b);$

$$Y_1 = \frac{10000 \times 12}{5{,}59} = 21467.$$

When a diagonal, s, sustains the parallelogram, so that by a cut, st, three members, Z_1, Y_1 and s are separated, we have for the definition of s the point of rotation, as before mentioned, in the intersection of Z_1 and Y_1; but Z_1 and Y_1 in their direction are parallel, and therefore without intersection at all. In this case (the same as for diagonals in girders with parallel top and bottom flanges) we

23.] suppose a point of rotation, O, at any distance in the direction (axis) x, and find thus from Fig. 23, where $x = \infty$, or infinite—$i.\,e.$, the lever of all forces, acting in a vertical direction upon the section $= \infty$.

$$0 = -s \cdot \infty \sin \varphi - D \cdot \infty + p \cdot \infty \ (\text{rot. } r \cdot O);$$

or, because ∞ is a factor of each part,

$$0 = -s \cdot \sin \varphi - 10000 + 10000.$$

In this equation, $s \cdot \sin \cdot \varphi$ (comp. Fig. 56 on semi-girders) is

24.] the vertical component of s (Fig. 24), and acts right-angled to the axis, x, like D and p.

The angle φ for our example $= 25°$;

$$\sin \varphi = 0{,}422 \ (\text{see table}),$$

and therefore $\quad 0 = -s \times 0{,}422 - 10000 + 10000,$

or $\qquad\qquad\qquad s = 0,$

showing that, as in Fig. 19, the diagonal, s, is without any strain and only useful for preventing dislocation. (Compare parabolic

25.] girders, to which this case is similar, because a parabola can be constructed through the sustaining points a, d, e and c, and therefore differs in this from Figs. 25 and 63.)

26.] For a reversed structure (Fig. 26) the strains will be the same, but of reversed signs.

In the following calculations of roofs and bridges it will be shown that the *Method of Moments* is thoroughly applicable, leading directly and in the most comprehensive manner to distinct results; but for a preliminary estimate of strain in the top and bottom chords at the centre of the structure the most simple way to define this strain may be stated by the following:

27,] As the flanged girder in Fig. 27, charged with an equally-distributed load, Q, will be exposed at its centre to the same
28.] exertion as the girder in Fig. 28, fixed at the centre, the moments will be for both, when $V =$ depth of girder and $l =$ length (the load being equally distributed).

$$\text{Mom} = \frac{Q}{2} \cdot \frac{l}{4} = V.x \text{ (rot. } r.o\text{)};$$

$$\frac{\frac{Q}{2} \cdot \frac{l}{4}}{V} = \frac{\frac{1}{8}Q.l}{V} = \text{compression or tension in flanges};$$

so $Q = 30000$ lbs.; $V = 5{,}59'$; and $l = 36'$.

$$\text{Mom} = \frac{30000}{2} \times \frac{36}{4} = 135000 = V.x,$$

and $\dfrac{135000}{5{,}59} = 24150$ lbs., the strain in the chords.

It is to be observed that the result is rather too high when applied upon a truss with few panels, as in Fig. 26, on account of the reactive pressure of the support, diminished by the partition of the direct load on this place.

On account of its being a very convenient method we recommend it; and in the following bridge skeletons we refer to it very frequently. (See D, Example I., and Sect II., note.)

29.] For a girder charged with a single weight at the centre (Fig. 29), we make a comparison with Fig. 30, and find for both

$$\text{Mom} = \frac{P}{2} \cdot \frac{l}{2} = V.x = \tfrac{1}{4} P.l,$$

30.] and $\dfrac{\tfrac{1}{4} P.l}{V} =$ horizontal strain;

i. e., compression or tension in the top or bottom chords, the formation of moments for a point of rotation, o, being very comprehensive.

When $P = 15000$ lbs.,

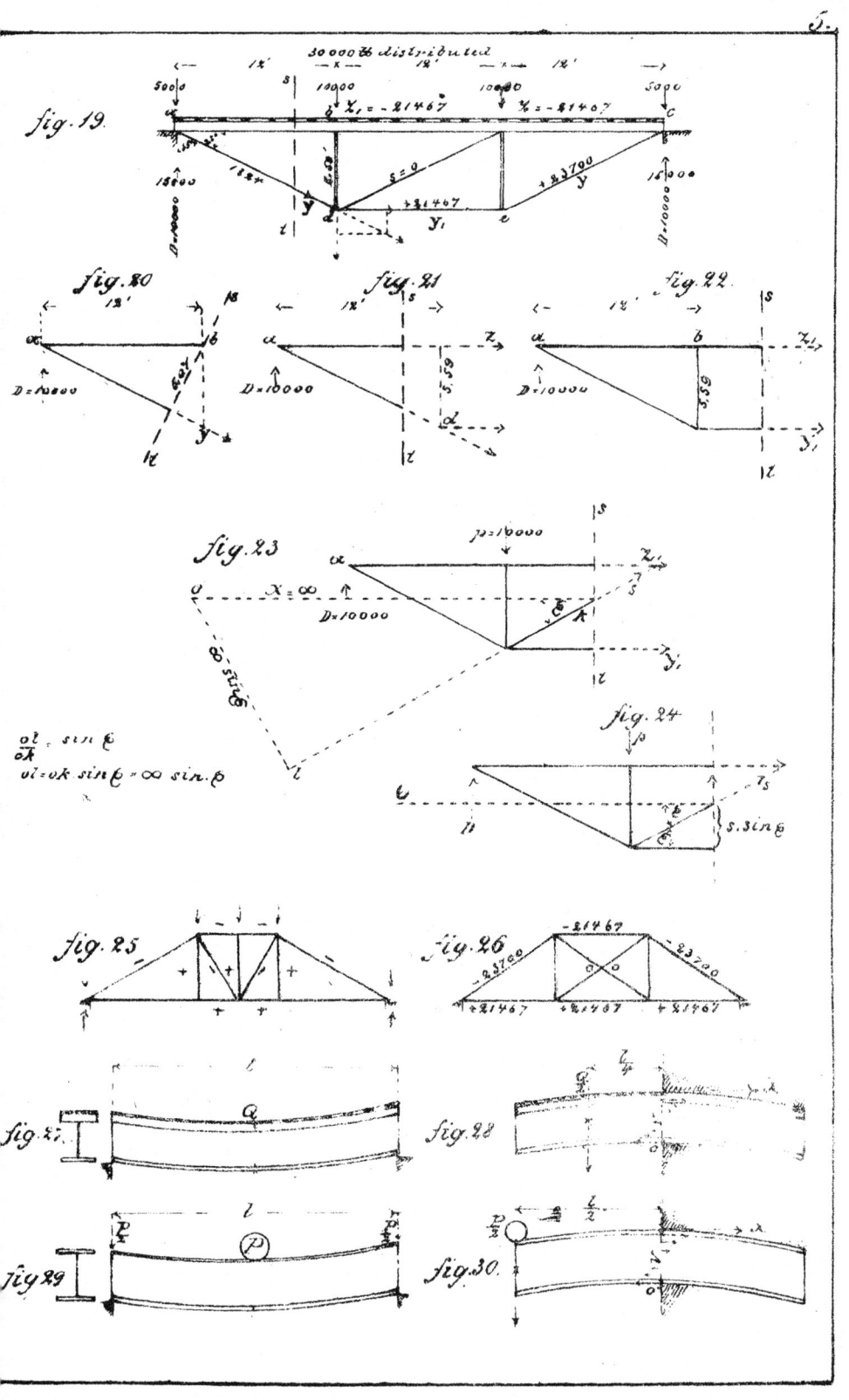

but $V = 5{,}59$, and $l = 36$ (as before),

so the $$\text{Mom} = \frac{15000}{2} \times \frac{36}{2} = 135000,$$

and $$\frac{\frac{15000}{2} \times \frac{36}{2}}{5{,}59} = 24150 \text{ lbs., the strain in flanges;}$$

showing that, for the same exertion, a beam loaded with a single weight, P, at the centre can bear only one-half of an equally-distributed load, Q.

[Plates 3, 4 and 5—embracing Figs. 13 to 30.]

B. ROOF CONSTRUCTION.

For small and not complicated roofs, experience is a common and in general, also, a sufficient guide. But experience is very limited, and not every constructor has opportunity and time to acquire it.

The true and acceptable guide for a safe practice will always be the calculation; and since, especially for complicated and more extensive combinations, the application of mechanical science has become unavoidable, the following compendium, leading from the simplest to the most complicated structures, will give for almost every purpose sufficient information.

Plate 6, Fig. 31ª.] By construction, when EG represents the weight at the centre of gravity, G (Fig. 31ª), the body will be at rest when the plane DF is right-angled to the line DE; CE being horizontal—i. e., right-angled to the vertical line EG.

Let EG be an assumed length, then in the parallelogram of forces the intensity of EK and EH is measured in proportion by the same rule.

31ᵇ.] For an angle, $\beta = 25°$ of a rafter with the horizontal line (Fig. 31ᵇ—similar to Fig. 16 reversed) leaning with the top end against a wall, the heel at A being morticed; we then have

$$\frac{cb}{ca} = \sin \beta = \frac{5{,}59}{13{,}24} = 0{,}422;$$

$$\sin^2 \beta = 0{,}17;$$

$$\sin 2\beta = \sin 50° = 0{,}766;$$

THE THEORY OF STRAINS.

$$\frac{ab}{ac} = \cos \beta = \frac{12}{13,24} = 0,906;$$

$$\cos^2 \beta = 0,82.$$

When W is an equally-distributed load of 20000 lbs., then

$$H = H_1 = \frac{W}{2} \times \frac{d}{h} = \frac{20000}{2} \times \frac{12}{5,59} = 21467 \text{ lbs.}$$

The vertical force, V, at the top of the rafter $= 0$, and the vertical pressure V_2 of the heel $= 20000$ lbs., or equal to the entire load.

Also the vertical force, V_1 at the centre $= 20000$ lbs.

The pressure in the rafter itself (compression) $=$

$$\frac{W}{2} \times \frac{l}{h} = 10000 \times \frac{13,24}{5,59} = 23685 \ (23700 \text{ lbs.}).$$

The entire pressure, R, of rafter toward the support,

$$R = \sqrt{V_2^2 + H_1^2} = 29300 \text{ lbs.}$$

Its direction can be constructed in making $K = 2h = 11,18$ feet, H_1 and V_2 forming the sides of the parallelogram.

When $P = 10000$ lbs., a single weight at centre of rafter,

$$H = H_1 = \frac{P}{2} \cdot \frac{d}{h} = 10733;$$

$$V = o,$$

and $\qquad V_2 = V_1 = 10000$ lbs.

[31°.] When in Fig. 31°, by FM the weight of the body $ABCD$ is represented, then FN, the force toward the wall, results in the horizontal and vertical forces CH and CV.

FL, the force acting perpendicular to the plane BI, in the direction BF.

G, the centre of gravity.

GF, vertical.

$CF \perp CB$, or $< FCB = 90°$.

$BI \perp FB$, then BI is the direction of the plane required to make the body at rest.

Also $\qquad FN = P = \frac{s}{l} G \cos \alpha;$

$$H = P \sin \alpha = \tfrac{1}{2} G \sin 2\alpha.$$

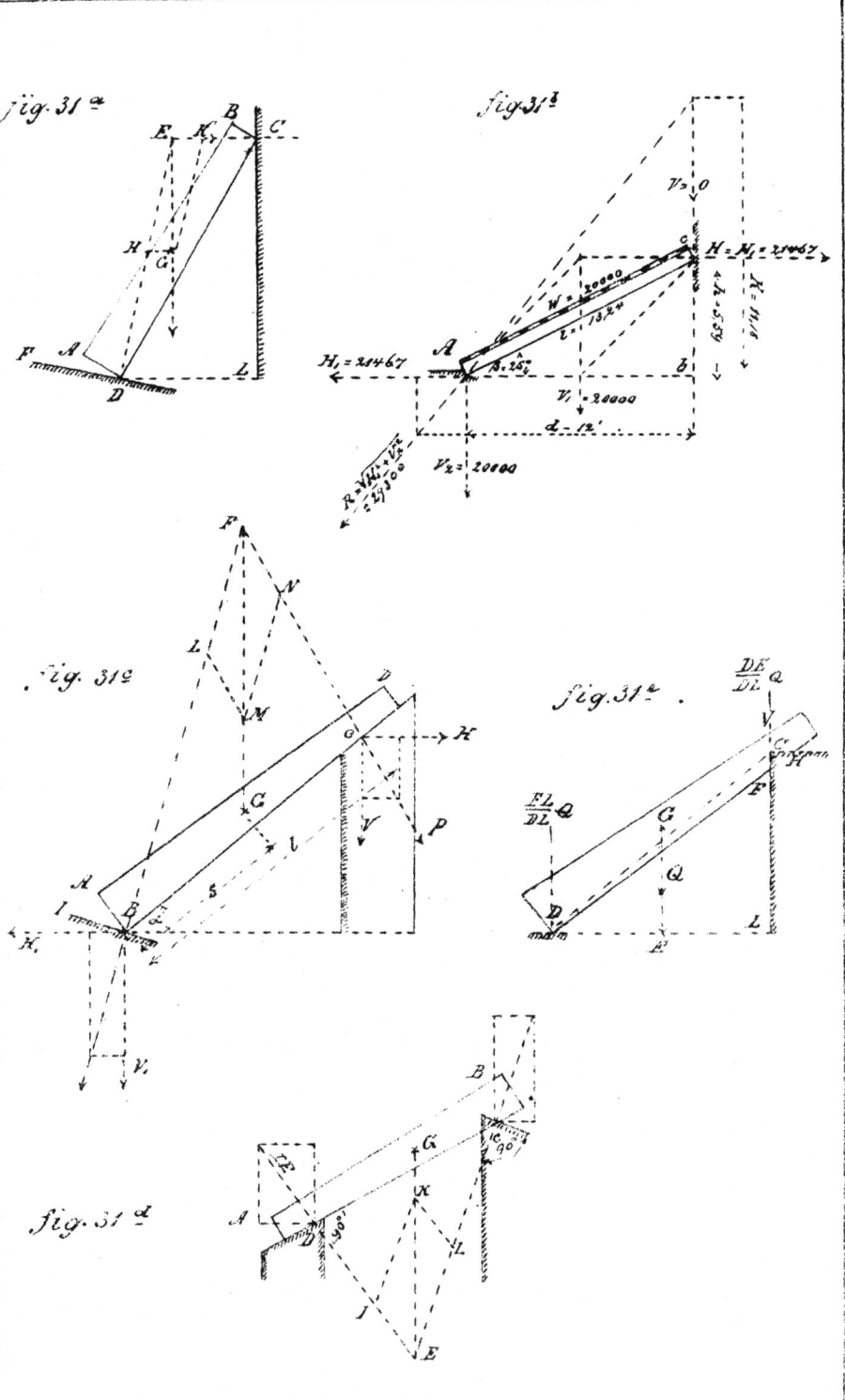

B. ROOF CONSTRUCTION.

31ᵈ.] Let the sloping body $ABCD$ (Fig. 31ᵈ) be supported by a wall at its lower end, D, which coincides with the surface of the body;

Let G be again the centre of gravity;

It is required to cut a notch out of the body at the upper end, C, so that it may rest upon the top of a wall which is made to fit the notch.

Make GE vertical;

From D draw $DE \perp$ to CD;

Join EC, and draw CF at right angles to it; then the notch at C being cut, the body $ABCD$ will be at rest.

31ᵉ.] A body, $ABCD$, resting on supports (Fig. 31ᵉ), will only produce the vertical strains $\dfrac{DE'}{DL} \cdot Q$ and $\dfrac{EL}{DL} \cdot Q$ at the supports.

Plate 7, Fig. 32.] For Figs. 32, 33 and 34 we have, again,

$$\frac{bc}{ac} = \sin \beta; \quad \frac{ab}{ac} = \cos \beta; \quad \frac{bc}{ab} = \tan \beta; \quad \frac{ab}{bc} = \cot \beta;$$

$$\sin 2\beta = \sin 50° = 0{,}766;$$

and when upon each rafter $W = 20000$ lbs., equally distributed, we have for Fig. 32,

$$H = H_1 = \frac{W}{2} \cdot \frac{d}{h} = \frac{W}{2} \cdot \cot \beta = 21467 \text{ lbs.}$$

The compression in the rafter $= \dfrac{W}{2} \cdot \dfrac{l}{h} = 23685$ lbs.,

and, again, $\quad R = \sqrt{H_1^2 + V_2^2} = 29300$ lbs.

For an angle $\beta = 26°\ 34'$; the horizontal thrust will $= 20000$ lbs.—*i. e.*, the same as the entire weight. (Comp. Fig. 16.)

33.] For Fig. 33 is, as the rafter in a vertical direction, sustained on the top,

$$H = H_1 = \frac{W}{4} \cdot \sin 2\beta = 5000 \times 0{,}766 \times 3830;$$

$$V = \frac{W}{2} \cdot \cos^2 \beta = 10000 \times 0{,}82 = 8200;$$

$$V_2 = \frac{W}{2}(1 + \sin^2 \beta) = 10000(1 + 0{,}17) + 11700;$$

and the compression in the rafter,
$$\frac{W}{2} \cdot \sin \beta = 10000 \times 0{,}422 = 4220 \text{ lbs.}$$

For Fig. 34, when the rafter is sustained at the top by a vertical post,
$$H = H_1 = \frac{W}{4} \cdot \sin 2\beta = 3830;$$

34.]
$$V = W \cos^2 \beta = 20000 \times 0{,}82 = 16400;$$
$$V_2 = \frac{W}{2}(1 + \sin^2 \beta) = 10000(1 + 0{,}17) = 11700;$$

and the compression in the rafter =
$$\frac{W}{2} \cdot \sin \beta = 4220 \text{ lbs.}$$

In the cases in Figs. 33 and 34 the post relieves the tie-rod or (as here, in the absence of a tie) the wall from a part of the thrust of the rafters, and compared with the truss in the preceding we see that the king-post acts in a different way.

The different combinations of this single hanging-and-thrust construction may be disregarded, and by the following calculations the method of moments thoroughly applied.

A rafter being constructed in this way (Fig. 35), without connection between the point e and the horizontal tie-rod aa, there are two different systems, that of a trussed beam, aec, similar to Fig. 16,

35.] and that of a single triangle like Fig. 32, and it is as there for the same angle, β, and a load = 20000 lbs. upon each rafter; the horizontal thrust, H, at the top, as also the tension in the horizontal tie-rod = 21467 lbs. The trussed rafter is understood to be calculated like Fig. 16 in combination with Fig. 31^b.

When the weight of structure, snow and wind-pressure upon a
36.] roof (Fig. 36), for one square foot of horizontal projection, in all = 50 lbs., and the width between the supports or $AC =$ 40 feet, the distance of rafters = 10 feet, then 20000 lbs. is the entire load, or 10000 lbs. upon each rafter, supported at A, B, C, D and E.

The pressure of one-half of the weight, or 10000 lbs., on the supports is counteracted by the direct load of 2500 lbs. It is therefore the reacting force, D, only 7500 lbs. (See Howe Truss, Sect. I., D.)

For a section separated by st we can define at once the strains in

fig. 32

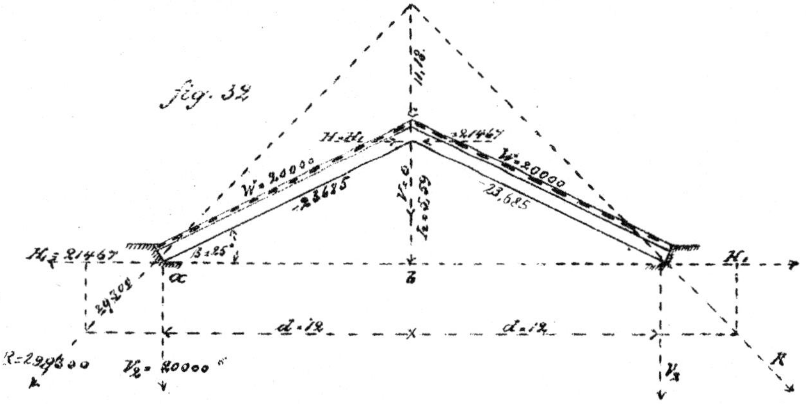

fig. 33

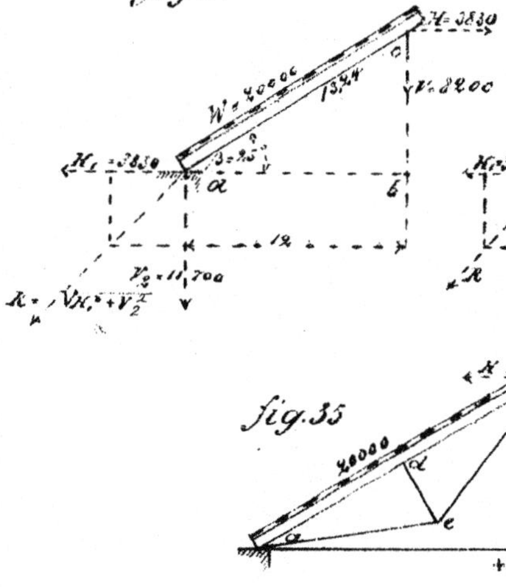

fig. 34

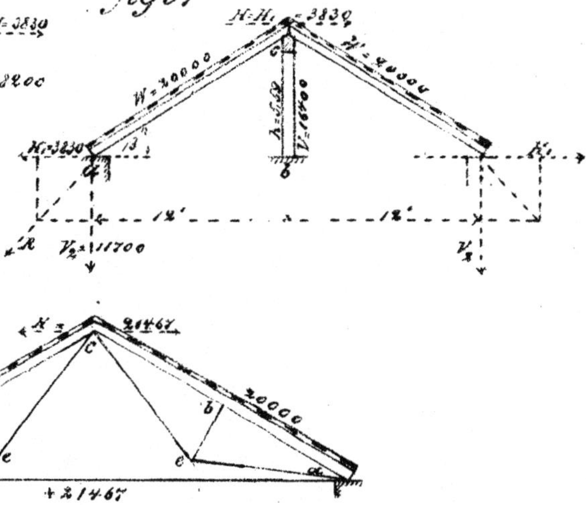

fig. 35

fig. 36.

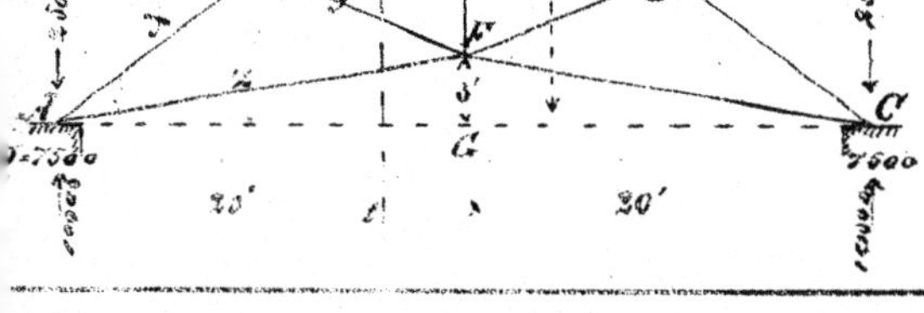

fig. 36ᵃ

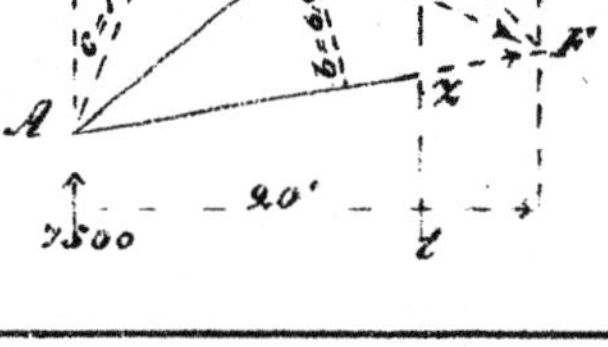

B. ROOF CONSTRUCTION.

z, y and x_1, so for x_1, considering the forces acting upon this section and the point of rotation in the intersection of y and z or F. (Fig. 36^a.)

36^a.] $0 = x_1 . a + D . 20 - 5000 \times 10.$

(Comp. Fig. 20, Equat. I.)

The arm or lever, a, can be measured near enough from a skeleton $= 9{,}6'$.

Besides, for the calculation of a we have for the angle ABG (Fig. 36),

$$AG = GB . \tang < ABG,$$

or $\tang . ABG = \dfrac{AG}{GB} = \dfrac{20}{15} = \dfrac{4}{3} = 1{,}333\,;$

i. e., $< ABG = 53° 7'$, and $\sin 53° 7' = 0{,}8\,;$

$a = BF \sin < ABG = 12 \times 0{,}8 = 9{,}6\,;$

therefore $0 = x_1 . 9{,}6 + 7500 \times 20 - 5000 \times 10\,;$

$$x_1 = -\dfrac{100000}{9{,}6} = -10412 \text{ lbs.}$$

For z (rot. r . E, Fig. 36^a),

$$0 = -z . 6 + 7500 \times 10,$$

or $z = +\dfrac{75000}{6} = +12500\,;$

and for y (rot. r . A, Fig. 36^a),

$$0 = y . c + 5000 . 10\,;$$
$$0 = y . 10{,}75 + 50000,$$

or $y = -\dfrac{50000}{10{,}75} = -4650.$

Plate 8, Fig. 36^b.] For the strain in x (rot. r . F, Fig. 36^b) is,

$$0 = x . 9{,}6 + 7500 \times 20,$$

or $x = -\dfrac{150000}{9{,}6} = -15625.$

In regard to the vertical V, we use for its definition the strain of the joining brace, $x_1 = -10412$, and make st a curved line; then we have, for a rot. r . D (Fig. 36^b),

$$0 = -V . 10 - (-10412) . 10{,}9,$$

or $0 = -V . 10 + 113490\,;$

36   THE THEORY OF STRAINS.

i.e., $$V = + \frac{113490}{10} = + 11349.$$

37.] The results are combined in Fig. 37.

38.] For Fig. 38, the entire load (equally distributed) again being 20000 lbs., the depth 15′, and between the supports 40′.

When here the cut st separates the line $x_1 y_1 z_1$, we have for x_1 (rot. in the intersection of $y_1 z_1$, or F, Fig. 39),

$$0 = x_1 \cdot 9{,}1 - 5000 \times 5\tfrac{1}{2} + 7500 \times 15\tfrac{1}{2};$$

39.] $$x_1 = -\frac{88750}{9{,}1} = 9752.$$

For y_1 (rot. $r \cdot A$), $0 = -y_1 \cdot 15 + 5000 \times 10$,

or $$y_1 = +\frac{50000}{15} = +3{,}333;$$

and for z_1 (rot. $r \cdot C$),

$$0 = -z_1 \cdot 15 - 5000 \times 10 = 7500 \times 20;$$

$$z_1 = +6{,}666.$$

40.] For a section, st, through x and z, we have for x (Fig. 40),

$$0 = x \cdot 9{,}1 + 7500 \times 15\tfrac{1}{2} \text{ (rot. } r \cdot F);$$

$$x = -\frac{116250}{9{,}1} = -12774;$$

and for z (rot. $r \cdot D$),

$$0 = -z \cdot 7{,}4 + 7500 \times 10;$$

or $$z = \frac{75000}{7{,}4} = 10135.$$

For y (rot. $r \cdot A$) is, $0 = y \cdot 12{,}5 + 5000 \times 10;$

$$y = -\frac{50000}{12{,}5} = -4000.$$

41.] The results combined in Fig. 41.

42.] When the figure before is changed in the depth, like Fig. 42, we have the following equation:

$$0 = x_1 \cdot 5{,}8 - 5000 \times 3{,}25 + 7500 \times 13{,}25 \text{ (rot. } r \cdot F, \text{Fig. 43)};$$

$$x_1 = -\frac{83125}{5{,}8} = -14332.$$

43.] For the definition of y_1, the intersection of x_1 and z_1 will be in G, and it is for G as rotation,

$$0 = -y_1 \cdot 8{,}25 + 5000 \times 6 + 7500 \times 4; \quad \text{(Fig. 43.)}$$

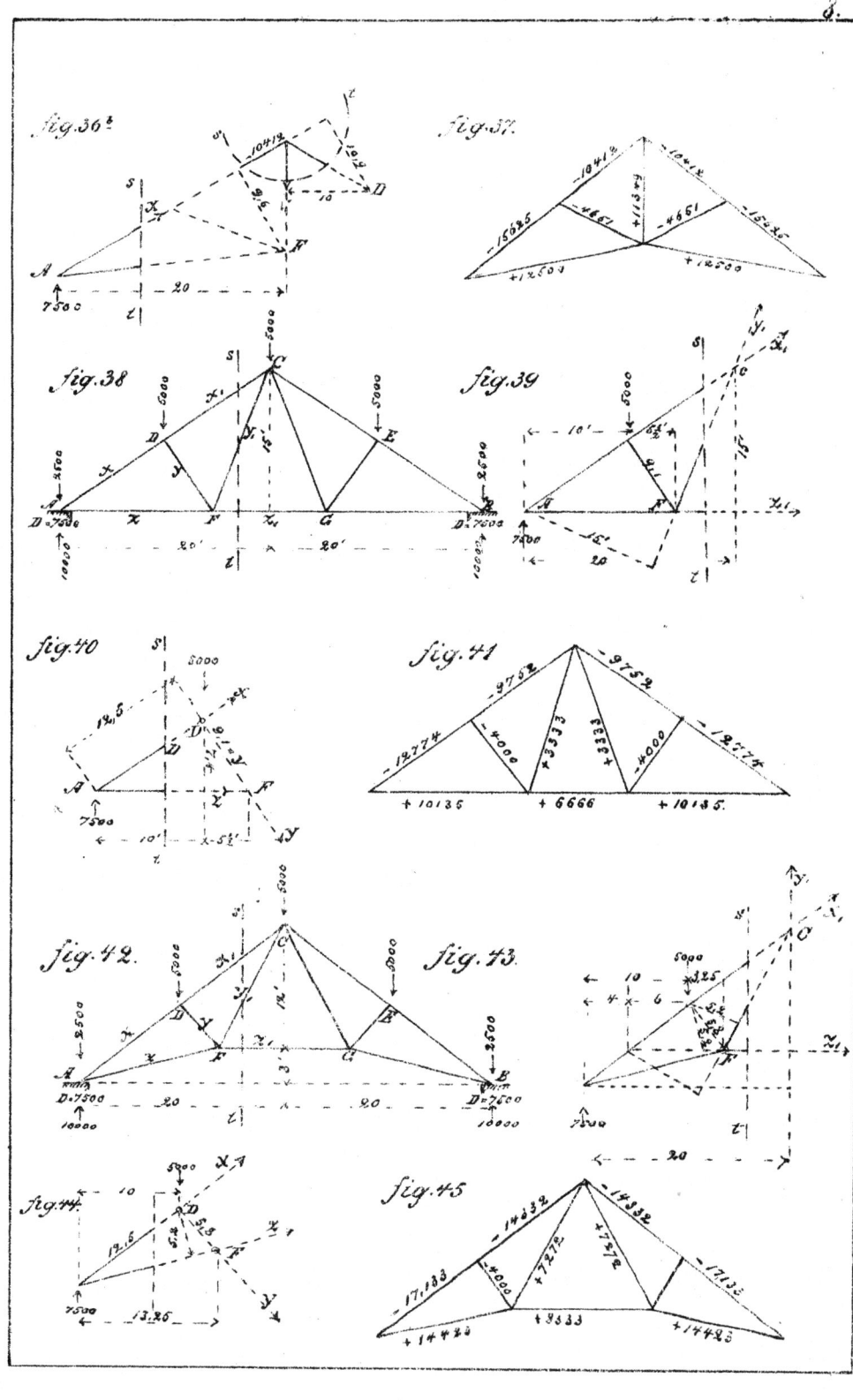

B. ROOF CONSTRUCTION.

$$y_1 = + \frac{60000}{8{,}25} = 7272.$$

For z_1 (rot. $r \cdot C$) we have

$$0 = - z_1 \cdot 12 - 5000 \times 10 + 7500 \times 20;$$

$$z_1 = + \frac{100000}{12} = + 8333.$$

44.] For a section, st, through x and z (Fig. 44), it is

$$0 = x \cdot 5{,}8 + 7500 \times 13{,}25 \text{ (rot. } r \cdot F);$$

$$x = - \frac{993750}{5{,}8} = - 17133;$$

and
$$0 = - z \cdot 5{,}2 + 7500 \times 10 \text{ (rot. } r \cdot D);$$

$$z = \frac{75000}{5{,}2} = + 14423;$$

and for y,
$$0 = y \cdot 12{,}5 + 5000 \times 10 \text{ (rot. } r \cdot A);$$

$$y = - \frac{50000}{12{,}5} = - 4000.$$

45.] The results combined in Fig. 45.

Plate 9,⎤ For the definition of X in Fig. 46, the point of rotation
Fig. 46.⎦ in E, or in the intersection of Y and Z, will be from
Fig 47.

47.]
$$0 = X \cdot x - P \cdot CE + D \cdot AE;$$

or
$$X = \frac{P \cdot CE - D \cdot AE}{x}.$$

For Y we choose A, or the intersection of X and Z, as the point of rotation, and the equation will be

$$0 = - Y \cdot y + P \cdot AC + Q \cdot AE,$$

or
$$Y = \frac{P \cdot AC + Q \cdot AE}{y},$$

and in the same way for Z, rot. $r \cdot H$.

$$0 = - Z \cdot z - Q \cdot EL - P \cdot CL + D \cdot AL,$$

or
$$Z = \frac{- Q \cdot EL - P \cdot CL + D \cdot AL}{z}.$$

It will not be necessary to show, by repetition of the foregoing, the equations for the other parts of the structure.

38   THE THEORY OF STRAINS.

48.] In more complicated systems (Fig. 48), it may happen that by a cut, *st* (which can be made curved as well as straight), different braces or rods are spared, like FG, DG and DE.

In this case it is possible to come to a direct result when *st* only can be laid so that all the braces or rods cut by *st* meet at one point, except that one whose strain is in question.

49.] So for the strain V in FG (rot. $r \cdot H$, Fig. 49),
$$0 = -V \cdot FH - R \cdot r;$$
$$V = -\frac{R \cdot r}{FH}.$$

50.] In the same manner the strain U in DG (rot. $r \cdot H$, Fig. 50),
$$0 = U \cdot u - R \cdot r;$$
$$U = \frac{R \cdot r}{u};$$
thus we find also the strain in KT and LT.

51.] Being by the foregoing in possession of a value for U in DG, we find for the strain X in DF, Y in DE, and Z in CE the following equations from Fig. 51:

$$0 = X \cdot DE + U \cdot v - Q \cdot NO - P \cdot MO + W \cdot AO \text{ (rot. } r \cdot E);$$
$$0 = Y \cdot AD + U \cdot l + Q \cdot AN + P \cdot AM \text{ (rot. } r \cdot A);$$
$$0 = -Z \cdot z + W \cdot AN - P \cdot MN \text{ (rot. } r \cdot D);$$

each one enabling us to obtain a direct result for the strain in question.

Plate 10, Fig. 52.] For a roof (Fig. 52), the weight of which, 11,3 lbs. per square foot of its horizontal plan, may be calculated 20 lbs. for wind pressure and snow, making together 31,3 lbs. per square foot.

The distance of rafters being $15\frac{1}{3}$ feet, the width, 100 feet, makes for each rafter $15\frac{1}{3} \times 100 \times 31,3 = 48000$ lbs. (approx.).

The load at each apex, therefore, will be $\frac{48000}{8} = 6000$ lbs., the distribution of which is shown by the skeleton.

For the reactive force on the supports is again
$$D = 24000 - 3000, \quad \text{or } D = 21000 \text{ lbs.}$$

There are, in all, seven times 6000 lbs. acting downward, and **twice** 21000 lbs. acting vertically upward upon the system.

fig. 46.

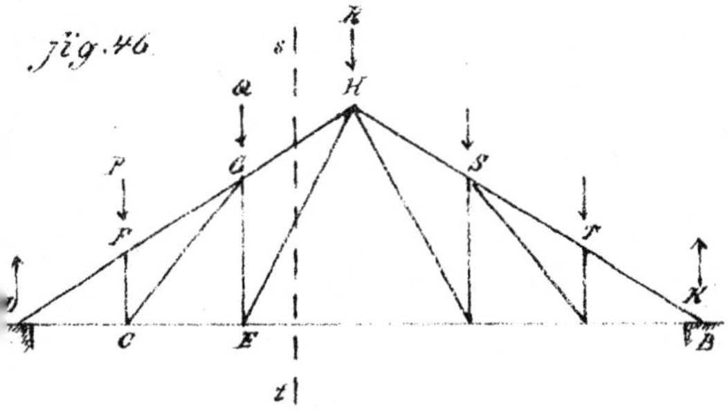

fig. 47.

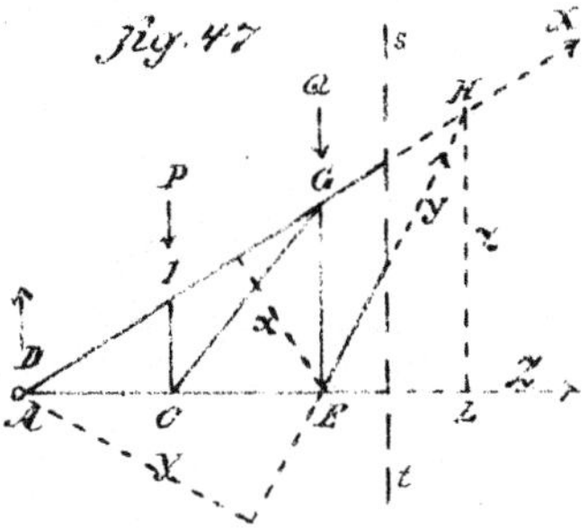

fig. 48.

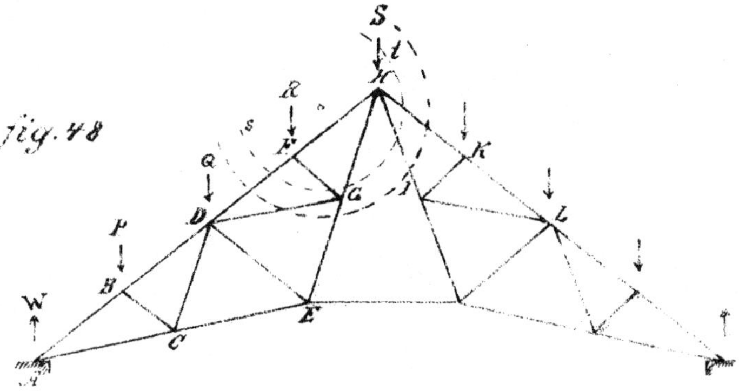

fig. 49.

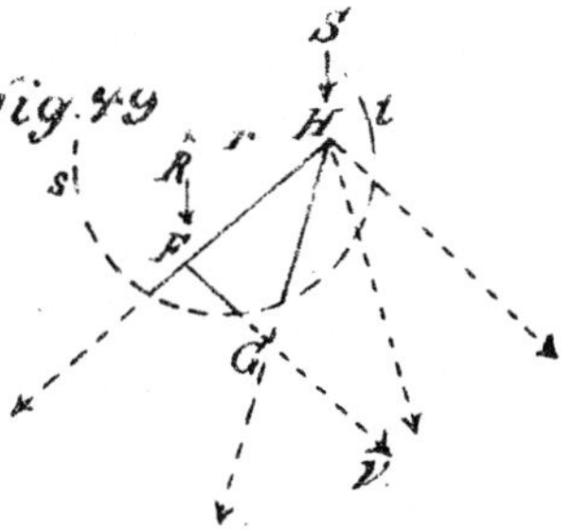

fig. 50.

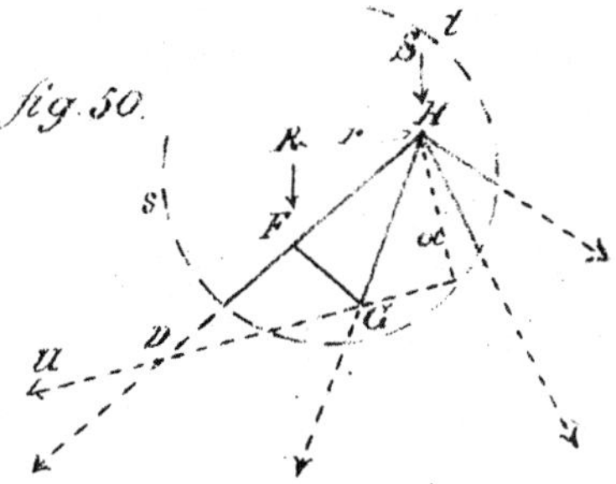

fig. 51.

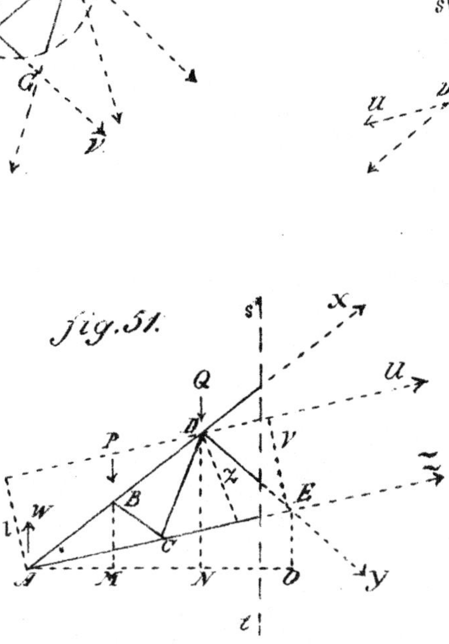

B. ROOF CONSTRUCTION.

53.] The section, A, s, t (Fig. 53), kept in equilibrium by the replaced forces, x, y and z, may be regarded first as a lever with the fulcrum at D; then the strain in x for the middle section is

$$0 = x \cdot 18{,}6 + 21000 \times 50 - 6000 \times 12{,}5 - 6000 \times 25 - 6000 \times 37{,}5,$$

or $x = 32300$ lbs.;

and in y, when A is the point of rotation,

$$0 = y \cdot 38{,}4 + 6000 \times 12{,}5 + 6000 \times 25 + 6000 \times 37{,}5 \text{ (rot. } A);$$

$$y = -11700 \text{ lbs.,}$$

and

$$0 = -z \cdot 15 + 21000 \times 37{,}5 - 6000 \times 12{,}5 - 6000 \times 25 \text{ (rot. } r \cdot E),$$

$$Z = +37500 \text{ lbs.}$$

54.] For V in Fig. 54 the rotation also round A is

$$0 = -V \cdot 37{,}5 + 6000 \times 12{,}5 = 6000 \times 25;$$

$$V = +6000 \text{ lbs.}$$

For the other members in Fig. 52,

$$0 = x_1 \cdot 13{,}9 + 21000 \times 37{,}5 - 6000 \times 12{,}5 - 6000 \times 25$$
(rot. $r \cdot F$);

$$x_1 = -40400;$$

$$0 = y_1 \cdot 23{,}5 + 6000 \times 12{,}5 + 6000 \times 25 \text{ (rot. } r \cdot A);$$

$$y_1 = -9570;$$

$$0 = -z_1 \cdot 10 + 21000 \times 25 - 6000 \times 12{,}5 \text{ (rot. } r \cdot G);$$

$$z_1 = +45000;$$

$$0 = -V_1 \cdot 25 + 6000 \times 12{,}5 \text{ (rot. } r \cdot A);$$

$$V_1 = +3000;$$

$$0 = x_2 \cdot 9{,}3 + 21000 \times 25 - 6000 \times 12{,}5 \text{ (rot. } r \cdot H);$$

$$x_2 = -48400;$$

$$0 = y_2 \cdot 9{,}3 + 6000 \times 12{,}5 \text{ (rot. } r \cdot A);$$

$$y_2 = -8100;$$

$$0 = -z_2 \cdot 5 + 21000 \times 12{,}5 \text{ (rot. } r \cdot I);$$

$$z_2 = +52500.$$

For the strain in x_3 we choose a convenient point for rotation in the line z, per Example D, Fig. 55.

55.] The equation in this case will be

$$0 = x_3 . 18,6 + 21000 \times 50;$$
$$x_3 = -56500.$$

The only strain not directly deducible is U in the vertical line CD at the centre.

As in Fig. 36, we use the strain of the joining brace,

$$x = -32300 \text{ lbs.}$$

56.] For B as the point of rotation (Fig. 56), our equation is

$$0 = -U.50 - 6000 \times 50 - (-32300).37,2;$$
$$U = 18000 \text{ lbs.}$$

57.] The results combined in Fig. 57.

58.] The weight and load of a roof (Fig. 58) being estimated, including wind-pressure and snow, to 50 lbs. per square foot of its horizontal plan, the distance of rafters being 12 feet, and the space between the walls 99 feet, which gives $50 . 12 . 99 = 59400$ lbs. for one rafter, or, in round figures, 60000 lbs.

The calculation of the top structure can be made as in the preceding example (Fig. 36).

58.] In the main construction are six supporting points, charged as in Fig. 58. The top structure transmits one-third of the entire load, or on each post 10000 lbs. to the apexes, ff.

Each wall has to bear 30000 lbs.; and after subtraction of the direct load the reactive force is 26666 lbs., or, by calculation,

$$D = \frac{6666(11+22)}{99} + \frac{13333(33+66)}{99} + \frac{6666(77+88)}{99};$$
$$D = 26666 \text{ lbs.}$$

59.] For the strain x_3 we have in Fig. 59,

$$0 = -x_3 . 21 - 13333 \times 16\tfrac{1}{2} - 6666(27\tfrac{1}{2} + 38\tfrac{1}{2}) + D.49\tfrac{1}{2}$$
(rot. $r . h$);

or, also,

$$0 = -x_3 . 21 - 6666(11+22) + 26666 \times 33 \text{ (rot. } r.f);$$

$$x_3 = +\frac{659967}{21} = +31427.$$

Further,

$$0 = Z_4 . 21 - 13333 \times 16\tfrac{1}{2} - 6666(27\tfrac{1}{2} + 38\tfrac{1}{2}) + D.49\tfrac{1}{2}$$
(rot. $r . g$).

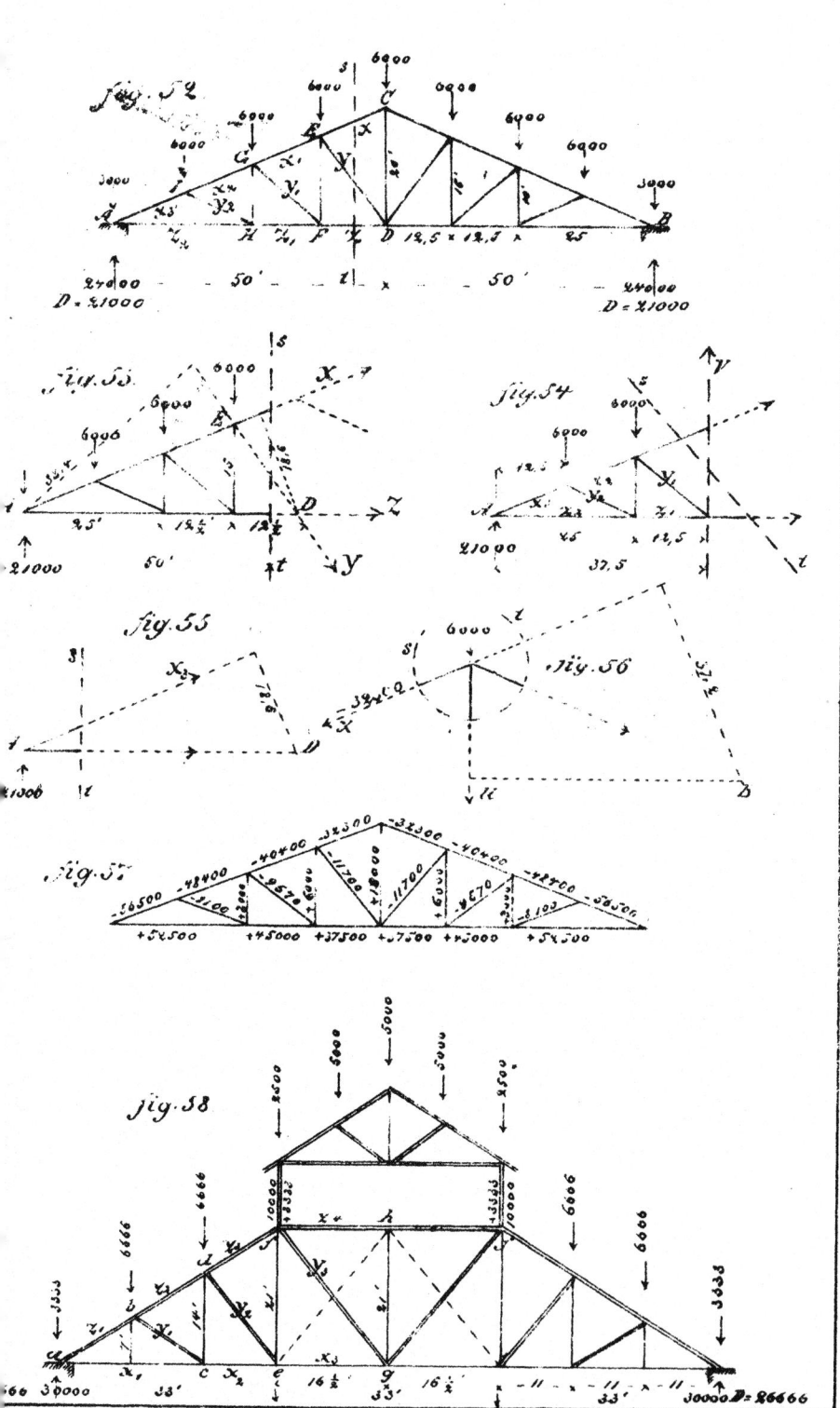

B. ROOF CONSTRUCTION. 41

$$Z_4 = -\frac{659967}{21} = -31427,$$

and $\quad 0 = y_3 \cdot 39{,}5 + 13333 \times 33 + 6666 \,(11 + 22)\, (\text{rot. } r \cdot a);$
$$Y_3 = -16708.$$

The tie-rod, gh, transmits the strain to the top flange, and is here sustained by the counter-brace, eh.

60.] From Fig. 60 is

$$0 = -x_2 \cdot 14 - 6666 \times 11 + D \cdot 22 \,(\text{rot. } r \cdot d);$$
$$x_2 = \frac{513304}{14} = 36665;$$

$$0 = z_3 \cdot 17\tfrac{3}{4} - 6666\,(11 + 22) + 26666 \times 33 \,(\text{rot. } r \cdot e);$$
$$z_3 = -\frac{660000}{17{,}75} = -37180;$$

$$0 = y_2 \cdot 26{,}7 + 6666 \times 11 + 6666 \times 22 \,(\text{rot. } r \cdot a);$$
$$y_2 = -8223.$$

61.] Fig. 61 gives the equations,

$$0 = -x_1 \cdot 7 + 26666 \times 11 \,(\text{rot. } r \cdot b);$$
$$x_1 = +41902;$$

$$0 = z_2 \cdot 13 - 6666 \times 11 + 26666 \times 22 \,(\text{rot. } r \cdot c);$$
$$z_2 = -39485;$$

$$0 = y_1 \cdot 13 + 6666 \times 11 \,(\text{rot. } r \cdot a);$$
$$y_1 = -5640;$$

and for z_1 we find from the same figure,

$$0 = z_1 \cdot 13 + 26666 \times 22;$$
$$z_1 = -45125.$$

62.] For the strain in tie-rods we find from Fig. 62.

$$0 = -V_3 \cdot 33 + 6666 \cdot (11 + 22) \,(\text{rot. } r \cdot a);$$
$$V_3 = +6666; \qquad (\text{Comp. Fig. 68.})$$

$$0 = -V_2 \cdot 22 + 6666 \times 11 \,(\text{rot. } r \cdot a);$$
$$V_2 = +3333;$$

$$0 = -V_1 \cdot 11 + 0 \,(\text{rot. } r \cdot a);$$
$$V_1 = 0 \text{ (and is therefore not essential)}.$$

THE THEORY OF STRAINS.

63.] The strain in V_4 at the centre rod, according to 8^b, can be defined thus:

$$V_4 = 2 \times \frac{21}{26,7} \times 16708 = 26200 \text{ lbs.}$$

The results are combined in Fig. 63.

64.] When in Fig. 64 the rafters are trussed—*i. e.*, stiffened by a king-post at *b*—there will be only four supporting points in the main construction, because the load in this case is transferred to the wall.

$$D = \frac{9999 \times 22}{99} + \frac{13333 \,(33 + 66)}{99} + \frac{9999 \times 77}{99} = 23332 \text{ lbs.}$$

Plate 12, Fig. 65.] Further in Fig. 65,

$0 = x_2 \cdot 21 - 13333 \times 16\tfrac{1}{2} - 9999 \times 27\tfrac{1}{2} + 23332 \times 49\tfrac{1}{2}$
  (rot. $r \cdot h$);
$$x_2 = 31427;$$

$0 = z_3 \cdot 21 - 13333 \times 16\tfrac{1}{2} - 9999 \times 27\tfrac{1}{2} + 23332 \times 49\tfrac{1}{2}$
  (rot. $r \cdot g$);
$$z_3 = -31427;$$

$0 = y_2 \cdot 39,5 + 9999 \times 22 + 13333 \times 33$ (rot. $r \cdot a$);
$$y_2 = -16708.$$

66.] And from Fig. 66,

$0 = -x_1 \cdot 14 + D \cdot 22 = -x_1 \cdot 14 + 23332 \times 22$ (rot. $r \cdot d$);
$$x_1 = +36665;$$

$0 = z_2 \cdot 17\tfrac{3}{4} + 23332 \times 33 - 9999 \times 11$ (rot. $r \cdot e$);
$$z_2 = -37180;$$

$0 = y_1 \cdot 26,75 + 9999 \times 22$ (rot. $r \cdot a$);
$$y_1 = -8223.$$

67.] For Z we have from Fig. 67,

$0 = Z_1 \cdot 13 + 23332 \times 22$ (rot. $r \cdot c$);
$$Z_1 = -39485.$$

68.] See the results in Fig. 68 combined.

The strain $V_4 = 26200$ lbs. can be defined independently of the Method of Moments by the parallelogram of forces, as in Fig. 63, already shown,

$$V_4 = 2\,(-16708)\,.\cos\alpha;$$

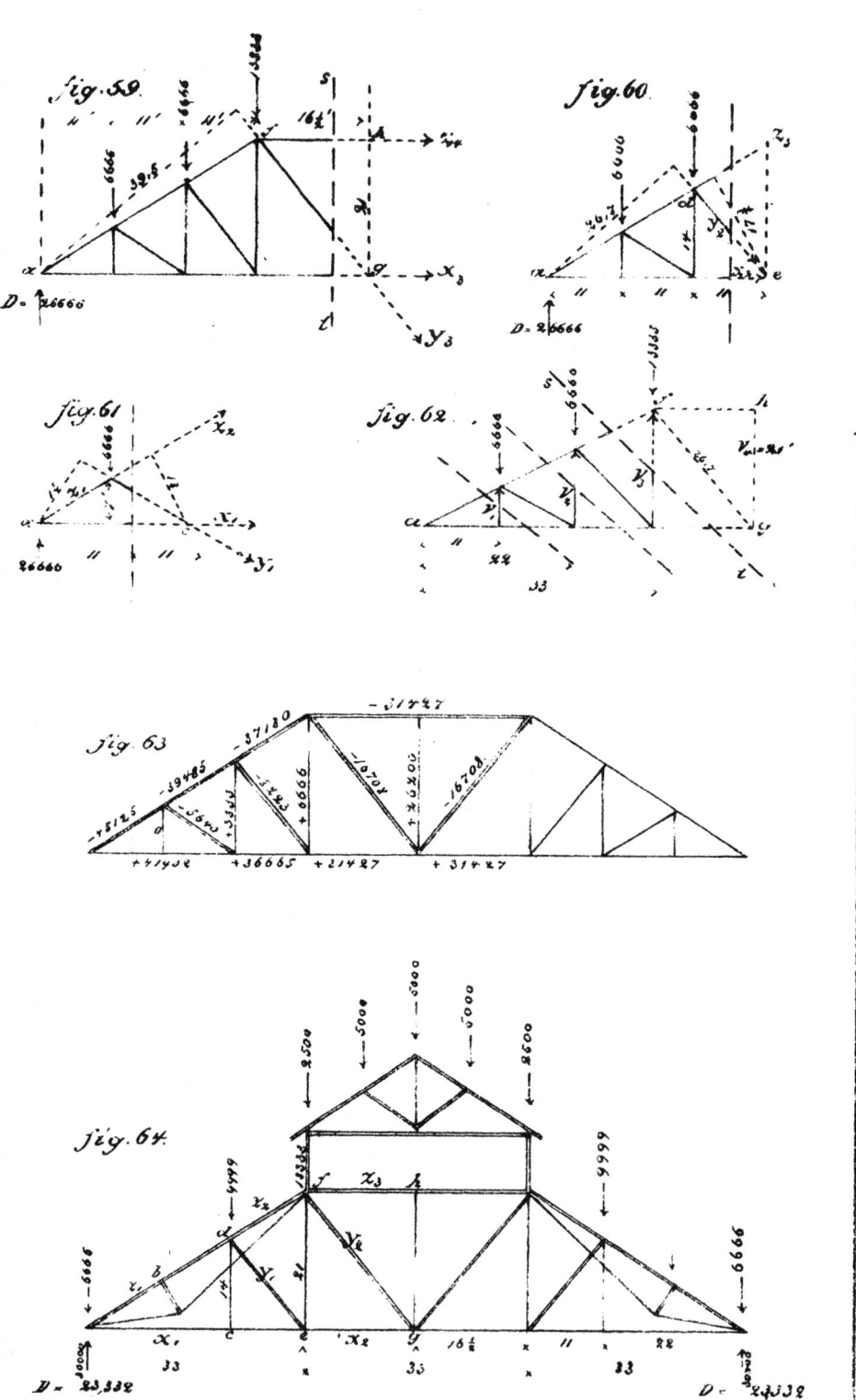

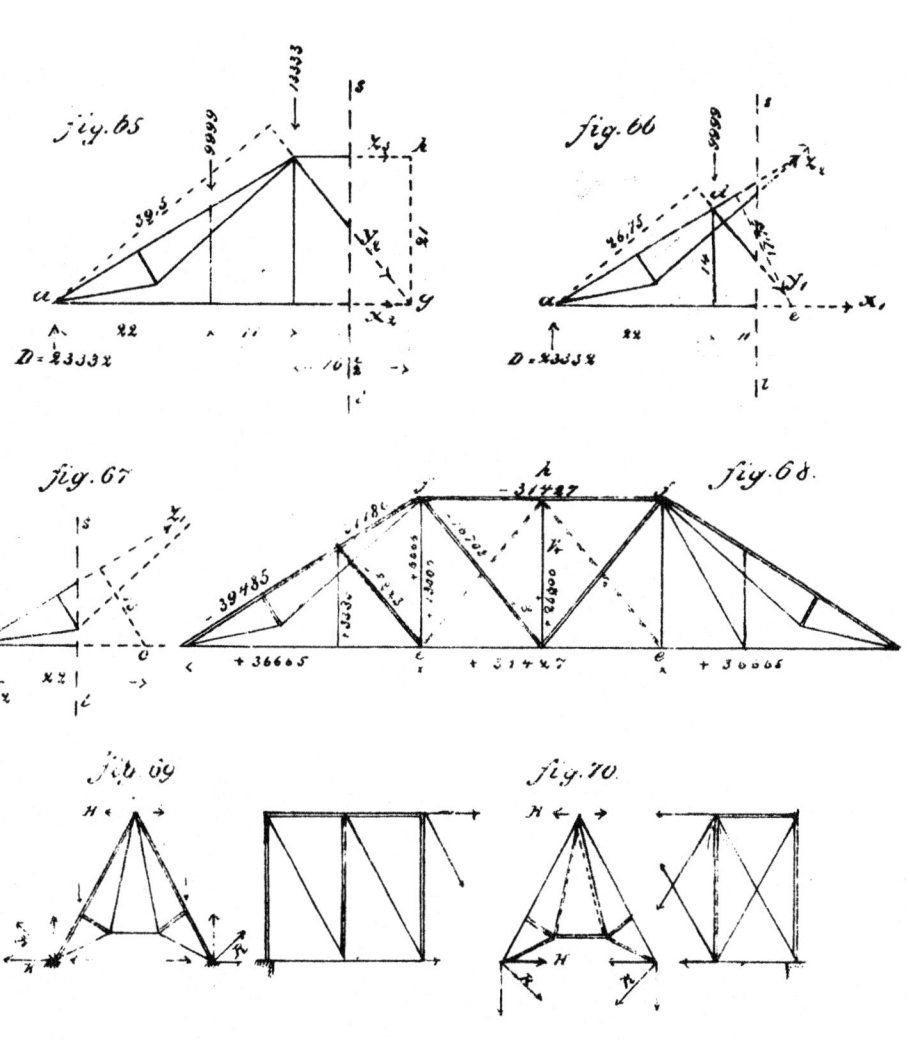

SEMI-GIRDERS LOADED AT THE EXTREMITY. 43

and when by means of counter-braces, e, h, the top chord is relieved from the strain, so that one-half to each side is transported to the tie-rods, e, f, then here the strain will increase to $13000 + 6666 = 19666$ lbs.

69,
70.] In a combination of rafters (Figs. 69, 70), the pressure of the end rafters upon the wall results in an outward horizontal and vertical force.

Different from this is the action of the intermediate rafters, being similar to an oblique bridge-truss, sustained at the top chord.

The horizontal force at the heels of the intermediate rafters is opposed to the horizontal force of the end rafters.

[Plates 6, 7, 8, 9, 10, 11 and 12—embracing Figs. 31 to 70.]

C. SEMI-GIRDERS.

I. *SEMI-GIRDERS LOADED AT THE EXTREMITY.*

Plate 13,
Fig. 71.] As the most simple presentation for a weight, W, the stress in struts and tie-rods is inscribed in Figs. 71 to 74, and the parallelogram of forces connected.

73.] To compute in Fig. 73 the stress in the lower flange, we have

$$\frac{de}{df} = \sec \alpha, \quad \text{and} \quad \frac{\frac{Z}{2}}{-W \cdot \sec \alpha} = -\sin \alpha,$$

or
$$\frac{Z}{2} = -W \cdot \sec \alpha \cdot \sin \alpha ;$$

$$Z = -W \cdot \sec \alpha \cdot \sin \alpha - W \cdot \sec \alpha \sin \alpha,$$

or
$$Z = -2W \cdot \sec \alpha \cdot \sin \alpha ;$$

and since
$$\sin \alpha = \frac{\tan \alpha}{\sec \alpha},$$

$$Z = -2W \cdot \sec \alpha \frac{\tan \alpha}{\sec \alpha} = -2W \cdot \tan \alpha$$

(much easier determined in Fig. 77 by the Method of Moments).

From Fig. 73 and the following we see that, for a load at the extremity, the diagonals are strained equally and alternately with tensile ($+$) and compressive ($-$) strains. (Comp. Fig. 23.)

But the strain in the flanges increases toward the support in each,
$$2W.\tang \propto,$$
where $\propto$ is the angle of diagonals with a vertical line.

75.] For a better presentation of this, see Fig. 75, and for the calculation apply the Method of Moments.

76, 77.] When by a cut, *st*, a section of the structure is separated, we have for the flanges as equation of equilibrium (Figs. 76 and 77),

$0 = -x_1.cb + W.ca$ (rot. $r.b$); | $0 = +z_1.h + W.2l$ (rot. $r.d$);

or for $cb = h$, and $ac = l$;

$x_1 = +W.\dfrac{l}{h} = +W.\tang \propto$; | $z_1 = -2W.\dfrac{l}{h} = -2W.\tang \propto$;

78, 79.] and by Figs. 76 and 79:

$0 = -x_2.h + W.3l$ (rot. $r.e$); | $0 = +z_2.h + W.4l$ (rot. $r.f$);

$x_2 = +3W.\dfrac{l}{h} = 3W.\tang \propto$. | $z_2 = -4W.\dfrac{l}{h} = -4W.\tang \propto$.

In the same manner is

$0 = -x_3.h + W.5l$ (rot. $r.g$); | $0 = +z_3.h + W.6l$ (rot. $r.h$);

$x_3 = 5W.\dfrac{l}{h}$ | $z_3 = -6W.\dfrac{l}{h}$.

CRANES.

Plate 14, Fig. A.] A wrought-iron crane (Fig. A), constructed of braces with link-joints, may be loaded at the extremity with 30000 lbs. $= P$; so is (for the dimensions noted in the skeleton) the horizontal strain, S, in a and b.

$$0 = -S.6 + P.12 \text{ (rot. } r.a);$$
$$S = 60000 \text{ lbs};$$

B.] and for the other members we have

$0 = -z_1.0{,}75 + 0$ (rot. in the intersection of y_1 and x_1 or g, Fig. B);

$$z_1 = 0;$$
$$o = y_1.1{,}1 - P.2{,}1 \text{ (rot. } r.i);$$
$$y_1 = +\frac{30000 \times 2{,}1}{1{,}1} = 57272;$$

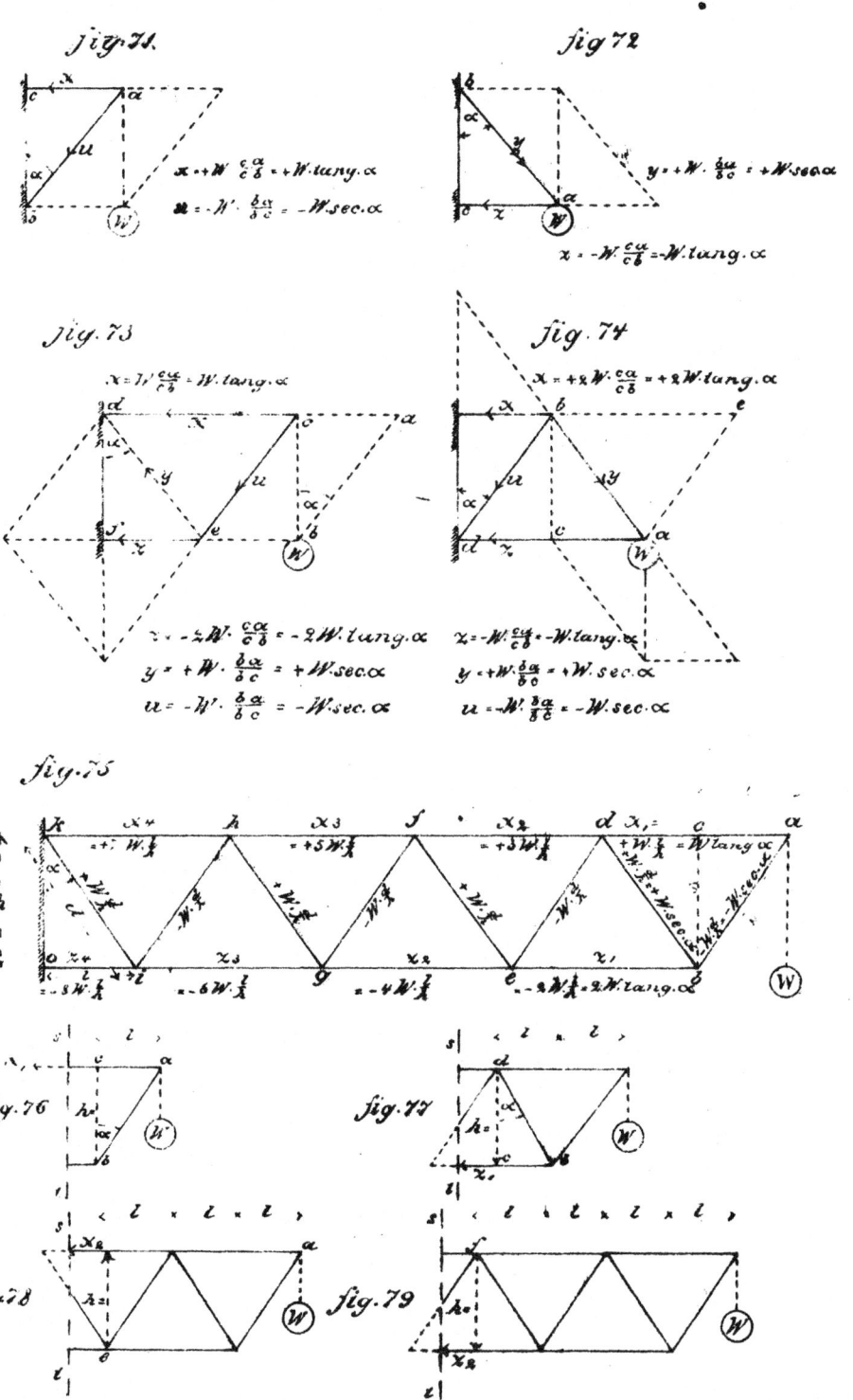

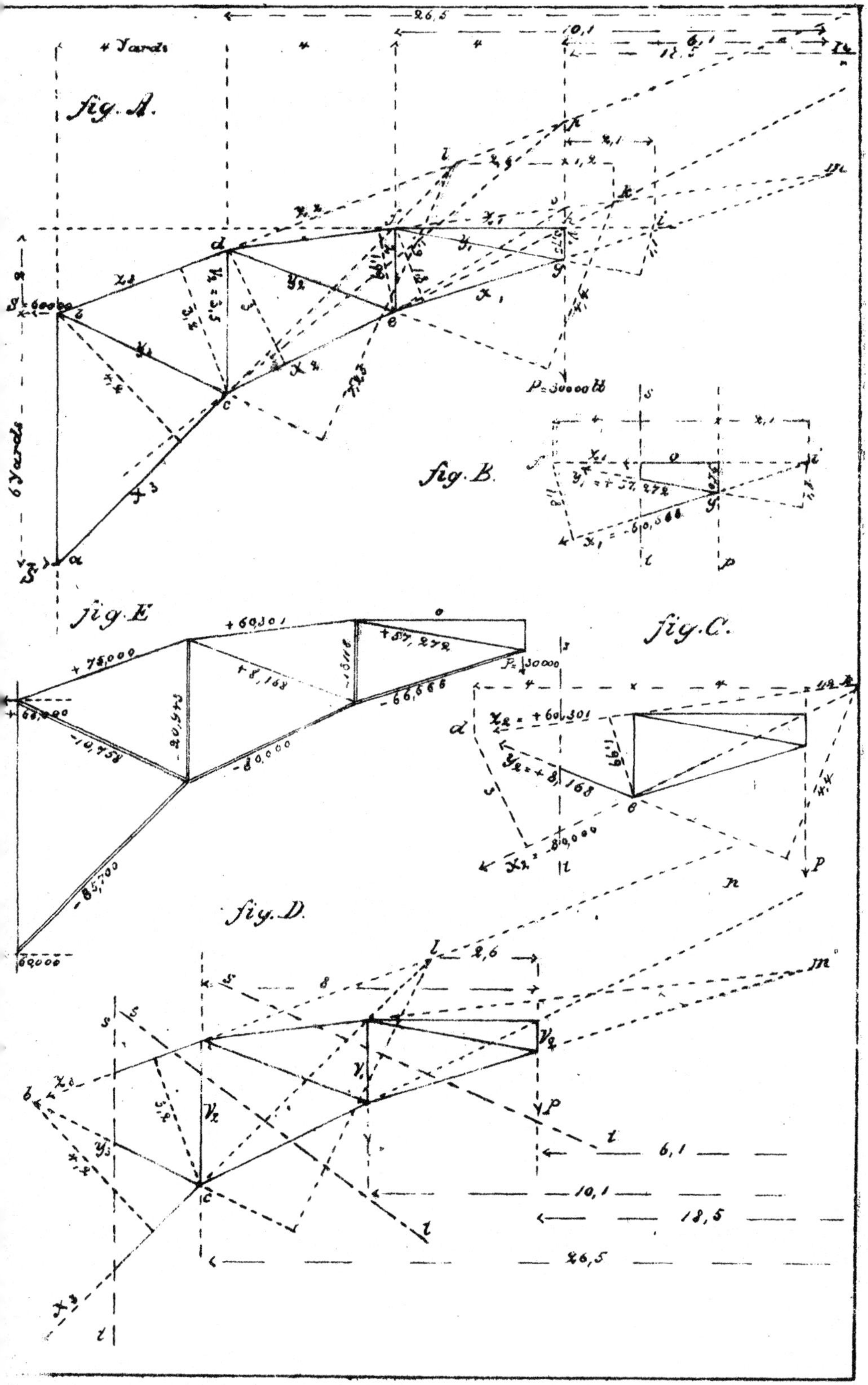

fig. A.
fig. B.
fig. C.
fig. D.
fig. E
4 Yards
6 Yards
26,5
10,1
18,5
6,1
P=30000 lb
+ 75,000
+ 60,301
+ 57,272
+ 8,168
+ 66,000
- 10,758
- 20,943
- 66,666
- 80,000
- 85,700
60000
30000
X_2 = + 60,301
y_2 = + 8,168
X_2 = - 80,000
y_1 = + 57,272
X_1 = - 66,666

$$0 = x_1 \cdot 1{,}8 + P \cdot 4 \text{ (rot. } f\text{)};$$
$$x_1 = -\frac{30000 \cdot 4}{1{,}8} = -66666;$$

C.] $$0 = -z_2 \cdot 1{,}99 + P \cdot 4 \text{ (rot. } r \cdot e, \text{ Fig. C)};$$
$$z_2 = \frac{120000}{1{,}99} = +60301;$$
$$0 = y_2 \cdot 4{,}4 - P \cdot 1{,}2 \text{ (rot. } r \cdot k\text{)};$$
$$y_2 = +8168;$$
$$0 = x_2 \cdot 3 + P \cdot 8 \text{ (rot. } r \cdot d\text{)};$$
$$x_2 = -80000;$$

D.] $$0 = -z_3 \cdot 3{,}2 + P \cdot 8 \text{ (rot. } r \cdot c, \text{ Fig. D)};$$
$$z_3 = 75000;$$
$$0 = x_3 \cdot 4{,}2 + P \cdot 12 \text{ (rot. } r \cdot b\text{)};$$
$$x_3 = 85700.$$

For y_3 the intersection l of x_3 and z_3 is to the left of the suspended weight, and the symbol reversed.

$$0 = y_3 \cdot 7{,}25 + P \cdot 2{,}6 \text{ (rot. } r \cdot l\text{)};$$
$$y_3 = -10758,$$

which would be $= 0$ when the intersection is in the vertical line of the suspended weight, as the lines oe and pc in Fig. A indicate.

For the verticals, V, we have from Fig. D,

$$0 = -V_1 \cdot 10{,}1 - P \cdot 6{,}1 \text{ (rot. } r \cdot m\text{)};$$
$$V_1 = 18118;$$
$$0 = -V_2 \cdot 26{,}5 - P \cdot 18{,}5 \text{ (rot. } r \cdot n\text{)};$$
$$V_2 = -20943.$$

E.] The results combined in Fig. E.*

II. *SEMI-GIRDERS LOADED AT EACH APEX.*

In Fig. 25 is occasionally explained how to compute the stress in diagonals, as there is no intersection of joining flanges, x and z, and as in the case here considered the diagonals receive at each loaded

---

* For most purposes the above will be sufficient. In Glynn's rudimentary treatise on the Construction of Cranes we find valuable and complete drawings.

46   THE THEORY OF STRAINS.

Plate 15,] apex an increment of strain, prior to the calculation
Fig. 80.] may be given the general thesis that *the strain in two diagonals whose intersection is at an unloaded point is the same in numerical value, but of opposite character.* (Fig. 80.)

(See IV. General Remarks.)

The strain in diagonals, meeting at a loaded point, is in numerical value different.

The strain in flanges increases from apex to apex in geometrical progression.

81.] In Fig. 81 suppose the angle φ of diagonals with a horizontal line $= 45°$, so, also, angle $\alpha = 45°$; and by the table, $\sec \alpha = 1,414$.

When, again, in the axis $x = \infty$ a point of rotation, o, is supposed, we have per example for diagonal, y_5.

$$0 = + y_5 . x \sin \varphi + \left(W + W + \frac{W}{2} \right) . x \text{ (rot. } r . o),$$

where $y_5 . \sin \varphi$ is the vertical component of y_5, or $= ab = a_1 b_1$ in the parallelogram of forces (Fig. 81), presenting by y_5 the resulting strain or diagonal. Divided by x, it follows:

$$0 = + y_5 \sin \varphi + \left(W + W + \frac{W}{2} \right);$$

and as $\varphi = 45°$, and $\sin 45° = 0,707$,

$$0 = + y_5 . 0,707 + \tfrac{5}{2} . W,$$

or $\qquad y_5 = -3,535 \, W.$

The same results from $-\tfrac{5}{2} W . \sec \alpha$, or $-\tfrac{5}{2} . W . 1,414$, which is also $= -3,535 \, W$.

82.] In the same manner in Fig. 82 for y_2, the direction of which, when separated by a cut, st, is reversed to the weight. (See Figs. 22 and 23.)

$$0 = - y_2 . \sin 45 + \frac{W}{2} \text{ (rot. } o\text{)};$$

$$y_2 = + \frac{\tfrac{1}{2} W}{0,707}, \quad \text{and } y_1 = - \frac{\tfrac{1}{2} W}{0,707};$$

and for the other diagonals,

$$0 = + y_3 . 0,707 + W + \frac{W}{2},$$

or $\qquad y_3 = - \dfrac{\tfrac{3}{2} W}{0,707}, \quad \text{and } y_4 = + \dfrac{\tfrac{3}{2} W}{0,707};$

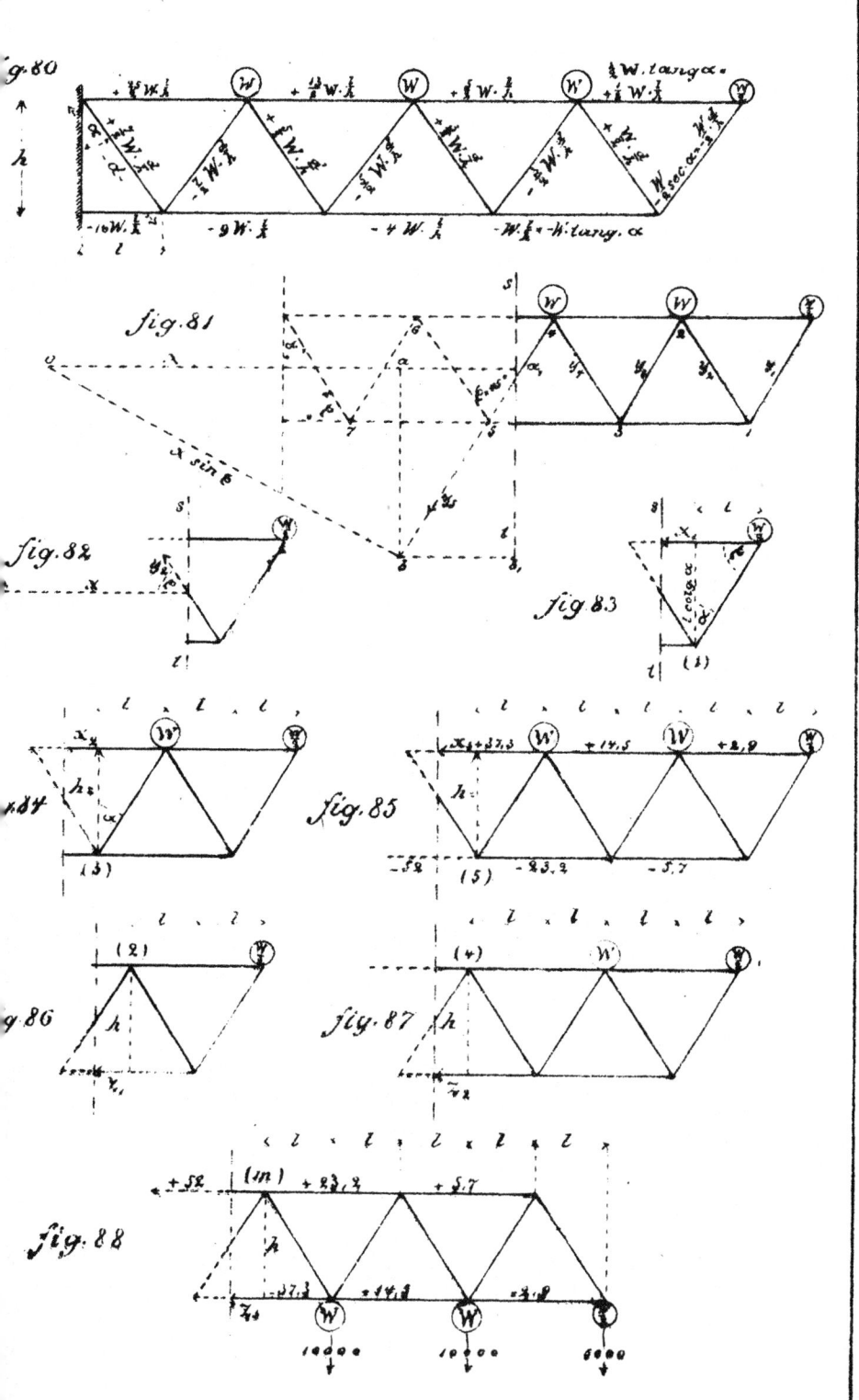

SEMI-GIRDERS LOADED AT EACH APEX.

$$y_5 = -\frac{\tfrac{5}{2}W}{0{,}707}, \quad \text{and } y_6 = +\frac{\tfrac{5}{2}W}{0{,}707};$$

$$0 = + y_7 \cdot 0{,}707 + W + W + W + \frac{W}{2},$$

or $\quad y_7 = -\dfrac{\tfrac{7}{2}W}{0{,}707}, \quad \text{and } y_8 = +\dfrac{\tfrac{7}{2}W}{0{,}707}.$

83.] For the strain in flanges we have from Fig. 83,

$$0 = -x_1 \cdot l \cdot \cot \alpha + \frac{W}{2} \cdot l \ (\text{rot. } r \cdot 1);$$

$$x_1 = \frac{\tfrac{1}{2}W\cdot l}{l\cdot\cot g\,\alpha}, \quad \text{or as } \frac{1}{\cot g\,\alpha} = \tan g\,\alpha\,,$$

$$x_1 = \tfrac{1}{2}W\cdot\tan g\,\alpha\,;$$

and when $W = 10$ tons, $< \varphi = 60°$; therefore $< \alpha = 30°$, and $\quad \tan g\,30° = 0{,}577$ ("Example Stoney");

$$x_1 = 5 \times 0{,}577 = + 2{,}9 \text{ tons};$$

or when, for an easier understanding, in Fig. 83,

$$l \cdot \cot g\,\alpha = h,$$

84.] we have for x_2 in Fig. 84,

$$0 = -x_2 \cdot h + W \cdot l + \frac{W}{2} \cdot 3\,l \ (\text{rot. } r\,.\,3);$$

$$x_2 = \frac{\tfrac{5}{2}W\cdot l}{h};$$

and as $\quad \dfrac{l}{h} = \tan g\,\alpha = 0{,}577,$

for our example,

$$x_2 = \tfrac{5}{2}\cdot W\cdot 0{,}577 = \tfrac{5}{2}\times 10 \times 0{,}577 = 14{,}5 \text{ tons.}$$

85.] So for x_3 in Fig. 85,

$$0 = -x_3 \cdot h + W \cdot l + W \cdot 3\,l + \frac{W}{2}\cdot 5\,l \ (\text{rot. } r\,.\,5);$$

$$x_3 = \tfrac{13}{2}\cdot W\cdot 0{,}577 = 37{,}3 \text{ tons,}$$

and so further.

86.] For the strain, z, in the lower flanges,

$$0 = + z_1 \cdot h + \frac{W}{2}\cdot 2\,l \ (\text{rot. } r\,.\,2 \text{ in Fig. 86});$$

$$z_1 = -W\cdot\frac{l}{h} = -10 \times 0{,}577 = -5{,}7 \text{ tons.}$$

87.] Fig. 87 gives

$$0 = + z_2 \cdot h + W \cdot 2l + \frac{W}{2} \cdot 4l \text{ (rot. } r \cdot 4\text{)};$$

$$z_2 = -4W \cdot \frac{l}{h} = -4 \times 10 \times 0{,}577 = -23{,}2 \text{ tons.}$$

In the same way for z_3,

$$0 = + z_3 \cdot h + W \cdot 2l + W \cdot 4l + \frac{W}{2} \cdot 6 \cdot l;$$

$$z_3 = -9W \cdot \frac{l}{h} = -52 \text{ tons.}$$

88.] In case the load should be connected to the lower apexes (Fig. 88), the equation of equilibrium, per example for z_3, would be

$$0 = + z_3 \cdot h + W \cdot l + W \cdot 3l + \frac{W}{2} \cdot 5l \text{ (rot. } r \cdot m\text{)};$$

$$z_3 = -\tfrac{13}{2} \cdot W \cdot \frac{l}{h} = -37{,}3 \text{ tons};$$

i. e., the strain is the same as in the flange of the reversed figure, but of opposite character. So also is the strain the same for the other flanges. (See Fig. 88.)

Remark.—In the given example the strains are determined without a certain length for h or l. This is easily explained by the relation which the angle φ or $\propto$ bears to h and l, as by the extension of one, the other will increase in the same ratio.

[Plates 13, 14 and 15—embracing Figs. 71 to 88.]

D. GIRDERS WITH PARALLEL TOP AND BOTTOM FLANGES.

(Calculated for a Permanent Load.)

I. STRAIN IN DIAGONALS AND VERTICALS.

The calculation is very similar to the preceding. Provided, again, the load to be connected to the upper or lower apexes for the application of the Method of Moments, we now consider as a special force the reaction of the supports toward the system.

D_1 may represent one-half the weight of loaded truss or the

STRAIN IN DIAGONALS AND VERTICALS.

pressure upon each support (prop), and diminished by the partition of load on this place directly sustained. (Comp. Fig. 21.) The reactive force of support wanted for our calculation will be signified by D.

To compute D, we refer to Fig. 4 in Sect. I., and define first for the following example its numerical value:

Plate 16,
Fig. 89. Through bridge (over-grade bridge), between supports, 48 feet;

8 panels, each 6 feet $= l$;

depth of truss $= 6$ feet $= h$, from centre to centre of top and bottom chords;

the weight of structure $= 3000$ lbs., and the load $= 15000$ lbs.;

gives a permanent load $= 18000$ lbs. per panel;

rolling load $= 0$. (See Sect. II.)

For the distribution of load, see Fig. 89.

Remark.—The strange impression which the arrangement of diagonals, unsymmetrical toward the centre, may first produce, will soon disappear after observation of the advantages for transformation upon succeeding systems.

Whole pressure of truss upon supports $= 8 \times 18000 = 144000$ lbs.;

$D_1 = 18000 \left(\frac{1}{8}+\frac{2}{8}+\frac{3}{8}+\frac{4}{8}+\frac{5}{8}+\frac{6}{8}+\frac{7}{8}\right) + 9000 \times \frac{8}{8} = 72000$ lbs.;

$D = 18000 \left(\frac{1}{8}+\frac{2}{8}+\frac{3}{8}+\frac{4}{8}+\frac{5}{8}+\frac{6}{8}+\frac{7}{8}\right) = 63000$ lbs.

The strain in the post, V_0, is 0, because $x_1 = 0$,

and $\qquad V_8 = -63000.$*

90.] Excepting the vertical component of y_1 (*i. e.*, $y_1 \sin \varphi$), for a section (Fig. 90), only $D = 63000$ lbs. is a second vertical force.

Both turn to the left around o in the axis x_0; therefore their symbol, —. (Comp. Fig. 22.)

---

* For a deck-bridge (under-grade bridge)—*i. e.*, when the upper apexes are loaded—would be
$$V_0 = -9000, \quad \text{and} \quad V_8 = -72000.$$

The angle of diagonals with a horizontal line will be 45°.

THE THEORY OF STRAINS.

$$0 = -y_1 \sin 45° - D \text{ (rot. } r \cdot o);$$

and as $\sin 45° = 0{,}7$,

$$0 = -y_1 \cdot 0{,}7 - 63000,$$

or $\qquad y_1 = -90000.$

91.] For V_1 in Fig. 91, only D is acting vertically upon this section.

D turns to the left around o, therefore

$$0 = + V_1 - D \text{ (rot. } r \cdot o);$$
$$0 = V_1 - 63000,$$

or $\qquad V_1 = + 63000.$

92.] According to the preceding, from Fig. 92,

$$0 = -y_2 \cdot 0{,}7 + 18000 - 63000 \text{ (rot. } r \cdot o);$$
$$y_2 = -64285;$$

93.] and from Fig. 93,

$$0 = + V_2 + 18000 - 63000 \text{ (rot. } r \cdot o);$$
$$V_2 = + 45000.$$

94.] Fig. 94 gives the equation,

$$0 = -y_3 \cdot 0{,}7 + 18000 +{,}18000 - 63000 \cdot$$
$$y_3 = -38570;$$

95.] and from Fig. 95 we have

$$0 = + V_3 + 18000 + 18000 - 63000;$$
$$V_3 = + 27000.$$

Now it will be unnecessary to farther accompany the remaining calculations with diagrams.

$$0 = -y_4 \cdot 0{,}7 + 18000 \times 3 - 63000;$$
$$y_4 = -12857;$$
$$0 = + V_4 + 18000 \times 3 - 63000;$$
$$V_4 = + 9000;$$
$$0 = -y_5 \cdot 0{,}7 + 18000 \times 4 - 63000;$$
$$y_5 = + 12857;$$
$$0 = + V_5 + 18000 \times 4 - 63000;$$
$$V_5 = -9000;$$
$$0 = -y_6 \cdot 0{,}7 + 18000 \times 5 - 63000;$$
$$y_6 = + 38570;$$

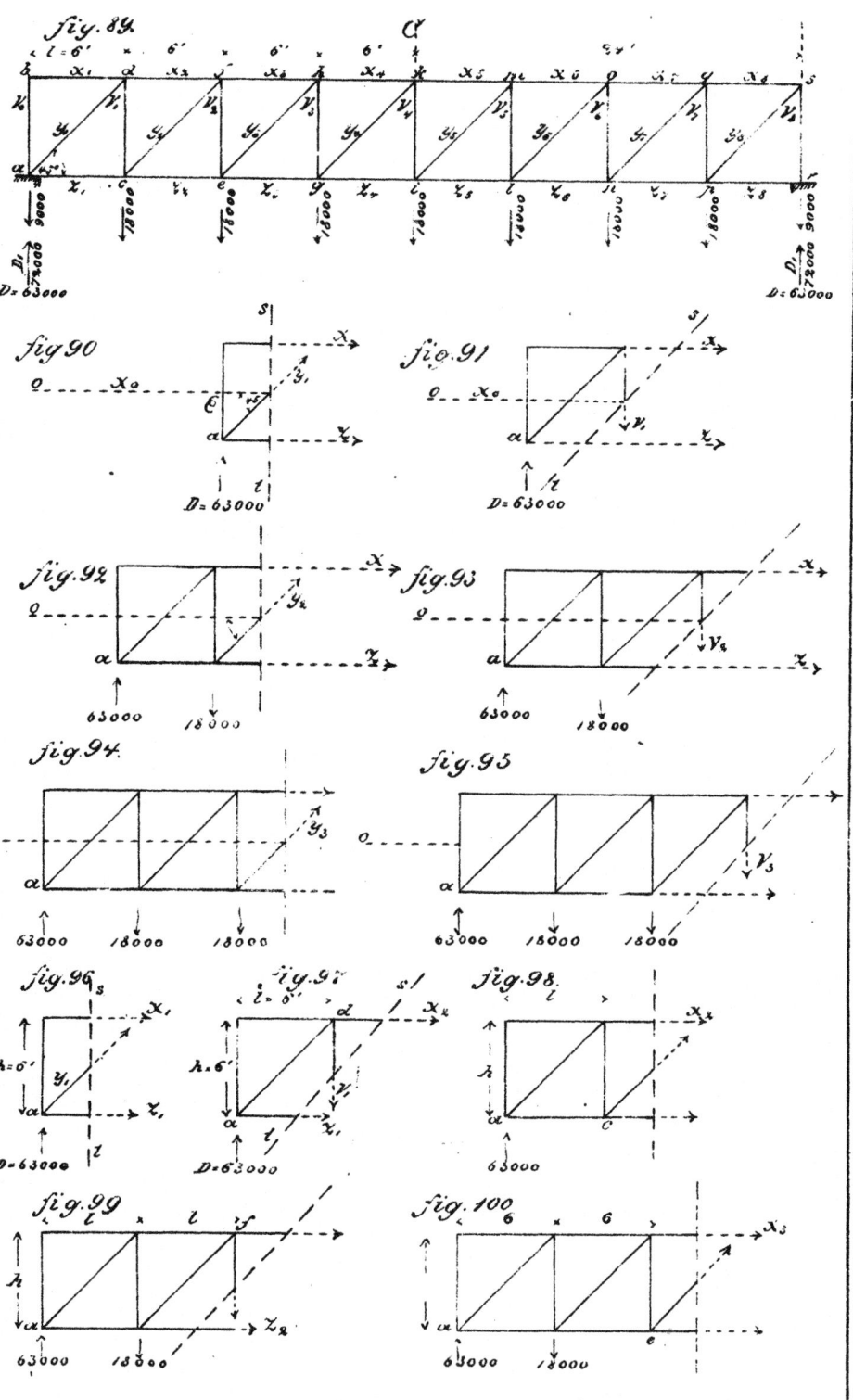

STRAIN IN FLANGES. 51

$$0 = + V_6 + 18000 \times 5 - 63000;$$
$$V_6 = - 27000;$$
$$0 = - y_7 \cdot 0{,}7 + 18000 \times 6 - 63000;$$
$$y_7 = + 64285;$$
$$0 = + V_7 + 18000 \times 6 - 63000;$$
$$V_7 = - 45000;$$
$$0 = - y_8 \cdot 0{,}7 + 18000 \times 7 - 63000;$$
$$y_8 = + 90000;$$
$$0 = + V_8 + 18000 \times 7 - 63000;$$
$$V_8 = - 63000.$$

II. *STRAIN IN FLANGES.*

The calculation of strain in flanges differs in so far from the preceding, and will give no difficulty in understanding, as here a suitable point of rotation—*i.e.*, an intersection of those members, separated by a cut, *st*, similar to that one for which we want to compute the strain—is directly presented by the apexes.

For a rough and preliminary control of strain in the top and bottom flanges at the centre of the truss, it is, as $72000 =$ one-half of the load, 6 feet $=$ depth, and 12 feet $=$ one-fourth of the space between the supports:

$$\frac{72000 \times 12}{6} = 144000 \text{ lbs., the horizontal strain in each flange.}$$

(Comp. Sect. I., Fig. 28.)

96.] For Fig. 96 we have the equation of equilibrium,

$$0 = x_1 \cdot h + D \cdot 0 \text{ (rot. in the intersection of } y_1 \text{ and } z_1 \text{ or } a);$$
$$x_1 = 0;$$

97.] and for Fig. 97,

$$0 = - z_1 \cdot h + D \cdot l \text{ (rot. in the intersection of } V_1 \text{ and } x_2 \text{ or } d);$$
$$z_1 = D \cdot \frac{l}{h} = 63000.$$

98.] In the same way for Fig. 98,

$$0 = x_2 \cdot h + D \cdot l \text{ (rot. } r \cdot c);$$
$$0 = x_2 \cdot 6 + 63000 \times 6;$$
$$x_2 = - 63000;$$

THE THEORY OF STRAINS.

99.] and for Fig. 99,
$$0 = -z_2 . h - 18000 . l + D . 2l \text{ (rot. } r.f);$$
$$0 = -z_2 . 6 - 18000 \times 6 + 63000 \times 12;$$
$$z_2 = +108000.$$

100.] $0 = x_3 . 6 - 18000 \times 6 + 63000 \times 12$ (rot. $r.e$, Fig. 100);
$$x_3 = -108000.$$

Plate 17, Fig. 101. $0 = -z_3 . 6 - 18000 (6+12) + 63000 \times 18$ (rot. $r.h$, Fig. 101);
$$z_3 = +135000.$$

In the same way for the other flanges,
$$0 = x_4 . 6 - 18000 (6+12) + 63000 \times 18 \text{ (rot. } r.g, \text{ Fig 89)};$$
$$x_4 = -135000;$$
$$0 = -z_4 . 6 - 18000 (6+12+18) + 63000 \times 24 \text{ (rot. } r.k);$$
$$z_4 = +144000;$$
$$0 = x_5 . 6 - 18000 (6+12+18) + 63000 \times 24 \text{ (rot. } r.i);$$
$$x_5 = -144000;$$
$$0 = -z_5 . 6 - 18000 (6+12+18+24) + 63000 \times 30 \text{ (rot. } r.m);$$
$$z_5 = +135000;$$
$$0 = x_6 . 6 - 18000 \times 60 + 63000 \times 30 \text{ (rot. } r.l);$$
$$x_6 = -135000;$$
$$0 = -z_6 . 6 - 18000 \times 90 + 63000 \times 36 \text{ (rot. } r.o);$$
$$z_6 = +108000;$$
$$0 = -x_7 . 6 - 18000 \times 90 + 63000 \times 36 \text{ (rot. } r.n);$$
$$x_7 = -108000;$$
$$0 = -z_7 . 6 - 18000 \times 126 + 63000 \times 42 \text{ (rot. } r.q);$$
$$z_7 = +63000;$$
$$0 = -x_8 . 6 - 18000 \times 126 + 63000 \times 42 \text{ (rot. } r.p);$$
$$x_8 = 63000;$$
$$0 = -z_8 . 6 - 18000 \times 168 + 63000 \times 48 \text{ (rot. } r.s);$$
$$z_8 = 0.$$

102.] From the calculation of the first panel for a reversed system (Fig. 102), it will be perceived that here the results are the same as before, and so also for the other panels:

$$0 = + y_1 . \sin 45° - D \,(\text{rot.}\, r . o);$$
$$0 = y_1 . 0{,}7 - 63000;$$
$$y_1 = \frac{63000}{0{,}7} = + 90000;$$

$0 = + x_1 . h + D . l$ (rot. in the intersection of y_1 and z_1, or c);
$$0 = x_1 . 6 + 63000 \times 6;$$
$$x_1 = - 63000;$$

$0 = - z_1 . h + D . 0$ (rot. in the intersection of y_1 and x_1, or b);
$$z_1 = 0.$$

103.] The results of the foregoing are combined in Fig. 103, the compressive strains being represented by double lines.

III. TRANSFORMATIONS.

104.] Truss symmetrical to the centre, with vertical tie-rods and oblique braces. (Howe's system, Fig. 104.)

105.] Pratt truss (Fig. 105), with oblique tie-rods and vertical braces, in which the vertical anchors, a, b, on the abutment can be spared, the same as in Fig. 114.*

IV. GENERAL REMARKS.

106.] For Howe's system (deck-bridge, Fig. 106), there will be in the vertical end post a compression = 9000 lbs., at the centre post 0, and for the reversed system at the centre post, 18000.

Further specification of this and the reversed and combined system, also for the isometrical truss, will be found in the connected tables (Figs. 108 to 117), forming thus a useful guide, especially for the strain in flanges.

The strain in flanges being a maximum for a full load is to be calculated always for a full load, also in the case of a combined (permanent and rolling) load, and it will be treated accordingly in the following pages.

The influence of a *rolling* load upon braces and tie-rods, being so far unconsidered, is very essential, as there is at the centre a tendency to horizontal dislocation, which is prevented in the Howe

---

* Keystone Bridge Company, Pittsburg.

truss by counter-braces, in the isometrical truss by counter-rods, and in other bridges by panel-rods or braces.

In regard to the connecting of a load, we will only remark that for both permanent and rolling loads it is quite the same for the diagonals and horizontal flanges whether the load is connected on the top (deck-bridge) or on the bottom (through-bridge) or to the vertical posts.

But for the post itself in the last case we have to consider the thesis, that

The vertical component of diagonals is equal to the strain in verticals—only of opposite character—when they meet at an unloaded point.

When, therefore, the load is connected between the top and bottom of the vertical brace, both top and bottom apexes are unloaded points; hence the strain in the upper and lower part of the vertical is the vertical strain (vertical component) of the adjoining diagonal, only of opposite character.

So, for example, would be for the post V_7, in Fig. 105, in the lower part,

$$- 90000 \cdot \sin 45°,$$

or $\qquad - 90000 \times 0{,}7 = - 63000,$

which is the vertical component of the adjoining diagonal, the symbol being reversed.

107.] In the upper part would be (Fig. 107),

$$- 64285 \times 0{,}7 = - 45000 \text{ lbs. (according to the same thesis)}.$$

In general, we can derive the strain in the verticals from the diagonals without difficulty. So for the same post, V_7, from Fig. 105,

$$V_7 = - y_1 \cdot \cos 45 = - 64285 \times 0{,}7 = - 45000,$$

and $\qquad V_6 = - 38570 \times 0{,}7 = - 27000\,;$

$\qquad V_5 = - 12857 \times 0{,}7 = - 9000.$

DIRECTIONS FOR THE CALCULATION OF COMPLEX SYSTEMS.

For complex systems, as shown in the post bridge,[*] the Linville, etc. (Fig. 107^a to 107^c), the calculation may be made for each system separately, to derive the strain in braces and tie-rods. For

---

[*] Atlantic Bridge Works, New York.

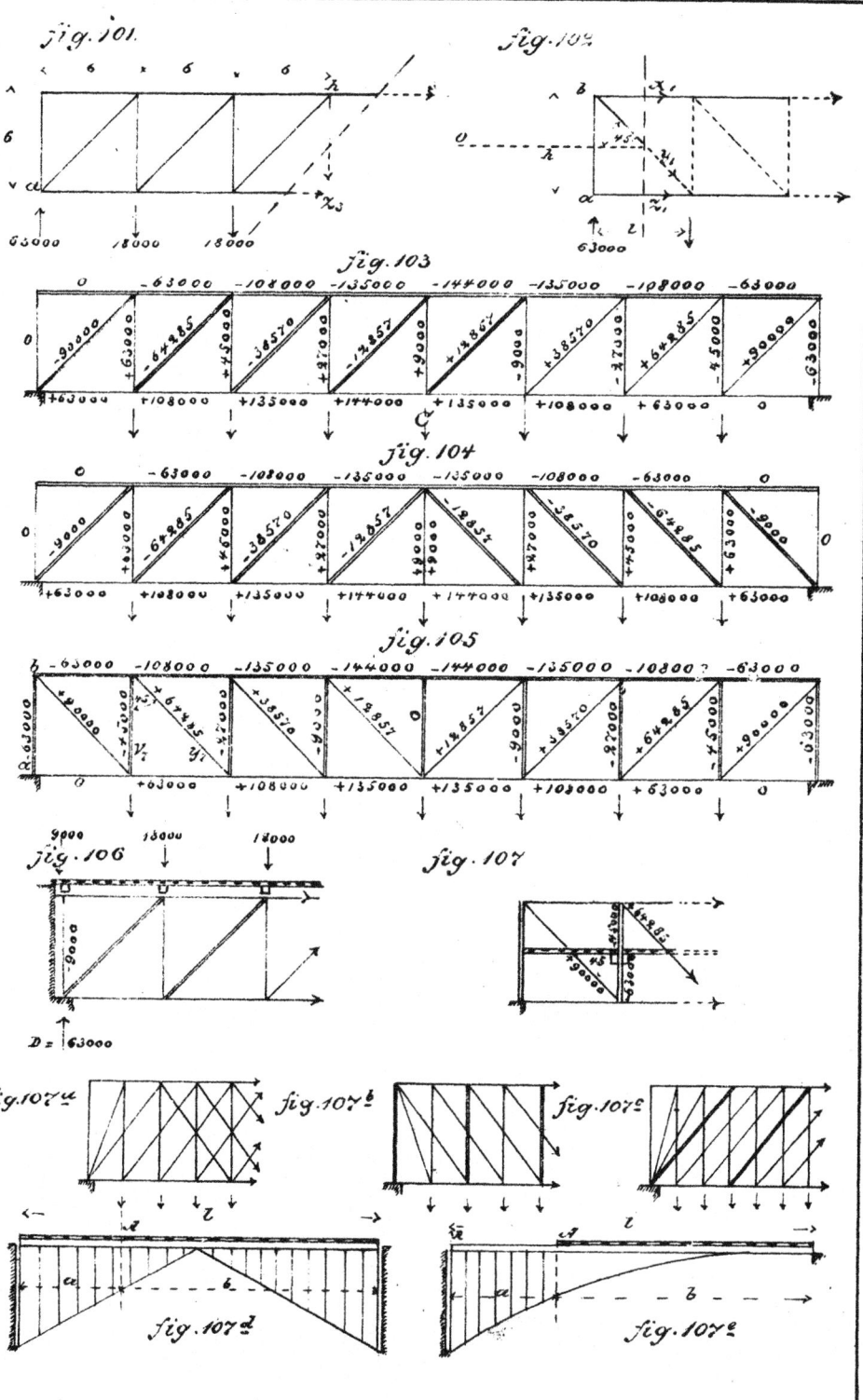

GENERAL REMARKS.

the strain in flanges, in laying the skeletons together, the covering parts of the flanges can be added, as shown in Sect. II. on the isometrical truss, Fig. 146.*

In the same way, by observation of the angles, this method can be applied to lattice systems.

107^c.] When, in Fig. 107^d, q is the weight per unit of length (foot), so, for an equally-distributed load, is $\frac{q \cdot l}{2}$ the shearing strain on the abutment, and at a point, A, the shearing strain =

$$q \cdot \frac{a+b}{2} - q \cdot a = \frac{q}{2}(b-a);$$

but at the centre = 0.

107^d.] When the greater segment of a girder is loaded (Fig. 107^e), the shearing strain at a point, A, is

$$q \cdot \frac{b^2}{2 \cdot l} = \text{the reaction, } R, \text{ of the abutment.}$$

This is the shearing strain throughout the segment a, and increases, when the load moves forward, in the same ratio as the ordinates of a parabola.

Subtracting the former quantity from the latter—*i. e.,*

$$\frac{q \cdot b^2}{2 \cdot l} - \frac{q}{2} \cdot (b-a) = q \cdot \frac{a^2}{2 \cdot l},$$

showing that the shearing strain is greater when, instead of the whole girder, the greater segment is loaded; and this quantity is the shearing strain throughout the segment b when the shorter segment, a, is loaded. (Mr. Stoney.)†

[Plates 16 and 17—embracing Figs. 89 to 107.]

---

* Isometrical Truss Bridge Company, Pottstown, Pa.

† Mr. Shreve, in Van Nostrand's "Eclectic Engineering Magazine," No. xx., August, 1870; Vol. III., page 193.

E. COMPARATIVE TABLES OF RESULTING STRAINS FOR A PERMANENT LOAD.

(*To Derive the Strains without Special Calculation.*)

I. SYSTEM OF RIGHT-ANGLED TRIANGLES.

a. *Single System*—oblique braces, vertical tie-rods, Fig. 108. (Howe truss.)

1. Through Bridge (over-grade bridge).

p signifies the load and weight for one-half panel; therefore $2p$ is the vertical strain at each apex.

For a full load, denoting the number of panels in one-half of the girder with n (here $= 5$), and the respective panels from centre of truss toward the end with x,

$$H_0 = +2p; \qquad H_x = +(2x+1).p; \qquad H_n = o;$$

$$D_x = -(2x-1)p \cdot \frac{d}{h}; \qquad S_x = +[n^2 - (x-1)^2]\, p \cdot \frac{b}{h};$$

$$P_x = -S(x+1) = -(n^2 - x^2)\, p \cdot \frac{b}{h};$$

2. Deck Bridge (under-grade bridge).

Plate 18, Fig. 108. Here the tension in the vertical connections (tie-rods) will be diminished each $2p$; *i. e.*, in the skeleton (Fig. 108),

$$H_0 = o; \qquad H = +p; \qquad H_2 = +3p; \qquad H_3 = +5p, \text{ etc.}$$

The vertical post on the abutment will have the compression $= -p$.

In the strain in flanges and oblique braces there will be no difference.

b. *Single System*—vertical braces, oblique tie-rods. (Fig. 109.)

1. Through Bridge.

For a full load,

$$H_0 = o; \qquad H_x = -(2x-1).p;$$

$$D_x = +(2x-1)\,p\,\frac{d}{h}; \qquad p_x = -[n^2 - (x-1)^2]\, p \cdot \frac{b}{h};$$

SYSTEM OF RIGHT-ANGLED TRIANGLES.

$$S_x = + P(x+1) = + (n^2 - x^2) p \cdot \frac{b}{h}.$$

2. Deck Bridge.

[109.] The strain in the vertical braces will be increased each $-2p$, so that in the skeleton (Fig. 109),

$$H_0 = -2p; \quad H_1 = -3p; \quad H_2 = -5p, \text{ and so on.}$$

The compression in the vertical post on the abutment will be increased by p; therefore

$$H_5 = -10p.$$

c. Combined System.

[110ª.] 1. For a full load by a through bridge (Fig. 110ª), the tension in the vertical connections all the same, or

$$H_x = + p.$$

The vertical post on the abutment has the compression,

$$H_n = -(n - \tfrac{1}{2}) p.$$

For any one panel the tension and compression in the crossing diagonals, and also the strain in the upper or lower flange, is the same—*i. e.*,

$$D_x = \pm (x - \tfrac{1}{2}) p \cdot \frac{d}{h};$$

$$P_x = S_x = \pm \left(n^2 - \frac{x^2 + (x-1)^2}{2} \right) \cdot p \cdot \frac{b}{h}.$$

2. For a deck-bridge changes the tension $+ p$ in the vertical connections to compression, or $- p$.

[110ª.] The compression in the vertical post on the abutment will be increased by $-p$; therefore in the above skeleton,

$$H_5 = -5\tfrac{1}{2} \cdot p.$$

3. For the system of right-angled triangles, when the connecting [110ª.] of cross-beams is not on the top or bottom, but between both on the verticals, the calculation for the part of the vertical above the connection is the same as under 1, and for the lower part of the vertical beneath the connection, the same as under 2.

For the rest the calculation is as under 1.

II. SYSTEM OF ISOSCELES BRACING.

(Load Permanent and Equally Distributed.)

a. *Single System* (triangular truss).

Plate 19,] 1. A loaded apex at the centre. (Fig. 111.)
Fig. 111.] The number of panels extended as occasion requires.

In general, each pair of diagonals from centre to abutment increases by $W \cdot \dfrac{d}{h}$ (*i. e.*, $W \sec \alpha$).

112.] 2. An unloaded apex at the centre. (Fig. 112.)

Each pair of diagonals from centre to abutment increases by $W \cdot \dfrac{d}{h}$.

When each diagonal represents one panel $= b$, and the number of panels $= n$ for one-half of the truss, counting from centre to abutment, there results the strain in flanges for an even 113.] n, say $n = 6$, and a loaded apex at the centre (Fig. 113), or 114.] an unloaded apex at the centre (Fig. 114).

For an uneven n, say $n = 7$, and a loaded apex at the centre 115.] (see Fig. 115); and for an uneven n, say $n = 7$, but an un- 116.] loaded apex at the centre (see Fig. 116).

b. *Combined System* (isometrical truss).

117.] A loaded apex at the centre, and $n = 6$ (Fig. 117).

For a full load in the xth panel the tension in the tie-rod or $D_x = + x \cdot \dfrac{W}{4} \cdot \dfrac{d}{h}$, and the compression of diagonal, $D_z = -(x-1) \dfrac{W}{4} \cdot \dfrac{d}{h}$.

The strains for this figure (where $n = 6$) will also be obtained by laying the figures 113 and 114 (A and B) together, making there $\dfrac{W}{4}$, instead of $\dfrac{W}{2}$, and adding the strains in flanges where they cover each other.

[Plates 18 and 19—embracing Figs. 108 to 117.]

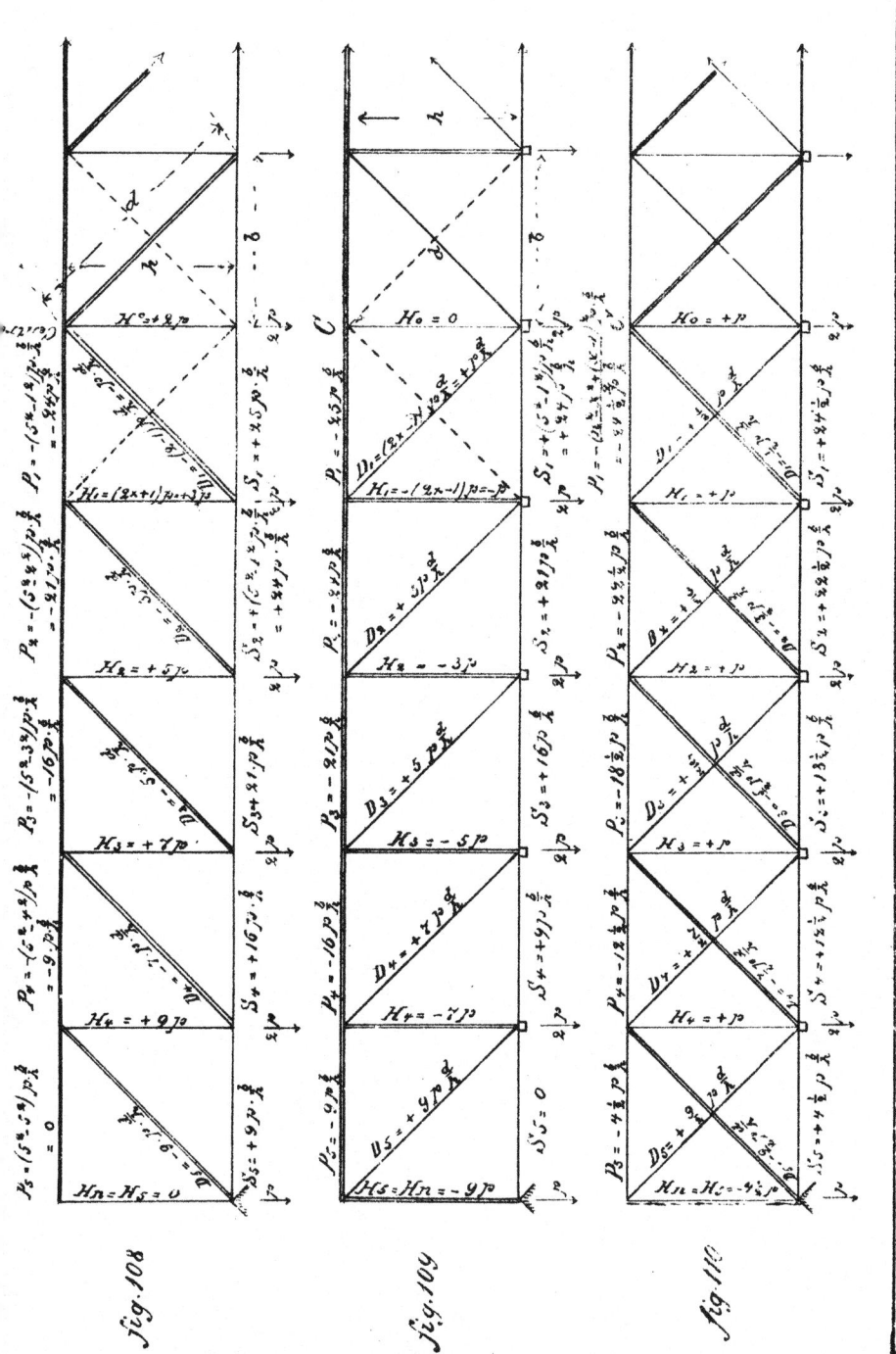

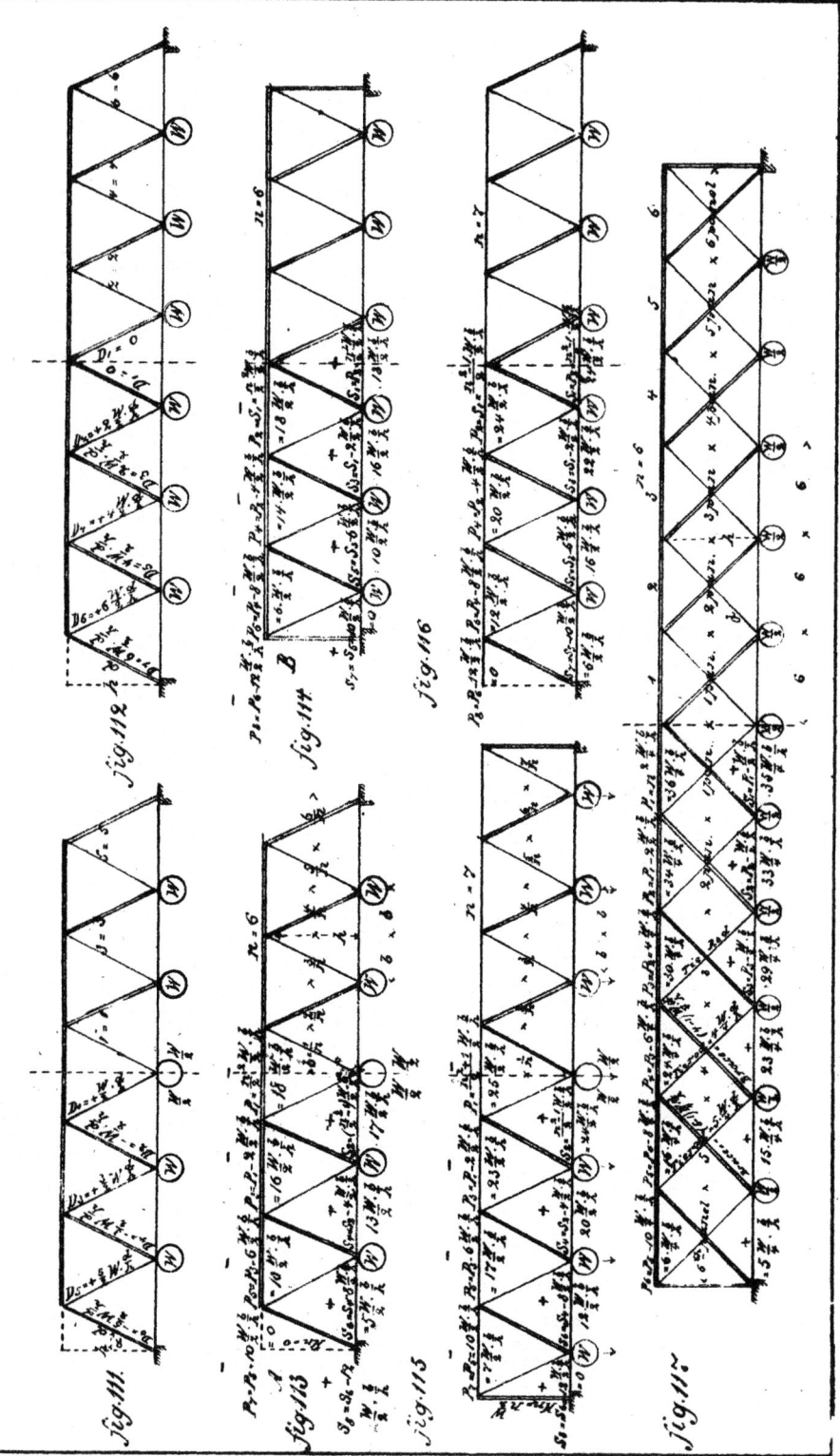

SECTION II.

GIRDERS CALCULATED FOR COMBINED (PERMANENT AND ROLLING) LOAD.

A. GIRDERS WITH PARALLEL TOP AND BOTTOM FLANGES.

I. *THE RIGHT-ANGLED SYSTEM.*

For the strain in flanges I refer to the preceding. It needs no repetition, as the strain in flanges is the largest for a full (permanent) load. (Figs. 108 to 117.)

As mentioned at the close of Sect. I. (General Remarks), the influence of a rolling load upon braces and tie-rods is very essential, and it is greatest when a traversing train of uniform density reaches the centre of the bridge.

Plate 20, Fig. 118.] For explanation we choose the diagonal y_3 in Fig. 118. q is the rolling load (traversing train) for one panel; p is the permanent load (weight of structure); so, again, is (see Figs. 81 and 94),

$$0 = -y_3 \cdot \sin \varphi - D \cdot \infty + \left(\frac{p}{2} + \frac{q}{2}\right) \infty + (p+q) \infty + (p+q) \infty,$$

or I. $\quad 0 = -y_3 \cdot \sin \varphi - D + (p+q) + (p+q) + \left(\frac{p}{2} + \frac{q}{2}\right)$

(rot. $r \cdot o$).

As before, $y_3 \cdot \sin \varphi$ is the vertical component of y_3, and D is the reaction of abutment, or

$D_1 = (p+q) \; (\tfrac{1}{8} + \tfrac{2}{8} + \tfrac{3}{8} + \tfrac{4}{8} + \tfrac{5}{8} + \tfrac{6}{8} + \tfrac{7}{8} + \tfrac{4}{8})$. (Fig. 119.)

II. $D = (p+q) \; (\tfrac{1}{8} + \tfrac{2}{8} + \tfrac{3}{8} + \tfrac{4}{8} + \tfrac{5}{8} + \tfrac{6}{8} + \tfrac{7}{8})$. (See Fig. 89.)

We include the value of D_1 in Equation I., so that the influence of each fraction of rolling load and permanent load upon D may be visible in its proper place.

III. $0 = -y_3 . \sin \varphi - (p+q) [(\frac{1}{8} + \frac{2}{8} + \frac{3}{8} + \frac{4}{8} + \frac{5}{8}) + (\frac{6}{8} - 1) + (\frac{7}{8} - 1) + (\frac{4}{8} - \frac{1}{2})]$,

or $0 = -y_3 . \sin \varphi - (p+q) [(\frac{1}{8} + \frac{2}{8} + \frac{3}{8} + \frac{4}{8} + \frac{5}{8}) - (1 - \frac{6}{8}) - (1 - \frac{7}{8})]$;

and now, separating the members containing the permanent load, p, from those containing the rolling load, q, and separating also the positive and negative members of the movable load,

$0 = -y_3 . \sin \varphi - p [\frac{1}{8} + \frac{2}{8} + \frac{3}{8} + \frac{4}{8} + \frac{5}{8} - (1 - \frac{6}{8}) - (1 - \frac{7}{8})]$;
$\quad - q (\frac{1}{8} + \frac{2}{8} + \frac{3}{8} + \frac{4}{8} + \frac{5}{8}) + q [(1 - \frac{6}{8}) + (1 - \frac{7}{8})]$.

In this equation may be neglected at one time the positive part, and at another time the negative part, of the movable load, q, and the maximum and minimum strain for y will be obtained, viz.:

I. $0 = -y_3 . \sin \varphi - p (\frac{1.5}{8} - \frac{2}{8} - \frac{1}{8}) - q . \frac{1.5}{8}$ (max. compr.).

II. $0 = -y_3 . \sin \varphi - p (\frac{1.5}{8} - \frac{2}{8} - \frac{1}{8}) + q (\frac{2}{8} + \frac{1}{8})$ (min. compr.),

or when the factor of q is greater than the factor of p, then it will be the maximum tension in this diagonal.

In Equation III. the fraction to the right is

$$(p + q) (\tfrac{4}{8} - \tfrac{1}{2}) = 0;$$

120.] therefore we introduce again D instead of D_1, and find from Fig. 120, under the same supposition of $x = \infty$ for the vertical rod V_3,

$$0 = + V_3 \infty - D \infty + (p + q) \infty,$$

or $\qquad 0 = + V_3 - D + (p + q) + (p + q)$,

differing from the equation for y only in so far as here is V instead of $-y \sin \varphi$.

Example.—Calculation of diagonals and verticals for a combined load:

121.]   Length of truss = 48 feet;   (Fig. 121.)
       8 panels, each 6 feet = l;
       height = 6 feet = h;
       permanent load = 3000 lbs. per panel = p;
       rolling load = 15000 lbs. per panel = q.

THE RIGHT-ANGLED SYSTEM.

The load being connected to the lower apexes, the pressure, D, of supports from Fig. 89 = 63000 lbs.

122.] Fig. 122 gives the equations,

$$0 = -y_1 \cdot \sin 45 - D \text{ (rot. } r.o\text{)};$$
$$0 = -y_1 \cdot 0{,}7 - 63000;$$

or
$$y_1 = -\frac{63000}{0{,}7} = -90000.$$

123.] From Fig. 123 we have

$$0 = -y_2 \cdot 0{,}7 - D + (p+q),$$

and including D combined with $p+q$ on its proper place,

$$0 = -y_2 \cdot 0{,}7 - (p+q)\,[\tfrac{1}{8} + \tfrac{2}{8} + \tfrac{3}{8} + \tfrac{4}{8} + \tfrac{5}{8} + \tfrac{6}{8} + (\tfrac{7}{8}-1)],$$

or $0 = -y_2 \cdot 0{,}7 - (p+q)\,[\tfrac{1}{8} + \tfrac{2}{8} + \tfrac{3}{8} + \tfrac{4}{8} + \tfrac{5}{8} + \tfrac{6}{8} - (1-\tfrac{7}{8})];$

$0 = -y_2 \cdot 0{,}7 - p\,(\tfrac{1}{8} + \tfrac{2}{8} + \tfrac{3}{8} + \tfrac{4}{8} + \tfrac{5}{8} + \tfrac{6}{8} - \tfrac{1}{8}) - q\,(\tfrac{1}{8} + \tfrac{2}{8} + \tfrac{3}{8} + \tfrac{4}{8} + \tfrac{5}{8} + \tfrac{6}{8}) - q\,(-\tfrac{1}{8});$

$$0 = -y_2 \cdot 0{,}7 - p \cdot \tfrac{20}{8} - q \cdot \tfrac{21}{8} + q \cdot \tfrac{1}{8},$$

and from this the two equations,

1.) $0 = -y_2 \cdot 0{,}7 - p \cdot \tfrac{20}{8} - q \cdot \tfrac{21}{8},\quad$ or $y_2 \cdot 0{,}7 = -3000 \times \tfrac{20}{8} - 15000 \times \tfrac{21}{8}.$

2.) $0 = -y_2 \cdot 0{,}7 - p \cdot \tfrac{20}{8} + q \cdot \tfrac{1}{8},\quad$ or $y_2 \cdot 0{,}7 = -3000 \times \tfrac{20}{8} + 15000 \times \tfrac{1}{8}.$

$\quad$ I. $y_2 = -66964$ (max. compr.);

$\quad$ II. $y_2 = -8036$ (min. compr.).

124.] Fig. 124 gives

$$0 = -y_3 \cdot 0{,}7 - D + (p+q) + (p+q);$$

$0 = -y_3 \cdot 0{,}7 - (p+q)\,[\tfrac{1}{8} + \tfrac{2}{8} + \tfrac{3}{8} + \tfrac{4}{8} + \tfrac{5}{8} + (\tfrac{6}{8}-1) + (\tfrac{7}{8}-1)];$

$0 = -y_3 \cdot 0{,}7 - (p+q)\,[\tfrac{1}{8} + \tfrac{2}{8} + \tfrac{3}{8} + \tfrac{4}{8} + \tfrac{5}{8} - (1-\tfrac{6}{8}) - (1-\tfrac{7}{8})];$

$0 = -y_3 \cdot 0{,}7 - (p+q)\,(\tfrac{1}{8} + \tfrac{2}{8} + \tfrac{3}{8} + \tfrac{4}{8} + \tfrac{5}{8} - \tfrac{2}{8} - \tfrac{1}{8});$

$$0 = -y_3 \cdot 0{,}7 - p \cdot \tfrac{12}{8} - q \cdot \tfrac{15}{8} + q \cdot \tfrac{3}{8};$$

1.) $0 = -y_3 \cdot 0{,}7 - p \cdot \tfrac{12}{8} - q \cdot \tfrac{15}{8};$

2.) $0 = -y_3 \cdot 0{,}7 - p \cdot \tfrac{12}{8} + q \cdot \tfrac{3}{8}.$

62 THE THEORY OF STRAINS.

$\quad$ I. $\ y_3 = -46608;$

$\quad$ II. $\ y_3 = +1608.$

For further equations, sketches will not be necessary, and they may be written in reduced forms.

$$0 = -y_4 \cdot 0{,}7 - D + (p+q) + (p+q) + (p+q);$$
$$0 = -y_4 \cdot 0{,}7 - (p+q)(\tfrac{1}{8} + \tfrac{2}{8} + \tfrac{3}{8} + \tfrac{4}{8} - \tfrac{3}{8} - \tfrac{2}{8} - \tfrac{1}{8});$$
$$0 = -y_4 \cdot 0{,}7 - p \cdot \tfrac{4}{8} - q \cdot \tfrac{10}{8} + q \cdot \tfrac{6}{8}.$$
$\quad$ 1.) $\ 0 = -y_4 \cdot 0{,}7 - p \cdot \tfrac{4}{8} - q \cdot \tfrac{10}{8};$

$\quad$ 2.) $\ 0 = -y_4 \cdot 0{,}7 - p \cdot \tfrac{4}{8} + q \cdot \tfrac{6}{8}.$

$\qquad$ I. $\ y_4 = +13930;$

$\qquad$ II. $\ y_4 = -28930.$

$$0 = -y_5 \cdot 0{,}7 - D + (p+q) + (p+q) + (p+q) + (p+q) + (p+q);$$
$$0 = -y_5 \cdot 0{,}7 - (p+q)(\tfrac{1}{8} + \tfrac{2}{8} + \tfrac{3}{8} - \tfrac{4}{8} - \tfrac{3}{8} - \tfrac{2}{8} - \tfrac{1}{8});$$
$$0 = -y_5 \cdot 0{,}7 + p \cdot \tfrac{4}{8} - q \cdot \tfrac{6}{8} + q \cdot \tfrac{10}{8}.$$
$\quad$ 1.) $\ 0 = -y_5 \cdot 0{,}7 + p \cdot \tfrac{4}{8} - q \cdot \tfrac{6}{8};$

$\quad$ 2.) $\ 0 = -y_5 \cdot 0{,}7 + p \cdot \tfrac{4}{8} + q \cdot \tfrac{10}{8}.$

$\qquad$ I. $\ y_5 = -13930;$

$\qquad$ II. $\ y_5 = +28930.$

$$0 = -y_6 \cdot 0{,}7 - (p+q)(\tfrac{1}{8} + \tfrac{2}{8} - \tfrac{5}{8} - \tfrac{4}{8} - \tfrac{3}{8} - \tfrac{2}{8} - \tfrac{1}{8});$$
$$0 = -y_6 \cdot 0{,}7 + p \cdot \tfrac{12}{8} - q \cdot \tfrac{3}{8} + q \cdot \tfrac{15}{8}.$$
$\quad$ 1.) $\ 0 = -y_6 \cdot 0{,}7 + p \cdot \tfrac{12}{8} - q \cdot \tfrac{3}{8};$

$\quad$ 2.) $\ 0 = -y_6 \cdot 0{,}7 + p \cdot \tfrac{12}{8} + q \cdot \tfrac{15}{8}.$

$\qquad$ I. $\ y_6 = -1608;$

$\qquad$ II. $\ y_6 = +46608.$

$$0 = -y_7 \cdot 0{,}7 - (p+q)(\tfrac{1}{8} - \tfrac{6}{8} - \tfrac{5}{8} - \tfrac{4}{8} - \tfrac{3}{8} - \tfrac{2}{8} - \tfrac{1}{8});$$
$$0 = -y_7 \cdot 0{,}7 + p \cdot \tfrac{20}{8} - q \cdot \tfrac{1}{8} + q \cdot \tfrac{21}{8}.$$
$\quad$ 1.) $\ 0 = -y_7 \cdot 0{,}7 + p \cdot \tfrac{20}{8} - q \cdot \tfrac{1}{8};$

$\quad$ 2.) $\ 0 = -y_7 \cdot 0{,}7 + p \cdot \tfrac{20}{8} + q \cdot \tfrac{21}{8}.$

THE RIGHT-ANGLED SYSTEM.

$$\text{I.} \quad y_7 = + 8036;$$
$$\text{II.} \quad y_7 = + 66964.$$

$$0 = -y_8 \cdot 0{,}7 - (p+q)(-\tfrac{7}{8} - \tfrac{6}{8} - \tfrac{5}{8} - \tfrac{4}{8} - \tfrac{3}{8} - \tfrac{2}{8} - \tfrac{1}{8});$$
$$0 = -y_8 \cdot 0{,}7 + p \cdot \tfrac{28}{8} + q \cdot \tfrac{28}{8}.$$

1.) $\quad y_8 = \dfrac{p+q}{0{,}7} \times \tfrac{28}{8}.$

$$\text{I.} \quad y_8 = + 90000.$$

In the preceding examples, as already stated, the value of vertical V can be easily obtained from the strain in the diagonals; so for V_3, making the character (symbol) reversed.

$$V_3 = + y_3 \cdot 0{,}7 = 46608 \times 0{,}7 = + 32625,$$
and $\quad V_3 = - y_3 \cdot 0{,}7 = - 1608 \times 0{,}7 = - 1125;$

but the usual way is here preferable.

$$V_0 = 0;$$
$$V_8 = - 63000;$$

and for a deck-bridge would be

$$V_0 = - 9000;$$
$$V_8 = - 72000.$$

125.] $\quad 0 = V_1 - D \text{ (rot. } r.o);$ (Fig. 125.)
$$V_1 = + 63000.$$

126.] $\quad 0 = V_2 - D + (p+q);$ (Fig. 126.)

$$0 = V_2 - (p+q)[\tfrac{1}{8} + \tfrac{2}{8} + \tfrac{3}{8} + \tfrac{4}{8} + \tfrac{5}{8} + \tfrac{6}{8} + (\tfrac{7}{8} - 1)];$$
$$0 = V_2 - (p+q)[\tfrac{1}{8} + \tfrac{2}{8} + \tfrac{3}{8} + \ldots + \tfrac{6}{8} - (1 - \tfrac{7}{8})];$$
$$0 = V_2 - (p+q)(\tfrac{1}{8} + \tfrac{2}{8} + \tfrac{3}{8} + \ldots + \tfrac{6}{8} - \tfrac{1}{8});$$
$$0 = V_2 - p \cdot \tfrac{20}{8} - q \cdot \tfrac{21}{8} + q \cdot \tfrac{1}{8}.$$

1.) $0 = V_2 - p \cdot \tfrac{20}{8} - q \cdot \tfrac{21}{8},\ $ or $V_2 = - 3000 \times \tfrac{20}{8} - 15000 \times \tfrac{21}{8};$
2.) $0 = V_2 - p \cdot \tfrac{20}{8} + q \cdot \tfrac{1}{8},\ $ or $V_2 = 3000 \times \tfrac{20}{8} + 15000 \times \tfrac{1}{8}.$

$$\text{I.} \quad V_2 = + 46875 \text{ (max. tension)};$$
$$\text{II.} \quad V_2 = + 5625.$$

64   THE THEORY OF STRAINS.

127.] $0 = V_3 - D + (p+q) + (p+q);$ (Fig. 127.)

$0 = V_3 - (p+q)[\tfrac{1}{8} + \tfrac{2}{8} + \tfrac{3}{8} + \tfrac{4}{8} + \tfrac{5}{8} + (\tfrac{6}{8} - 1) + (\tfrac{7}{8} - 1)];$

$0 = V_3 - (p+q)[\tfrac{1}{8} + \tfrac{2}{8} + \tfrac{3}{8} + \tfrac{4}{8} + \tfrac{5}{8} - (1 - \tfrac{6}{8}) - (1 - \tfrac{7}{8})];$

$0 = V_3 - p(\tfrac{1}{8} + \tfrac{2}{8} + \tfrac{3}{8} + \tfrac{4}{8} + \tfrac{5}{8} - \tfrac{2}{8} - \tfrac{1}{8}) - q(\tfrac{1}{8} + \tfrac{2}{8} + \ldots + \tfrac{5}{8}) + q(\tfrac{2}{8} + \tfrac{1}{8});$

$0 = V_3 - p \cdot \tfrac{12}{8} + q \cdot \tfrac{15}{8} - q \cdot \tfrac{3}{8}.$

1.) $0 = V_3 - p \cdot \tfrac{12}{8} + q \cdot \tfrac{15}{8};$

2.) $0 = V_3 - p \cdot \tfrac{12}{8} - q \cdot \tfrac{3}{8}.$

I. $V_3 = +32625$ (max. tension).

II. $V_3 = -1125$ (max. compr.).

$0 = V_4 - D + (p+q) + (p+q) + (p+q);$

$0 = V_4 - (p+q)(\tfrac{1}{8} + \tfrac{2}{8} + \tfrac{3}{8} + \tfrac{4}{8} - \tfrac{3}{8} - \tfrac{2}{8} - \tfrac{1}{8});$

$0 = V_4 - p \cdot \tfrac{4}{8} - q \cdot \tfrac{10}{8} + q \cdot \tfrac{6}{8}.$

1.) $0 = V_4 - p \cdot \tfrac{4}{8} - q \cdot \tfrac{10}{8};$

2.) $0 = V_4 - p \cdot \tfrac{4}{8} + q \cdot \tfrac{6}{8}.$

I. $V_4 = +20250;$

II. $V_4 = -9750.$

$0 = V_5 - D + (p+q) + (p+q) + (p+q) + (p+q);$

$0 = V_5 - (p+q)(\tfrac{1}{8} + \tfrac{2}{8} + \tfrac{3}{8} - \tfrac{4}{8} - \tfrac{3}{8} - \tfrac{2}{8} - \tfrac{1}{8});$

$0 = V_5 + p \cdot \tfrac{4}{8} - q \cdot \tfrac{6}{8} + q \cdot \tfrac{10}{8}.$

1.) $0 = V_5 + p \cdot \tfrac{4}{8} + q \cdot \tfrac{10}{8};$

2.) $0 = V_5 + p \cdot \tfrac{4}{8} - q \cdot \tfrac{6}{8}.$

I. $V_5 = -20250;$

II. $V_5 = +9750.$

$0 = V_6 - (p+q)(\tfrac{1}{8} + \tfrac{2}{8} - \tfrac{5}{8} - \tfrac{4}{8} - \tfrac{3}{8} - \tfrac{2}{8} - \tfrac{1}{8});$

$0 = V_6 + p \cdot \tfrac{12}{8} - q \cdot \tfrac{3}{8} + q \cdot \tfrac{15}{8};$

1.) $0 = V_6 + p \cdot \tfrac{12}{8} - q \cdot \tfrac{3}{8};$

2.) $0 = V_6 + p \cdot \tfrac{12}{8} + q \cdot \tfrac{15}{8}.$

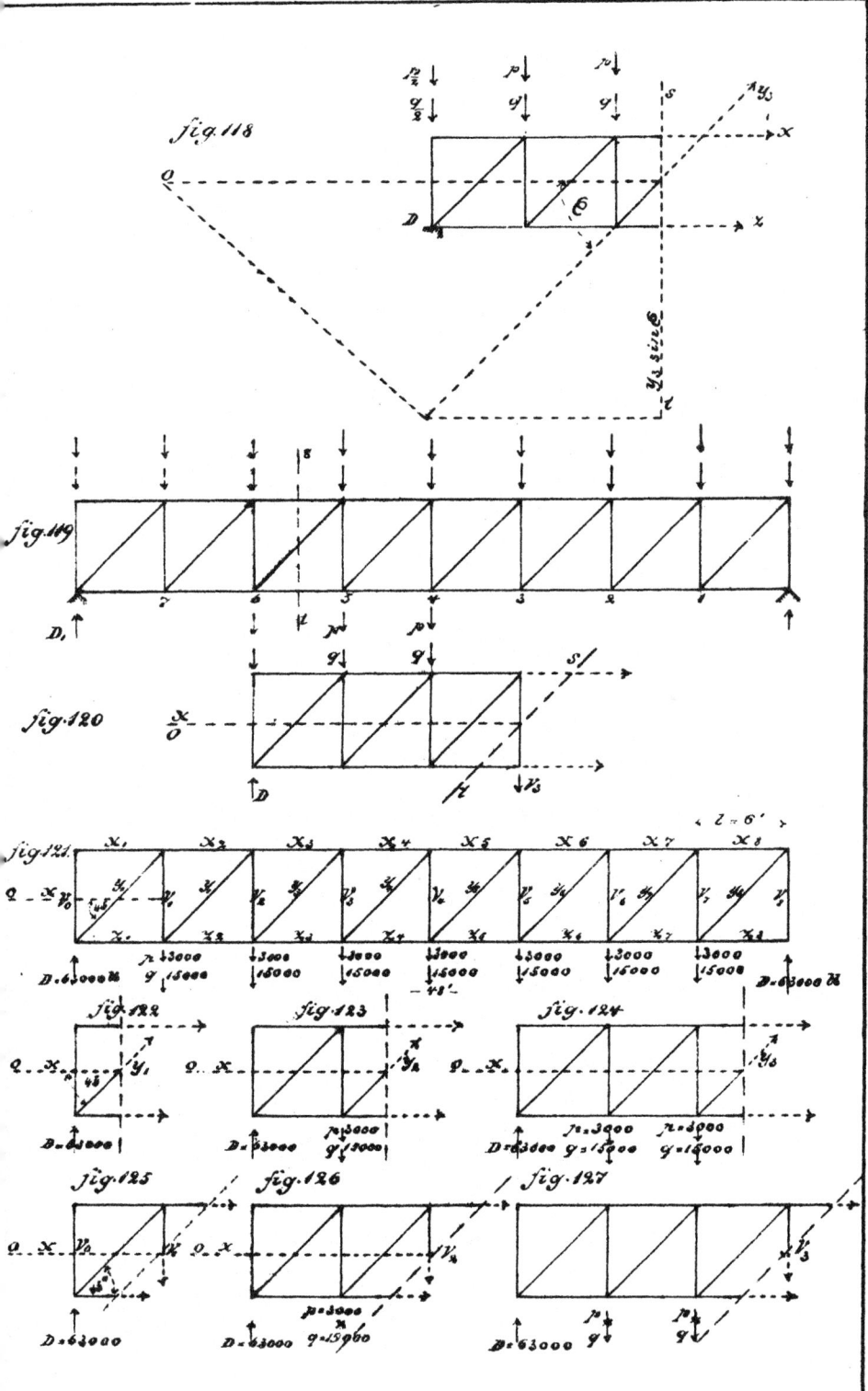

THE RIGHT-ANGLED SYSTEM. 65

$$\text{I. } V_6 = -32625;$$
$$\text{II. } V_6 = +1125.$$

$$0 = V_7 - (p+q)\,(\tfrac{1}{8} - \tfrac{6}{8} - \tfrac{5}{8} - \tfrac{4}{8} - \tfrac{3}{8} - \tfrac{2}{8} - \tfrac{1}{8});$$
$$0 = V_7 + p\cdot\tfrac{20}{8} - q\cdot\tfrac{1}{8} + q\cdot\tfrac{21}{8}.$$

1.) $0 = V_7 + p\cdot\tfrac{20}{8} + q\cdot\tfrac{21}{8}$;

2.) $0 = V_7 + p\cdot\tfrac{20}{8} - q\cdot\tfrac{1}{8}$.

$$\text{I. } V_7 = -46875 \text{ (max. compr.)};$$
$$\text{II. } V_7 = -5625.$$

$$0 = V_8 - (p+q)\,(-\tfrac{7}{8} - \tfrac{6}{8} - \tfrac{5}{8} - \tfrac{4}{8} - \tfrac{3}{8} - \tfrac{2}{8} - \tfrac{1}{8});$$
$$V_8 = -18000 \times \tfrac{28}{8} = -63000.$$

Plate 21, Fig. 128.] The results are combined in the skeleton (Fig. 128); and the strain in flanges, from the example in Sect. I., D., is repeated.

129.] In the symmetrical skeleton (Fig. 129) the tensile strains in the braces are replaced by counter-braces. The verticals are exposed only to tensile strain.

130.] In the same way the skeleton can easily be transformed to a reversed system (Pratt Truss, Fig. 132); but the uniformity in calculation may here, also, be first shown. (Fig. 130.)

$V_8 = -D$, or $0 = -V_8 - (p+q)\,(\tfrac{1}{8} + \tfrac{2}{8} + \tfrac{3}{8} + \tfrac{4}{8} + \tfrac{5}{8} + \tfrac{6}{8} + \tfrac{7}{8})$;
$$V_8 = -(p+q)\,\tfrac{28}{8} = -63000.$$

131.] $\qquad 0 = +y_8\cdot 0{,}7 - D;$ \qquad (Fig. 131.)

$$y_8 = +\frac{63000}{0{,}7} = 90000.$$

132.] The compressive strains of the diagonals in skeleton 132 are replaced by counter-rods.

The verticals or posts are only exposed to compressive strain.

For a deck-bridge, as before shown, the only difference in compression will be in the end-post, which, in Fig. 129 $= -9000$ lbs., and in Fig. 132 $= -72000$ lbs.

[Plates 20 and 21—embracing Figs. 118 to 132.]

II. ISOSCELES BRACING.

1. TRIANGULAR TRUSS.

Plate 22,
Fig. 133.] In Fig. 133, the load on the bottom is sustained one-half by the lower apexes, and one-half, by means of vertical tie-rods, by the upper apexes, distributing the load on the top and bottom chords to equal parts.

The length $= 259$ feet;

the number of triangles, 27;

the depth $= \dfrac{18{,}5}{2}$ tang $60° = 9{,}25 \times 1{,}73 = 16$ feet.

For a more simple calculation the length of 9,25, or one-half of the side of the triangle, may be called 1, or unit; then

The side of the triangle $= 2$;

the height $= 1{,}73$;

the whole length of girder $= 28$.

134.] The load and weight being each 5 tons for every connecting point, the position of the acting forces on the girder will be seen in Fig. 134.

For the calculation of horizontal strains, x and z, in the upper and lower chords, we have for the section, AMN, with M at one time, and N at another, as the point of rotation, and the value of

$$D = 10\left(\tfrac{1}{28} + \tfrac{2}{28} + \ldots + \tfrac{27}{28}\right) = 135 \text{ tons.}$$

The value of $D = 135$ tons, introduced.

135.] $0 = x_4 \cdot 1{,}73 + 135 \times 7 - 10(1 + 2 + 3 + \ldots + 6)$; (Fig. 135.)

$0 = -z_4 \cdot 1{,}73 + 135 \times 8 - 10(1 + 2 + 3 + \ldots + 7)$.

These equations give the result,

$x_4 = -425$ tons;

$z_4 = +462$ "

In the same way for the other strains in x and z.

$0 = x_1 \cdot 1{,}73 + 135 \times 1$;

fig. 128, fig. 129, fig. 130, fig. 131, fig. 132

ISOSCELES BRACING.

$$x_1 = -78 \text{ tons.}$$
$$0 = -z_1 \cdot 1{,}73 + 135 \times 2 - 10 \cdot 1;$$
$$z_1 = +150 \text{ tons.}$$
$$0 = x_2 \cdot 1{,}73 + 135 \times 3 - 10(1+2);$$
$$x_2 = -216 \text{ tons.}$$
$$0 = -z_2 \cdot 1{,}73 + 135 \times 4 - 10(1+2+3);$$
$$z_2 = +277 \text{ tons};$$
$$0 = x_3 \cdot 1{,}73 + 135 \times 5 - 10(1+2+3+4);$$
$$x_3 = -338 \text{ tons};$$
$$0 = -z_3 \cdot 1{,}73 + 135 \times 6 - 10(1+2+3+4+5);$$
$$z_3 = +381 \text{ tons.}$$

Further, also,
$$x_5 = -494 \text{ tons};$$
$$z_5 = +520 \text{ ``}$$
$$x_6 = -540 \text{ ``}$$
$$z_6 = +555 \text{ ``}$$
$$x_7 = -564 \text{ ``}$$
$$z_7 = +566 \text{ ``}$$

Remark.—For an approximate calculation of strain in the top and bottom flanges at the centre, when $10 \times 28 =$ entire load, or $140 =$ one-half of the load,

$$\frac{140 \times \frac{28}{4}}{1{,}73} = 566 \text{ tons.}$$

Calculation of Strains y and u in Diagonals.

The angle of diagonals with a horizontal line being 60°, for the strain in diagonals and tie-rods we have

$$y \cdot \sin 60°, \quad \text{and } u \cdot \sin 60°,$$

or
$$y \cdot 0{,}866, \quad \text{and } u \cdot 0{,}866.$$

68 THE THEORY OF STRAINS.

136,] So for y_4 and u_4 in Figs. 136 and 137,
137.]
$$o = y_4 \cdot 0{,}866 - D + 5 \times 6 + 5 \times 6;$$
$$o = -u_4 \cdot 0{,}866 - D + 5 \times 7 + 5 \times 7.$$

In substituting the permanent and rolling load,

$$D = 5\left(\tfrac{1}{28} + \tfrac{2}{28} + \tfrac{3}{28} + \ldots + \tfrac{27}{28}\right) + 5\left(\tfrac{1}{28} + \tfrac{2}{28} + \tfrac{3}{28} \ldots + \tfrac{27}{28}\right);$$

and combining each time the share of each separate load of the pressure, D, with those directly-produced vertical strains, as in the Howe truss already shown, these equations will be

$$0 = y_4 \cdot 0{,}866 - 5\left[\left(\tfrac{1}{28} + \tfrac{2}{28} + \ldots + \tfrac{21}{28}\right) - \left(1 - \tfrac{22}{28}\right) - \left(1 - \tfrac{23}{28}\right) - \ldots \left(1 - \tfrac{27}{28}\right)\right] - 5\left(\tfrac{1}{28} + \tfrac{2}{28} + \ldots + \tfrac{21}{28}\right)$$
$$+ 5\left[\left(1 - \tfrac{22}{28}\right) + \left(1 - \tfrac{23}{28}\right) + \ldots \left(1 - \tfrac{27}{28}\right)\right];$$

$$0 = -u_4 \cdot 0{,}866 - 5\left[\left(\tfrac{1}{28} + \tfrac{2}{28} + \ldots + \tfrac{20}{28}\right) - \left(1 - \tfrac{21}{28}\right) - \left(1 - \tfrac{22}{28}\right) - \ldots \left(1 - \tfrac{27}{28}\right)\right] - 5\left(\tfrac{1}{28} + \tfrac{2}{28} + \ldots + \tfrac{20}{28}\right)$$
$$+ 5\left[\left(1 - \tfrac{21}{28}\right) + \left(1 - \tfrac{22}{28}\right) + \ldots \left(1 - \tfrac{27}{28}\right)\right];$$

and omitting in these equations at one time the positive $(+)$ members and at another time the negative $(-)$ members which were produced by the rolling load, we have

$$0 = y_4 \cdot 0{,}866 - 5\left(\tfrac{1}{28} + \tfrac{2}{28} + \ldots + \tfrac{21}{28} - \tfrac{6}{28} - \tfrac{5}{28} - \tfrac{4}{28} - \ldots \tfrac{1}{28}\right) + 5\left(\tfrac{1}{28} + \tfrac{2}{28} + \ldots \tfrac{21}{28}\right);$$
$$y_4 = +91 \text{ tons (max.)};$$

$$0 = y_4 \cdot 0{,}866 - 5\left(\tfrac{1}{28} + \tfrac{2}{28} + \ldots + \tfrac{21}{28} - \tfrac{6}{28} - \tfrac{5}{28} - \ldots \tfrac{1}{28}\right) + 5\left(\tfrac{6}{28} + \tfrac{5}{28} + \ldots \tfrac{1}{28}\right);$$
$$y_4 = +39 \text{ tons}.$$

$$0 = -u_4 \cdot 0{,}866 - 5\left(\tfrac{1}{28} + \tfrac{2}{28} + \ldots \tfrac{20}{28} - \tfrac{7}{28} - \tfrac{6}{28} - \ldots \tfrac{1}{28}\right) + 5\left(\tfrac{7}{28} + \tfrac{6}{28} + \ldots \tfrac{1}{28}\right);$$
$$u_4 = -32 \text{ tons}.$$

$$0 = -u_4 \cdot 0{,}866 - 5\left(\tfrac{1}{28} + \tfrac{2}{28} + \ldots \tfrac{20}{28} - \tfrac{7}{28} - \tfrac{6}{28} - \ldots \tfrac{1}{28}\right) - 5\left(\tfrac{1}{28} + \tfrac{2}{28} + \ldots \tfrac{20}{28}\right);$$
$$u_4 = -81 \text{ tons (min.)}.$$

In the same manner as for y_4 and u_4 the equations for the other diagonals are,

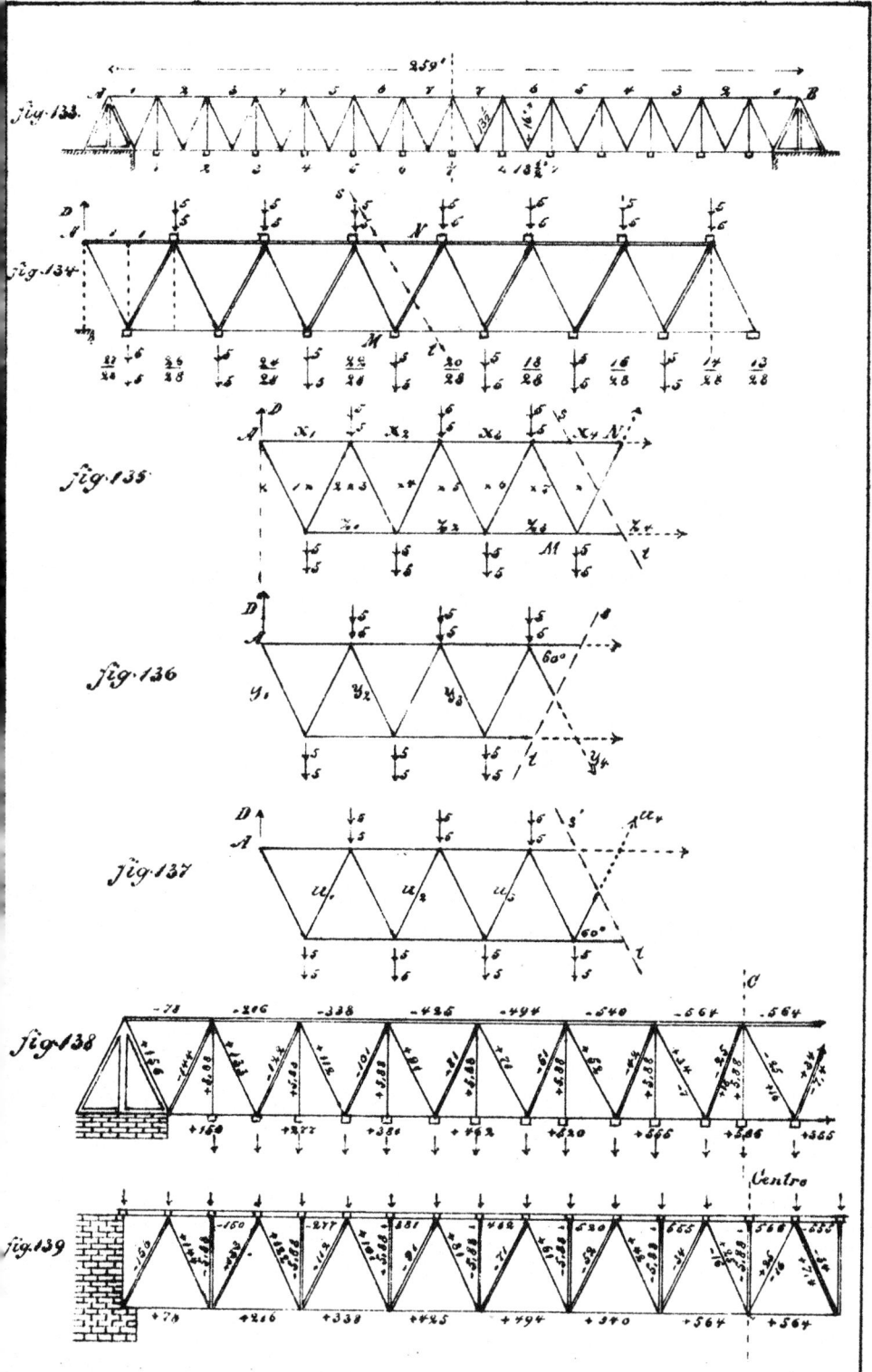

ISOMETRICAL TRUSS.

$0 = y_1 \cdot 0{,}866 - 5 \left(\tfrac{1}{28} + \tfrac{2}{28} + \ldots \tfrac{27}{28}\right) - 5 \left(\tfrac{1}{28} + \tfrac{2}{28} + \ldots \tfrac{27}{28}\right);$

$\qquad y_1 = + 156$ tons, and $y_1 = + 78$ tons.

$0 = - u_1 \cdot 0{,}866 - 5 \left(\tfrac{1}{28} + \tfrac{2}{28} + \ldots \tfrac{26}{28} - \tfrac{1}{28}\right) - 5 \left(\tfrac{1}{28} + \tfrac{2}{28} + \ldots \tfrac{26}{28}\right) + 5 \left(\tfrac{1}{28}\right);$

$\qquad u_1 = - 72$ tons, and $u_1 = - 144$ tons.

$0 = y_2 \cdot 0{,}866 - 5 \left(\tfrac{1}{28} + \tfrac{2}{28} + \ldots \tfrac{25}{28} - \tfrac{2}{28} - \tfrac{1}{28}\right) - 5 \left(\tfrac{1}{28} + \tfrac{2}{28} + \ldots \tfrac{25}{28}\right) + 5 \left(\tfrac{2}{28} + \tfrac{1}{28}\right);$

$\qquad y_2 = + 133$ tons, and $y_2 = + 66$ tons;

$0 = - u_2 \cdot 0{,}866 - 5 \left(\tfrac{1}{28} + \tfrac{2}{28} + \ldots \tfrac{24}{28} - \tfrac{3}{28} - \tfrac{2}{28} - \tfrac{1}{28}\right) - 5 \left(\tfrac{1}{28} + \tfrac{2}{28} + \ldots \tfrac{24}{28}\right) + 5 \left(\tfrac{3}{28} + \tfrac{2}{28} + \tfrac{1}{28}\right);$

$\qquad u_2 = - 59$ tons, and $u_2 = - 122$ tons.

Further,

$\qquad y_3 = + 112,\qquad$ and $y_3 = + 53;$

$\qquad u_3 = - 46,\qquad$ and $u_3 = - 101;$

$\qquad y_5 = + 71,\qquad$ and $y_5 = + 24;$

$\qquad u_5 = - 17,\qquad$ and $u_5 = - 61;$

$\qquad y_6 = + 52,\qquad$ and $y_6 = + 9;$

$\qquad u_6 = - 0{,}8,\qquad$ and $u_6 = - 42;$

$\qquad y_7 = + 34,\qquad$ and $y_7 = - 7{,}4;$

$\qquad u_7 = + 16,\qquad$ and $u_7 = - 25.$

For the other half of the truss the numbers are the same.

The suspenders bear, besides 5 tons moving load, a part of the permanent load; so that, when the weight of track = 24,75 tons, there is for each rod $\dfrac{24{,}75}{28} = 0{,}88$ tons more, or 5,88 tons.

138.] The results of the above calculations in skeleton 138.

139.] When the + and — signs in this skeleton are changed, it represents a truss for a deck-bridge. The suspenders in this case will be studs.

2. ISOMETRICAL TRUSS.

Plate 23,] Calculation of a 143-feet span through bridge. (Fig. 140.)
Fig. 140.

$p =$ permanent load per panel $= 5,5$ tons for two ribs.
$q =$ rolling   "   " $= 17,5$ "   "   "
$\qquad\qquad$ Together $= \overline{23,0}$ tons.

Depth of truss $= 22,52$ feet;
length of diagonals $= 26$ feet;
length of panels $= 13$ feet.

141.] The weight and load of bridge acting upon the system, being $23 \times 10 = 230$ tons, makes for two ribs, but one single system $= \frac{230}{2} = 115$ tons, and it will be similar in Fig. 141.

$$D_1 = (p+q)(\tfrac{1}{11} + \tfrac{3}{11} + \tfrac{5}{11} + \tfrac{7}{11} + \tfrac{9}{11}) + \frac{p+q}{2} \cdot \tfrac{11}{11},$$

or $D = (p+q)(\tfrac{1}{11} + \tfrac{3}{11} + \tfrac{5}{11} + \tfrac{7}{11} + \tfrac{9}{11}) = 52,27$ tons on the left, and $D = 62,73$ tons on the right support.

On account of the symmetry of the systems (one left = the other right), we need only to make a calculation both for diagonals and flanges for one system, adding for the strain in flanges the covering parts of the two combined diagrams. (See Fig. 146.)

a. Calculation of Diagonals.

141.] For the diagonals we have again, as in the foregoing examples (see Howe Truss, Fig. 118), as example for y_4, Fig. 141,

$0 = -y_4 \cdot \sin 60° - D + (p+q) + (p+q) + (p+q)$ (rot. $r \cdot o$);

$0 = -y_4 \cdot 0,866 - (p+q)[\tfrac{1}{11} + \tfrac{3}{11} + (\tfrac{5}{11} - 1) + (\tfrac{7}{11} - 1) + (\tfrac{9}{11} - 1)]$,

or $0 = -y_4 \cdot 0,866 - (p+q)[\tfrac{1}{11} + \tfrac{3}{11} - (1 - \tfrac{5}{11}) - (1 - \tfrac{7}{11}) - (1 - \tfrac{9}{11})]$;

$0 = -y_4 \cdot 0,866 - (p+q)(\tfrac{1}{11} + \tfrac{3}{11} - \tfrac{6}{11} - \tfrac{4}{11} - \tfrac{2}{11})$;

$0 = -y_4 \cdot 0,866 + p \cdot \tfrac{8}{11} - q \cdot \tfrac{4}{11} + q \cdot \tfrac{12}{11}$.

1.) $0 = -y_4 \cdot 0,866 + p \cdot \tfrac{8}{11} - q \cdot \tfrac{4}{11}$;

2.) $0 = -y_4 \cdot 0,866 + p \cdot \tfrac{8}{11} + q \cdot \tfrac{12}{11}$.

I. $y_4 = -2,72$ tons (max. compr.);

II. $y_4 = +26,6$ "   (max. tens.);

CALCULATION OF DIAGONALS.

and according to the theorem in Sect. II., Fig. 80, the strains in diagonals joining at an unloaded point are of the same numerical amount, but of opposite character.

I. $u_4 = + 2{,}72$ tons (max. tens.);

II. $u_4 = + 26{,}6$ " (max. compr.).

In the same way,
$$0 = - y_1 \cdot 0{,}866 - D;$$
$$y_1 = - \frac{52{,}25}{0{,}866} = - 60;$$
$$u_1 = + 60;$$

$0 = - y_2 \cdot 0{,}866 - (p+q) \left[\frac{1}{11} + \frac{3}{11} + \frac{5}{11} + \frac{7}{11} + (\frac{9}{11} - 1)\right];$

$0 = - y_2 \cdot 0{,}866 - p \cdot \frac{14}{11} - q \cdot \frac{16}{11} + q \cdot \frac{2}{11};$

$\qquad y_2 = - 37{,}4, \quad$ and $y_2 = - 4{,}41;$
$\qquad u_2 = + 37{,}4, \quad$ and $u_2 = + 4{,}41;$

$0 = - y_3 \cdot 0{,}866 - (p+q) \left[\frac{1}{11} + \frac{3}{11} + \frac{5}{11} + (\frac{7}{11} - 1) + (\frac{9}{11} - 1)\right];$

$0 = - y_3 \cdot 0{,}866 - p \cdot \frac{3}{11} - q \cdot \frac{9}{11} + q \cdot \frac{6}{11};$

$\qquad y_3 = - 18{,}3, \quad$ and $y_3 = + 10;$
$\qquad u_3 = + 18{,}3, \quad$ and $u_3 = - 10;$

$0 = - y_5 \cdot 0{,}866 - (p+q) \left[\frac{1}{11} + (\frac{3}{11} - 1) + (\frac{5}{11} - 1) + (\frac{7}{11} - 1) + (\frac{9}{11} - 1)\right];$

$0 = - y_5 \cdot 0{,}866 + p \cdot \frac{19}{11} - q \cdot \frac{1}{11} + q \cdot \frac{20}{11};$

$\qquad y_5 = + 47{,}4, \quad$ and $y_5 = + 9{,}2;$
$\qquad u_5 = - 47{,}4, \quad$ and $u_5 = - 9{,}2;$

$0 = - y_6 \cdot 0{,}866 - (p+q) \left[(\frac{1}{11} - 1) + (\frac{3}{11} - 1) + (\frac{5}{11} - 1) + (\frac{7}{11} - 1) + (\frac{9}{11} - 1)\right];$

$0 = - y_6 \cdot 0{,}866 - (p+q) \left(- \frac{10}{11} - \frac{8}{11} - \frac{6}{11} - \frac{4}{11} - \frac{2}{11}\right);$

$\qquad y_6 = + 72{,}1$ tons.

142.] The results for the combined system in skeleton 142.

Remark.—For the compression in the vertical posts o, a and $11 \cdot m'$ on the abutments, we have

$$0{,}866 \times 72{,}1 = 62{,}5 \text{ tons.}$$

72   THE THEORY OF STRAINS.

And for an approximate estimate of strain at the centre of chords,
$23 \times 11 = 253$ the entire weight and load of bridge;
$126{,}5 =$ one-half the weight and load;

$$\frac{126{,}5 \times \frac{143}{4}}{22{,}52} = 200 \text{ tons.}$$

b. CALCULATION OF TOP AND BOTTOM CHORDS (FLANGES).

143.] $0 = x_1 \cdot 22{,}52 + D \cdot o$ (rot. $r \cdot a$, Fig. 143);

$$x_1 = 0;$$

$$0 = -z_1 \cdot 22{,}52 + D \cdot 13 \text{ (rot. } r \cdot 1\text{, Fig. 143);}$$

$$z_1 = \frac{52{,}27 \times 13}{22{,}52} = +30{,}1;$$

$$0 = x_2 \cdot 22{,}52 + D \cdot 26 \text{ (rot. } r \cdot c\text{, Fig. 143);}$$

$$x_2 = -\frac{52{,}27 \times 26}{22{,}52} = -60{,}3;$$

$$0 = -z_2 \cdot 22{,}52 + D \cdot 39 - 23 \times 13 \text{ (rot. } r \cdot 3\text{);}$$

$$z_2 = +\frac{52{,}27 \times 39 - 23 \times 13}{22{,}52} = +77{,}2;$$

144.] $0 = x_3 \cdot 22{,}52 + D \cdot 52 - 23 \times 26$ (rot. $r \cdot e$, Fig. 144);

$$x_3 = -\frac{52{,}27 \times 52 + 23 \times 26}{22{,}52} = -94{,}1;$$

145.] $0 = -z_3 \cdot 22{,}52 + D \cdot 65 - 23(13 + 39)$ (rot. $r \cdot 5$, Fig. 145);

$$z_3 = \frac{52{,}27 \times 65 - 23 \times 52}{22{,}52} = +97{,}8;$$

$$0 = x_4 \cdot 22{,}52 + D \cdot 78 - 23(26 + 52) \text{ (rot. } r \cdot g\text{);}$$

$$x_4 = -\frac{52{,}27 \times 78 + 23 \times 78}{22{,}52} = -101{,}3;$$

$$0 = -z_4 \cdot 22{,}52 + D \cdot 91 - 23(13 + 39 + 65) \text{ (rot. } r \cdot 7\text{);}$$

$$z_4 = \frac{52{,}27 \times 91 - 23 \times 117}{22{,}52} = +91{,}7;$$

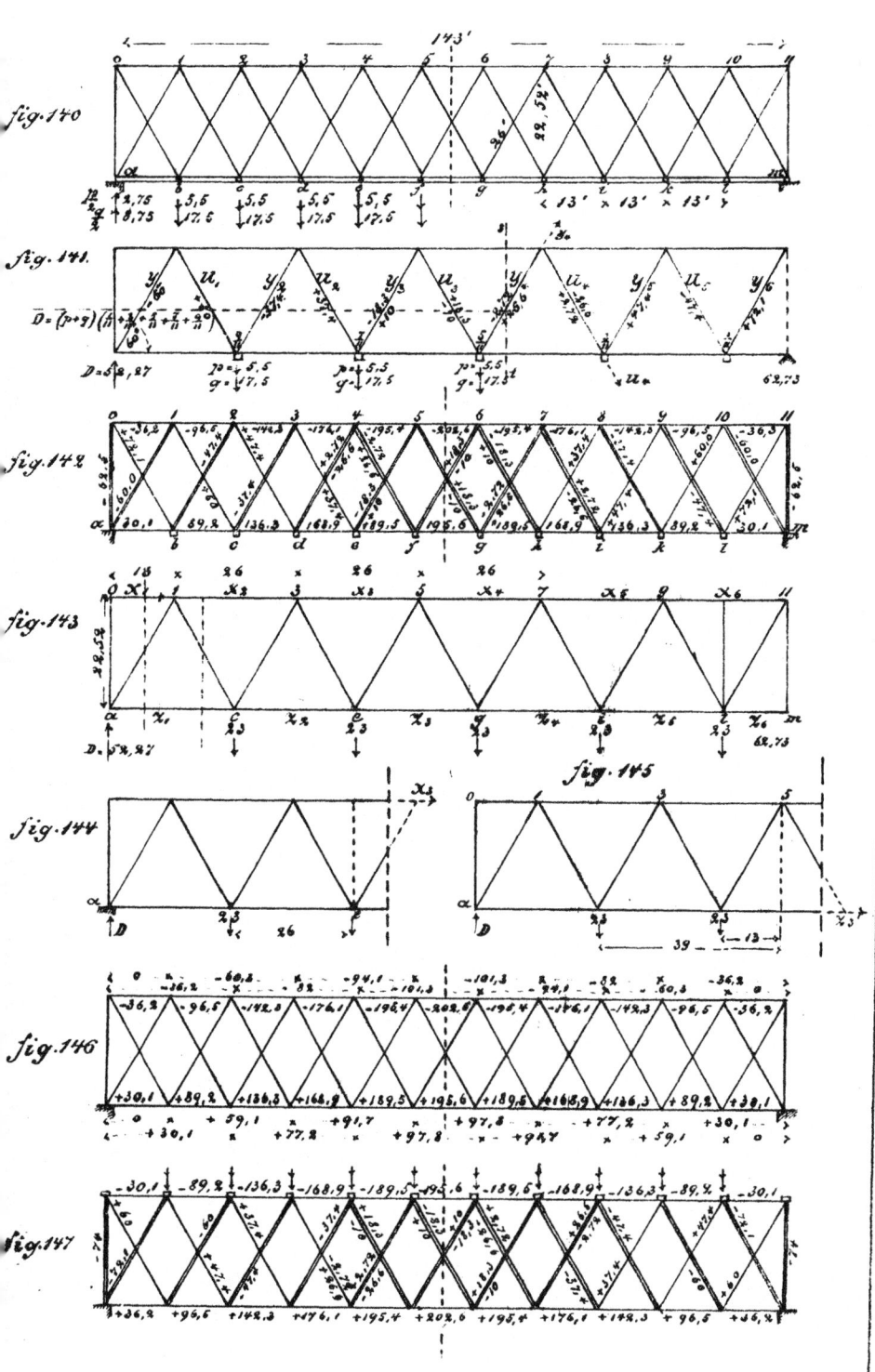

CAMBER IN TRUSSES.

$$0 = x_5 \cdot 22{,}52 + D \cdot 104 - 23\,(26 + 52 + 78)\ (\text{rot. } r \cdot i);$$

$$x_5 = -\frac{52{,}27 \times 104 + 23 \times 156}{22{,}52} = -82{,}0\,;$$

$$0 = -z_5 \cdot 22{,}52 + D \cdot 117 - 23\,(13 + 39 + 65 + 91);$$

$$z_5 = \frac{52{,}27 \times 117 - 23 \times 208}{22{,}52} = +59{,}1\,;$$

$$0 = x_6 \cdot 22{,}52 + D \cdot 130 - 23\,(26 + 52 + 78 + 104)$$

$$x_6 = -\frac{52{,}27 \times 130 + 23 \times 260}{22{,}52} = -36{,}2\,;$$

$$0 = -z_6 \cdot 22{,}52 + D \cdot 143 - 23\,(13 + 39 + 65 + 91 + 117);$$

$$z_6 = \frac{52{,}27 \times 143 - 23 \times 325}{22{,}52} = 0.$$

146.] The results of strain in the top and bottom flanges by the addition of strain for each single system are combined in Fig. 146.

147.] For a deck-bridge the strains in diagonals and flanges result from Fig. 147.

B. CAMBER IN TRUSSES, WITH PARALLEL TOP AND BOTTOM CHORDS.

After the definition of the resulting strains, it is a matter of importance to prevent deflection, which should be provided for in "laying out" the truss.

In the suspension truss (Fig. 10) no special attention to certain camber is required, each pair of tie-rods with combined vertical post forming an independent system, regulated by tie-bolts at the foot of the post.

Plate 24,] In other trusses the difference in the length of
Fig. 148.] diagonals and verticals would form arch-shaped chords, as demonstrated by Fig. 148[a, b].

This arrangement having some difficulties on account of the difference in the length of braces, another and better plan is frequently adopted in making the division of panels in the bottom chord smaller than in the top chord.

149ª.] In this case the vertical connections will lose their parallel direction and intersect at a certain point in the vertical centre line. (Fig. 149.)

Approximately, this can be done by experience, though not sufficiently, in case a certain camber is prescribed.

For a correct calculation the annexed tables, showing the length of arches for degrees, minutes and seconds, will be useful. (See Tables, p. 77, *et seq.*)

Example.—(Truss, Fig. 140.)

Distance of the distinguished points $AB = 143$ feet;

depth of truss $= 22,52$ feet;

number of panels $= 11$.

First we find the radius in Fig. 149ª, according to Sect. I., Fig. B,

The distance AB being $2 \times 71,5 = 143$ feet;

the distance $CI = \dfrac{AD^2}{CD} + CD$,

or $\qquad CI = \dfrac{71,5^2}{0,33333} + 0,33333$;

Diameter $CI = 15336,09 + 0,33333 = 15336,423$;

" $EH = 15336,423 + 2 \times 22,52 = 15381,463$;

or, also, $\qquad$ radius $AM = 7668,211$ feet;

" $FM = 7690,731$ "

By means of the radii for a small camber ($\frac{1}{500}$ of the length), in general the difference of length of the top and bottom flanges may be derived approximately by the difference of the chords AB and FG, viz.:

$$\dfrac{Fd}{AD} = \dfrac{FM}{AM}, \quad \text{or } Fd = AD \cdot \dfrac{FM}{AM};$$

$$Fd = 71,5 \times \dfrac{7690,731}{7668,211};$$

$$Fd = 71,709;$$

i. e., $\qquad FG = 143,418$;

CAMBER IN TRUSSES.   75

and when $AB = 143{,}000$ subtracted,

the difference of chords $= 0{,}418$ ft. $= 5{,}016$ in.,

which, when divided by 11 (*i. e.*, by the number of panels),

$$\frac{5{,}016}{11} = 0{,}456 \text{ in.};$$

therefore, for a camber of 4 inches, the top flanges ought to be made 0,456 inches longer than the bottom flanges; the latter being 13 feet, the top flanges ought to be 13 feet and $\frac{7}{16}$ inches.

For 4 inches camber, a truss of 100 feet length, 9½ feet depth, and 9 panels, the top flanges ought to be 0,339 inches longer than the bottom flanges.

Also, a truss with 14 panels, 9½ feet depth, 5½ feet in bottom flanges, and 5 feet 6¼ inches in top flanges, will have a camber of nearly 6 inches.

A truss of 27 panels, 4 feet depth, 2¼ feet in bottom flanges, and $\frac{1}{48}$ more in top flanges, will give a camber of nearly 2 inches.

In the preceding calculation the definition of the angle a at the centre, M, is avoided, otherwise, by geometrical rule, the arch is in relation to the whole circle as its angle at the centre is to $360°$;

i. e., $\quad \dfrac{\text{arc}}{2 \cdot r \cdot \pi} = \dfrac{a}{360°}, \quad$ or $\quad \dfrac{\text{arc}}{\text{diam.} \times 3{,}14} = \dfrac{a}{360°},$

Now, when not the bottom chord, AB, but for a small camber the arch ACB is accepted to 143 feet, and the defined diameter of the preceding is retained, being in reality smaller, then

$$\frac{143}{15336{,}423 \times 3{,}141} = \frac{a}{360},$$

or $\quad a° = \dfrac{360 \times 143}{15336{,}423 \times 3{,}141} = 1{,}068° = 1° \, 4{,}08';$

therefore for the arch $ACB = x$,

$$\frac{x}{15336{,}423 \times 3{,}141} = \frac{1{,}063}{360},$$

or $\quad x = 142{,}909,$

76 THE THEORY OF STRAINS.

and for the arch $FEG = y$,
$$\frac{y}{15381{,}463 \times 3{,}141} = \frac{1{,}068}{360},$$
or $\quad\quad\quad\quad y = 143{,}329;$

$y - x = 143{,}329 - 142{,}909 = 0{,}420$ feet $= 5{,}04$ inches, the difference in the arches, which, divided by 11, (*i. e.*, by the number of panels),

$\dfrac{5{,}04}{11} = 0{,}458$ inches, the difference in the top and bottom flanges, as before.

More accurate still is the following calculation:

$$\frac{AD}{AM} = \sin\frac{a}{2} = \frac{71{,}5}{7668{,}211} \; 0{,}009342,$$

which gives by tables of nat. sin., cos., etc.,

$$\frac{a}{2} = 32{,}117' \text{ (approx.)}, \text{ or } a = 1°\, 4{,}234' = 1°\, 4'\, 14''.$$

The annexed tables show

$$\begin{aligned}
\text{For } 1° \text{ the figure } & \;0{,}017453 \\
\text{`` } 4' \text{ `` } & \;0{,}001164 \\
\text{`` } 14'' \text{ `` } & \;0{,}000068 \\ \hline
& \;0{,}018685
\end{aligned}$$

which, by multiplication with the radius, $AM = r$, gives arc, $ACB = 0{,}018685 \times 7668{,}211 = 143{,}2805$ feet, and with the radius, $FM = R$,

Arc $FEG = 0{,}018685 \times 7690{,}731 = 143{,}7013$ feet.

The difference of arches, therefore,

$$143{,}7013 - 143{,}2805 = 0{,}4208 \text{ feet.}$$

This result divided by the number of panels $= 11$.

$$\frac{0{,}4208}{11} = 0{,}038 \text{ feet, or } 0{,}456 \text{ inches.}$$

Thus $\quad\dfrac{143{,}2805}{11} = 13{,}025$ feet (the bottom flanges),

and $\quad 13{,}025 + 0{,}038 = 13{,}063$ feet (the top flanges).

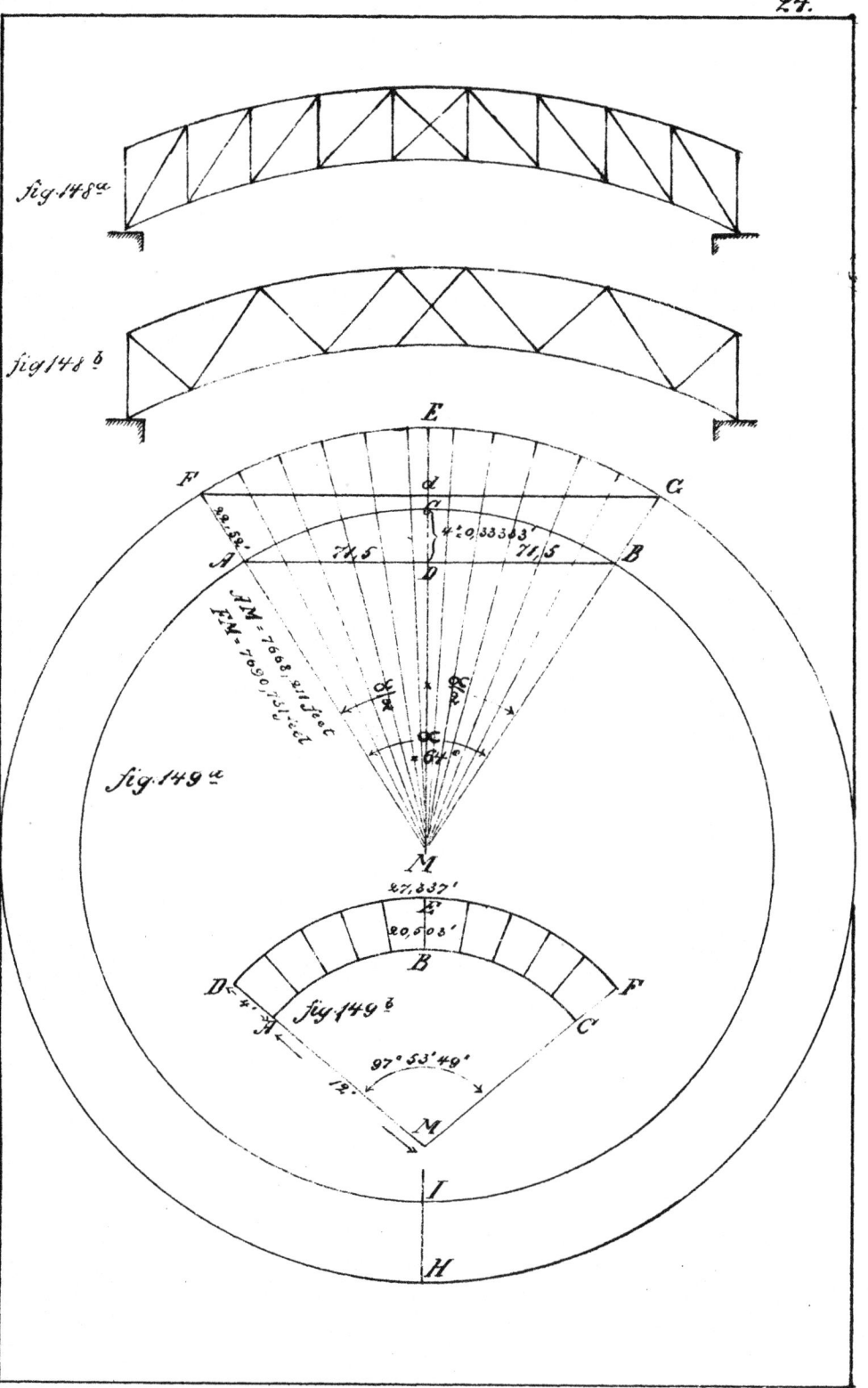

LENGTH OF ARCHES FOR DEGREES, MINUTES, ETC.

TABLES CONTAINING THE LENGTH OF ARCHES FOR DEGREES, MINUTES AND SECONDS, FOR A RADIUS AS UNIT.

LENGTH OF ARCHES FOR EVERY DEGREE.

1	0.017453	46	0.802852	91	1.588250	136	2.373648	181	3.159046
2	0.034907	47	0.820305	92	1.605703	137	2.391101	182	3.176499
3	0.052360	48	0.837758	93	1.623156	138	2.408554	183	3.193953
4	0.069813	49	0.855211	94	1.640610	139	2.426008	184	3.211406
5	0.087267	50	0.872665	95	1.658063	140	2.443461	185	3.228859
6	0.104720	51	0.890118	96	1.675516	141	2.460914	186	3.246312
7	0.122173	52	0.907571	97	1.692969	142	2.478368	187	3.263766
8	0.139626	53	0.925025	98	1.710423	143	2.495821	188	3.281219
9	0.157080	54	0.942478	99	1.727876	144	2.513274	189	3.298672
10	0.174533	55	0.959931	100	1.745329	145	2.530727	190	3.316126
11	0.191986	56	0.977384	101	1.762783	146	2.548181	191	3.333579
12	0.209440	57	0.994838	102	1.780236	147	2.565634	192	3.351032
13	0.226893	58	1.012291	103	1.797689	148	2.583087	193	3.368486
14	0.244346	59	1.029744	104	1.815142	149	2.600541	194	3.385939
15	0.261799	60	1.047198	105	1.832596	150	2.617994	195	3.403392
16	0.279253	61	1.064651	106	1.850049	151	2.635447	196	3.420845
17	0.296706	62	1.082104	107	1.867502	152	2.652901	197	3.438299
18	0.314159	63	1.099557	108	1.884956	153	2.670354	198	3.455752
19	0.331613	64	1.117011	109	1.902409	154	2.687807	199	3.473205
20	0.349066	65	1.134464	110	1.919862	155	2.705260	200	3.490659
21	0.366519	66	1.151917	111	1.937316	156	2.722714	201	3.508112
22	0.383972	67	1.169371	112	1.954769	157	2.740167	202	3.525565
23	0.401426	68	1.186824	113	1.972222	158	2.757620	203	3.543018
24	0.418879	69	1.204277	114	1.989675	159	2.775074	204	3.560472
25	0.436332	70	1.221731	115	2.007129	160	2.792527	205	3.577925
26	0.453786	71	1.239184	116	2.024582	161	2.809980	206	3.595378
27	0.471239	72	1.256637	117	2.042035	162	2.827433	207	3.612832
28	0.488692	73	1.274090	118	2.059489	163	2.844887	208	3.630285
29	0.506145	74	1.291544	119	2.076942	164	2.862340	209	3.647738
30	0.523599	75	1.308997	120	2.094395	165	2.879793	210	3.665191
31	0.541052	76	1.326450	121	2.111848	166	2.897247	211	3.682645
32	0.558505	77	1.343904	122	2.129302	167	2.914700	212	3.700098
33	0.575959	78	1.361357	123	2.146755	168	2.932153	213	3.717551
34	0.593412	79	1.378810	124	2.164208	169	2.949606	214	3.735005
35	0.610865	80	1.396263	125	2.181662	170	2.967060	215	3.752458
36	0.628319	81	1.413717	126	2.199115	171	2.984513	216	3.769911
37	0.645772	82	1.431170	127	2.216568	172	3.001966	217	3.787364
38	0.663225	83	1.448623	128	2.234021	173	3.019420	218	3.804818
39	0.680678	84	1.466077	129	2.251475	174	3.038673	219	3.822271
40	0.698132	85	1.483530	130	2.268928	175	3.054326	220	3.839724
41	0.715585	86	1.500983	131	2.286381	176	3.071780	221	3.857178
42	0.733038	87	1.518436	132	2.303835	177	3.089233	222	3.874631
43	0.750492	88	1.535890	133	2.321288	178	3.106686	223	3.892084
44	0.767945	89	1.553343	134	2.338741	179	3.124139	224	3.909538
45	0.785398	90	1.570796	135	2.356195	180	3.141592	225	3.926991

LENGTH OF ARCHES FOR EVERY DEGREE. (*Continued.*)

226	3.944444	261	4.555309	296	5.166175	331	5.777040
227	3.961897	262	4.572763	297	5.183628	332	5.794493
228	3.979351	263	4.590216	298	5.201081	333	5.811946
229	3.996804	264	4.607669	299	5.218535	334	5.829400
230	4.014257	265	4.625123	300	5.235988	335	5.846853
231	4.031711	266	4.642576	301	5.253441	336	5.864306
232	4.049164	267	4.660029	302	5.270894	337	5.881760
233	4.066617	268	4.677482	303	5.288348	338	5.899213
234	4.084070	269	4.694936	304	5.305801	339	5.916666
235	4.101524	270	4.712389	305	5.323254	340	5.934120
236	4.118977	271	4.729842	306	5.340708	341	5.951573
237	4.136430	272	4.747296	307	5.358161	342	5.969026
238	4.153884	273	4.764749	308	5.375614	343	5.986479
239	4.171337	274	4.782202	309	5.393067	344	6.003933
240	4.188790	275	4.799655	310	5.410521	345	6.021386
241	4.206244	276	4.817109	311	5.427974	346	6.038839
242	4.223697	277	4.834562	312	5.445427	347	6.056293
243	4.241150	278	4.852015	313	5.462881	348	6.073746
244	4.258603	279	4.869469	314	5.480334	349	6.091200
245	4.276057	280	4.886922	315	5.497787	350	6.108652
246	4.293510	281	4.904375	316	5.515240	351	6.126106
247	4.310963	282	4.921829	317	5.532694	352	6.143559
248	4.328417	283	4.939282	318	5.550147	353	6.161012
249	4.345870	284	4.956735	319	5.567600	354	6.178466
250	4.363323	285	4.974188	320	5.585054	355	6.195919
251	4.380776	286	4.991642	321	5.602507	356	6.213372
252	4.398230	287	5.009095	322	5.619960	357	6.230825
253	4.415683	288	5.026548	323	5.637414	358	6.248279
254	4.433136	289	5.044002	324	5.654867	359	6.265732
255	4.450590	290	5.061455	325	5.672320	360	6.283185
256	4.468043	291	5.078908	326	5.689773		
257	4.485496	292	5.096361	327	5.707227		
258	4.502950	293	5.113815	328	5.724680		
259	4.520403	294	5.131268	329	5.742133		
260	4.537856	295	5.148721	330	5.759587		

LENGTH OF ARCHES FOR EVERY MINUTE.

1	0.000291	16	0.004654	31	0.009018	46	0.013381
2	0.000582	17	0.004945	32	0.009308	47	0.013672
3	0.000873	18	0.005236	33	0.009599	48	0.013963
4	0.001164	19	0.005527	34	0.009890	49	0.014254
5	0.001454	20	0.005818	35	0.010181	50	0.014544
6	0.001745	21	0.006109	36	0.010472	51	0.014835
7	0.002036	22	0.006400	37	0.010763	52	0.015126
8	0.002327	23	0.006690	38	0.011054	53	0.015417
9	0.002618	24	0.006981	39	0.011345	54	0.015708
10	0.002909	25	0.007272	40	0.011636	55	0.015999
11	0.003200	26	0.007563	41	0.011926	56	0.016290
12	0.003491	27	0.007854	42	0.012217	57	0.016581
13	0.003782	28	0.008145	43	0.012508	58	0.016872
14	0.004072	29	0.008436	44	0.012799	59	0.017162
15	0.004363	30	0.008727	45	0.013090	60	0.017453

LENGTH OF ARCHES FOR EVERY SECOND.

1	0.000005	16	0.000078	31	0.000150	46	0.000223
2	0.000010	17	0.000082	32	0.000155	47	0.000228
3	0.000015	18	0.000087	33	0.000160	48	0.000233
4	0.000020	19	0.000092	34	0.000165	49	0.000238
5	0.000024	20	0.000097	35	0.000170	50	0.000242
6	0.000030	21	0.000102	36	0.000175	51	0.000247
7	0.000034	22	0.000107	37	0.000179	52	0.000252
8	0.000039	23	0.000112	38	0.000184	53	0.000257
9	0.000044	24	0.000116	39	0.000189	54	0.000262
10	0.000049	25	0.000121	40	0.000194	55	0.000267
11	0.000053	26	0.000126	41	0.000199	56	0.000272
12	0.000058	27	0.000131	42	0.000204	57	0.000276
13	0.000063	28	0.000136	43	0.000209	58	0.000281
14	0.000068	29	0.000141	44	0.000213	59	0.000286
15	0.000073	30	0.000145	45	0.000218	60	0.000291

Mode of Application.—When the angle, a, at the centre, M, of a part of a circle is known, then the radius must be multiplied with the sum of the figures attached to those degrees, minutes and seconds in the tables, and the length of the arch will be obtained.

149^b.] For example, we want to know the length of an arch for 97° 53′ 49″, when the radius of the circle is 12 feet. (Fig. 149^b.)

For a radius as unit, the arch for 97° = 1.692969
" " " " 53′ = 0.015417
" " " " 49″ = 0.000238
                                        —————
                                        1.708624

This, multiplied by the radius, 12, gives 20.503488 feet, the length of the arch ABC, and when multiplied by the radius, 16, the length of arch = 27.337984.

Reversed, when the length of an arch = 98.765432 feet, and the radius of the circle = 20 feet, then for the angle at centre, M,

$$\frac{98.765432}{20} = 4.938272$$

In the table where an arch = 282° = 4.921829
                                        —————
                          Remainder, 0.016443
" " " = 56′ = 0.016290
                                        —————
                          Remainder, 0.000153
" " " = 31″ = 0.000150
                                        —————
                          Balance,   0.000003

therefore the angle = 282° 56′ 31″.

[Plates 22, 23 and 24—embracing Figs. 133 to 149.]

C. PARABOLIC GIRDER OF 48 FEET, OR 16 METER, SPAN.

(With Single Diagonal System.)

Weight of girder = 500 kilograms per meter, or 1000 kilograms on each apex.

Plate 25,] Rolling load = 2500 kilograms per meter, or 5000
Fig. 150.] kilograms on each apex. (Fig. 150.)

151.] The following skeleton (Fig. 151) shows the distribution of weight and load:

For the reactive force, D, of abutments, we have

$$D = 1000\left(\tfrac{1}{8} + \tfrac{2}{8} + \tfrac{3}{8} + \tfrac{4}{8} + \tfrac{5}{8} + \tfrac{6}{8} + \tfrac{7}{8}\right) + 5000\left(\tfrac{1}{8} + \tfrac{2}{8} + \tfrac{3}{8} + \tfrac{4}{8} + \tfrac{5}{8} + \tfrac{6}{8} + \tfrac{7}{8}\right);$$

152.] For the strain in x_1 (Fig. 152) is

$$0 = x_1 \cdot \tfrac{7}{8} + D \cdot 2 \text{ (rot. } r \cdot C);$$

and when the value of D is substituted,

$$0 = x_1 \cdot \tfrac{7}{8} + 1000\left(\tfrac{1}{8} + \tfrac{2}{8} + \tfrac{3}{8} + \tfrac{4}{8} + \tfrac{5}{8} + \tfrac{6}{8} + \tfrac{7}{8}\right)2 + 5000\left(\tfrac{1}{8} + \tfrac{2}{8} + \tfrac{3}{8} + \tfrac{4}{8} + \tfrac{5}{8} + \tfrac{6}{8} + \tfrac{7}{8}\right) \cdot 2;$$

$$x_1 = -48000 \text{ kil.};$$

and for z_1 from the same figure,

$$0 = -z_1 \cdot 0{,}8 + D \cdot 2 \text{ (rot. } r \cdot B);$$

$$0 = -z_1 \cdot 0{,}8 + 1000\left(\tfrac{1}{8} + \tfrac{2}{8} + \ldots + \tfrac{7}{8}\right) \cdot 2 + 5000\left(\tfrac{1}{8} + \tfrac{2}{8} + \ldots + \tfrac{7}{8}\right) \cdot 2;$$

$$z_1 = +52500 \text{ kil.}$$

153.] For V we take as the point of rotation the intersection R of x_1 and z_2, and it is

$$0 = -V_1 \cdot 2{,}8 - D \cdot 0{,}8; \qquad \text{(Fig. 153.)}$$

$$0 = -V_1 \cdot 2{,}8 - 1000\left(\tfrac{1}{8} + \tfrac{2}{8} + \tfrac{3}{8} + \ldots + \tfrac{7}{8}\right) \cdot 0{,}8$$

$$- 5000\left(\tfrac{1}{8} + \tfrac{2}{8} + \tfrac{3}{8} + \ldots + \tfrac{7}{8}\right) \cdot 0{,}8;$$

$$V_1 = -6000 \text{ kil.};$$

154.] For x_2 (rot. $r \cdot E$, Fig. 154) is

$$0 = x_2 \cdot 1{,}5 + D \cdot 4 - 1000 \times 2 - 5000 \times 2,$$

PARABOLIC GIRDER OF 48 FEET SPAN.

or $\quad 0 = x_2 . 1,5 + 1000 \left(\frac{1}{8} + \frac{2}{8} + \ldots \frac{7}{8}\right).4 + 5000 \left(\frac{1}{8} + \frac{2}{8} + \ldots \frac{7}{8}\right).4 - 1000 \times 2 - 5000 \times 2;$

and now, according to the rule formerly given,

$$0 = x_2 . 1,5 + 1000 \left[\left(\frac{1}{8} + \frac{2}{8} + \ldots \frac{6}{8}\right).4 + \left(\frac{7}{8} \times 4 - 2\right)\right];$$
$$+ 5000 \left[\left(\frac{1}{8} + \frac{2}{8} + \ldots \frac{6}{8}\right).4 + \left(\frac{7}{8} \times 4 - 2\right)\right];$$
$$x_2 = -48000 \text{ kil.}$$

154.] For y_2 (rot. $r.R$, Fig. 154) is

$$0 = y_2 . 1,68 - 1000 \left(\frac{1}{8} + \frac{2}{8} + \ldots \frac{7}{8}\right).0,8 - 5000 \left(\frac{1}{8} + \frac{2}{8} + \ldots \frac{7}{8}\right).0,8 + 1000 \times 2,8 + 5000 \times 2,8;$$

$$0 = y_2 . 1,68 - 1000 \left[\left(\frac{1}{8} + \frac{2}{8} + \ldots \frac{6}{8}\right).0,8 - \left(2,8 - \frac{7}{8} \times 0,8\right)\right]$$
$$- 5000 \left(\frac{1}{8} + \frac{2}{8} + \ldots \frac{6}{8}\right).0,8 + 5000 \left(2,8 - \frac{7}{8} \times 0,8\right);$$

and omitting from the movable load at one time the members with the symbol $+$, and at another time with the symbol $-$,

$$0 = y_2 . 1,68 - 1000 \left[\left(\frac{1}{8} + \frac{2}{8} + \ldots \frac{6}{8}\right).0,8 - \left(2,8 - \frac{7}{8} \times 0,8\right)\right]$$
$$- 5000 \left(\frac{1}{8} + \frac{2}{8} + \ldots \frac{6}{8}\right).0,8,$$

or $\quad\quad\quad\quad y_2 = + 6250 \text{ kil.,}$

and $0 = y_2 . 1,68 - 1000 \left[\left(\frac{1}{8} + \frac{2}{8} + \ldots \frac{6}{8}\right).0,8 - \left(2,8 - \frac{7}{8} \times 0,8\right)\right]$
$$+ 5000 \left(2,8 - \frac{7}{8} \times 0,8\right);$$
$$y_2 = - 6250 \text{ kil.}$$

In omitting no member of the first equation, y_2 will $= 0$, as per example for a full load. (See remarks on Parabolic Girders and the Arched Truss.)

For z_2 (rot. $r.B$) and the members in the prescribed form directly arranged, will be from Fig. 154.

$$0 = z_2 . 0,835 + 1000 \left(\frac{1}{8} + \frac{2}{8} + \ldots + \frac{7}{8}\right) 2 + 5000 \left(\frac{1}{8} + \frac{2}{8} + \ldots \frac{7}{8}\right) 2;$$
$$z_2 = + 50300 \text{ kil.}$$

155.] For V_2 (rot. $r.S$) we find from Fig. 155,

$$0 = - V_2 . 8 - 1000 \left[\left(\frac{1}{8} + \frac{2}{8} + \ldots \frac{6}{8}\right).4 - \left(6 - \frac{7}{8} \times 4\right)\right]$$
$$- 5000 \left(\frac{1}{8} + \frac{2}{8} + \ldots \frac{6}{8}\right) + 5000 \left(6 - \frac{7}{8} \times 4\right);$$

F

82   THE THEORY OF STRAINS.

$$0 = -V_2 \cdot 8 - 1000\left[(\tfrac{1}{8} + \tfrac{2}{8} + \ldots \tfrac{6}{8}) \cdot 4 - (6 - \tfrac{7}{8} \times 4)\right] - 5000\,(\tfrac{1}{8} + \tfrac{2}{8} + \ldots \tfrac{6}{8}) \cdot 4;$$

$$V_2 = -7560 \text{ kil.},$$

and $$0 = -V_2 \cdot 8 - 1000\left[(\tfrac{1}{8} + \tfrac{2}{8} + \ldots \tfrac{6}{8}) \cdot 4 - (6 - \tfrac{7}{8} \times 4)\right] + 5000\,(6 - \tfrac{7}{8} \times 4);$$

$$V_2 = +560 \text{ kil.}$$

In the same way we find for the remaining,

$$0 = x_3 \cdot 1,875 + 1000\left[(\tfrac{1}{8} + \tfrac{2}{8} + \ldots \tfrac{5}{8}) \cdot 6 + (\tfrac{6}{8} \times 6 - 2) + (\tfrac{7}{8} \times 6 - 4)\right]$$
$$+ 5000\left[(\tfrac{1}{8} + \tfrac{2}{8} + \ldots \tfrac{5}{8}) \cdot 6 + (\tfrac{6}{8} \times 6 - 2) + (\tfrac{7}{8} \times 6 - 4)\right];$$

$$x_3 = -48000 \text{ kil.};$$

$$0 = y_3 \cdot 5{,}47 - 1000\left[(\tfrac{1}{8} + \tfrac{2}{8} + \ldots \tfrac{5}{8}) \cdot 4 - (8 - \tfrac{6}{8} \times 4) - (6 - \tfrac{7}{8} \times 4)\right]$$
$$- 5000\,(\tfrac{1}{8} + \tfrac{2}{8} + \ldots \tfrac{5}{8}) \cdot 4 + 5000\,(8 - \tfrac{6}{8} \times 4) + 5000\,(6 - \tfrac{7}{8} \times 4);$$

$$y_3 = +6850 \text{ kil.},$$

and $$y_3 = -6850 \text{ ``}$$

$$0 = -z_3 \cdot 1{,}474 + 1000\left[(\tfrac{1}{8} + \ldots \tfrac{6}{8}) \cdot 4 + (\tfrac{7}{8} \times 4 - 2)\right]$$
$$+ 5000\left[(\tfrac{1}{8} + \ldots \tfrac{6}{8}) \cdot 4 + (\tfrac{7}{8} \times 4 - 2)\right];$$

$$z_3 = +48900 \text{ kil};$$

$$0 = -V_3 \cdot 30 - 1000\left[(\tfrac{1}{8} + \ldots \tfrac{5}{8}) \cdot 24 - (28 - \tfrac{6}{8} \times 24) - (26 - \tfrac{7}{8} \times 24)\right]$$
$$- 5000\,(\tfrac{1}{8} + \ldots \tfrac{5}{8}) \cdot 24 + 5000\,(28 - \tfrac{6}{8} \times 24) + 5000\,(26 - \tfrac{7}{8} \times 24);$$

$$V_3 = +1500 \text{ kil.},$$

and $$V_3 = -8500 \text{ ``}$$

$$0 = x_4 \cdot 2 + 1000\left[(\tfrac{1}{8} + \ldots \tfrac{4}{8}) \cdot 8 + (\tfrac{5}{8} \times 8 - 2) + (\tfrac{6}{8} \times 8 - 4) + (\tfrac{7}{8} \times 8 - 6)\right]$$
$$+ 5000\left[(\tfrac{1}{8} + \ldots \tfrac{4}{8}) \cdot 8 + (\tfrac{5}{8} \times 8 - 2) + \tfrac{6}{8} \times 8 - 4) + (\tfrac{7}{8} \times 8 - 6)\right];$$

$$y_4 = -48000 \text{ kil.};$$

$$0 = y_4 \cdot 21{,}2 - 1000\left[(\tfrac{1}{8} + \ldots \tfrac{4}{8}) \cdot 24 - (30 - \tfrac{5}{8} \times 24) - (28 - \tfrac{6}{8} \times 24) - (26 - \tfrac{7}{8} \times 24)\right]$$

PARABOLIC GIRDER OF 48 FEET SPAN.

$$-5000\,(\tfrac{1}{8}+\ldots\tfrac{4}{8})\,.24+5000\,[(30-\tfrac{5}{8}\times 24)+(28-\tfrac{6}{8}\times 24)+(26-\tfrac{7}{8}\times 24)];$$

$$y_4 = +7080 \text{ kil.,}$$

and
$$y_4 = -7080 \text{ "}$$

$$0 = -z_1.1,873 + 1000\,[(\tfrac{1}{8}+\ldots\tfrac{5}{8})\,.6+(\tfrac{6}{8}\times 6-2)+(\tfrac{7}{8}\times 6-4)]$$
$$+5000\,[(\tfrac{1}{8}+\ldots\tfrac{5}{8})\,.6+(\tfrac{6}{8}\times 6-2)+(\tfrac{7}{8}\times 6-4)];$$

$$z_4 = +48100 \text{ kil.}$$

The equations now following are for the section of figure regarded to the right of the cut *st*.

$$0 = -V_4.32 + 1000\,[(\tfrac{1}{8}+\tfrac{2}{8}+\tfrac{3}{8})\,24 - (32-\tfrac{4}{8}\times 24) - (30-\tfrac{5}{8}\times 24) - (28-\tfrac{6}{8}\times 24) - (26-\tfrac{7}{8}\times 24)]$$
$$+5000\,(\tfrac{1}{8}+\tfrac{2}{8}+\tfrac{3}{8})\,24 - 5000\,[(32-\tfrac{4}{8}\times 24)+(30-\tfrac{5}{8}\times 24)+(28-\tfrac{6}{8}\times 24)+(26-\tfrac{7}{8}\times 24)];$$

$$V_4 = +1800 \text{ kil.,}$$

and
$$V_4 = -8800 \text{ "}$$

$$0 = -x_5.1,875 - 1000\,[(\tfrac{1}{8}+\ldots\tfrac{5}{8})\,6+(\tfrac{6}{8}\times 6-2)+(\tfrac{7}{8}\times 6-4)]$$
$$-5000\,[(\tfrac{1}{8}+\ldots\tfrac{5}{8})\,6+(\tfrac{6}{8}\times 6-2)+(\tfrac{7}{8}\times 6-4)];$$

$$x_5 = -48000 \text{ kil.;}$$

$$0 = y_5.21,88 + 1000\,[(\tfrac{1}{8}+\ldots\tfrac{4}{8})\,24 - (30-\tfrac{5}{8}\times 24) - (28-\tfrac{6}{8}\times 24) - 26-\tfrac{7}{8}\times 24)]$$
$$+5000\,(\tfrac{1}{8}+\ldots\tfrac{4}{8})\,24 - 5000\,[(30-\tfrac{5}{8}\times 24)+(28-\tfrac{6}{8}\times 24)+(26-\tfrac{7}{8}\times 24)];$$

$$y_5 = +6850 \text{ kil.,}$$

and
$$y_5 = -6850 \text{ "}$$

$$0 = z_5.1,996 - 1000\,[(\tfrac{1}{8}+\ldots\tfrac{4}{8})\,8+(\tfrac{5}{8}\times 8-2)+(\tfrac{6}{8}\times 8-4)+(\tfrac{7}{8}\times 8-6)]$$
$$-5000\,[(\tfrac{1}{8}+\ldots\tfrac{4}{8})\,8+(\tfrac{5}{8}\times 8-2)+(\tfrac{6}{8}\times 8-4)+(\tfrac{7}{8}\times 8-6)];$$

$$z_5 = +48100 \text{ kil.;}$$

$$0 = -V_5 \cdot 10 + 1000\,[(\tfrac{1}{8}+\ldots \tfrac{4}{8})\,4 - (10 - \tfrac{5}{8}\times 4) - (8 - \tfrac{6}{8}\times 4) - (6 - \tfrac{7}{8}\times 4)]$$
$$+ 5000\,[(\tfrac{1}{8}+\ldots \tfrac{4}{8})\,4 - 5000\,[(10 - \tfrac{5}{8}\times 4) + (8 - \tfrac{6}{8}\times 4) + 6 - \tfrac{7}{8}\times 4)];$$

$$V_5 = + 1500 \text{ kil.},$$
and $\qquad V_5 = - 8500$ "

$$0 = -x_6 \cdot 1{,}5 - 1000\,[(\tfrac{1}{8}+\ldots \tfrac{6}{8}) \cdot 4 + (\tfrac{7}{8}\times 4 - 2)] - 5000\,[(\tfrac{1}{8}+ \ldots \tfrac{6}{8})\,4 + (\tfrac{7}{8}\times 4 - 2)];$$

$$x_6 = - 48000 \text{ kil.};$$

$$0 = y_6 \cdot 6 + 1000\,[(\tfrac{1}{8}+\ldots \tfrac{5}{8})\,4 - (8 - \tfrac{6}{8}\times 4) - (6 - \tfrac{7}{8}\times 4)]$$
$$+ 5000\,(\tfrac{1}{8}+\ldots \tfrac{5}{8})\,4 - 5000\,[(8 - \tfrac{6}{8}\times 4) + (6 - \tfrac{7}{8}\times 4)];$$

$$y_6 = + 6250 \text{ kil.},$$
and $\qquad y_6 = - 6250$ "

$$0 = z_6 \cdot 1{,}84 - 1000\,[(\tfrac{1}{8}+\ldots \tfrac{5}{8})\,6 + (\tfrac{6}{8}\times 6 - 2) + (\tfrac{7}{8}\times 6 - 4)]$$
$$- 5000\,[(\tfrac{1}{8}+\ldots \tfrac{5}{8})\,6 + (\tfrac{6}{8}\times 6 - 2) + (\tfrac{7}{8}\times 6 - 4)];$$

$$z_6 = + 48900 \text{ kil.};$$

$$0 = -V_6 \cdot 4{,}8 + 1000\,[(\tfrac{1}{8}+\ldots \tfrac{5}{8})\,0{,}8 - (4{,}8 - \tfrac{6}{8}\times 0{,}8) - (2{,}8 - \tfrac{7}{8}\times 0{,}8)]$$
$$+ 5000\,(\tfrac{1}{8}+\ldots \tfrac{5}{8})\,0{,}8 - 5000\,[(4{,}8 - \tfrac{6}{8}\times 0{,}8) + (2{,}8 - \tfrac{7}{8}\times 0{,}8)];$$

$$V_6 = + 560 \text{ kil.},$$
and $\qquad V_6 = - 7560$ "

$$0 = -x_7 \cdot 0{,}875 - 1000\,(\tfrac{1}{8}+\ldots \tfrac{7}{8})\,2 - 5000\,(\tfrac{1}{8}+\ldots \tfrac{7}{8})\,2;$$
$$x_7 = - 48000 \text{ kil};$$

$$0 = y_7 \cdot 1{,}92 + 1000\,[(\tfrac{1}{8}+\ldots \tfrac{6}{8})\,0{,}8 - (2{,}8 - \tfrac{7}{8}\times 0{,}8)]$$
$$+ 5000\,(\tfrac{1}{8}+\ldots \tfrac{6}{8})\,0{,}8 - 5000\,(2{,}8 - \tfrac{7}{8}\times 0{,}8);$$

$$y_7 = + 5470 \text{ kil.},$$
and $\qquad y_7 = - 5470$ "

$$0 = z_7 \cdot 1{,}43 - 1000\,[(\tfrac{1}{8}+\ldots \tfrac{6}{8})\,4 + (\tfrac{7}{8}\cdot 4 - 2)] - 5000\,[(\tfrac{1}{8}+ \ldots \tfrac{6}{8})\,4 + (\tfrac{7}{8}\times 4 - 2)];$$

$$z_7 = + 50300 \text{ kil.};$$

-150
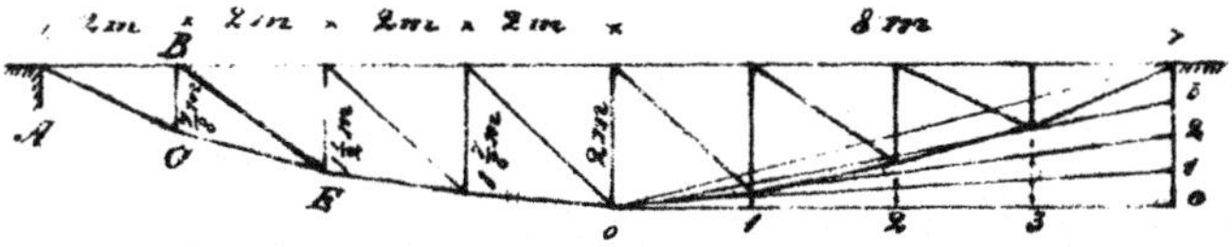

.151
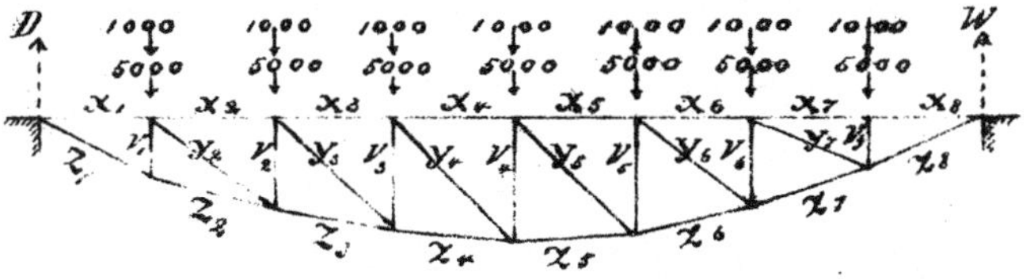

.152
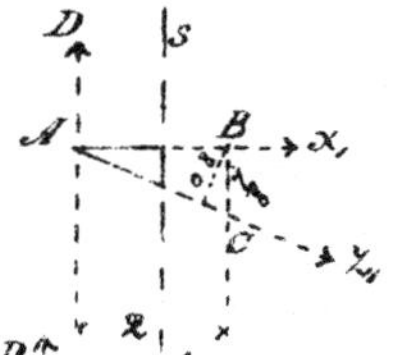

fig.153
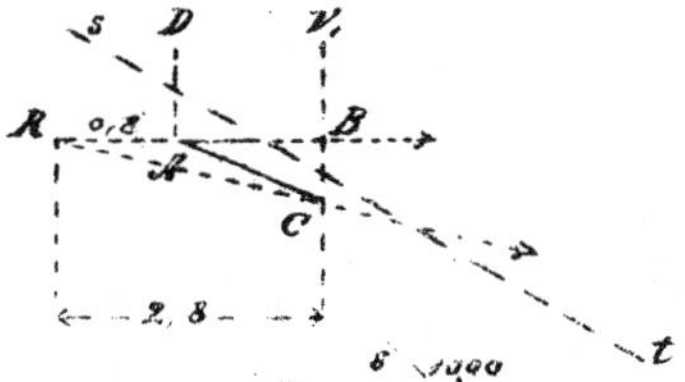

-154
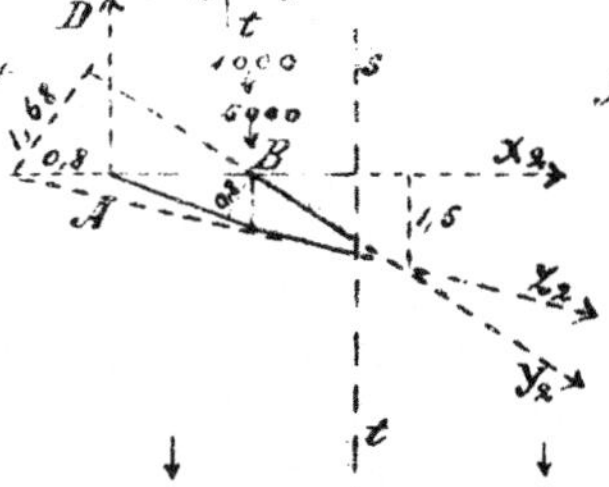

fig 155
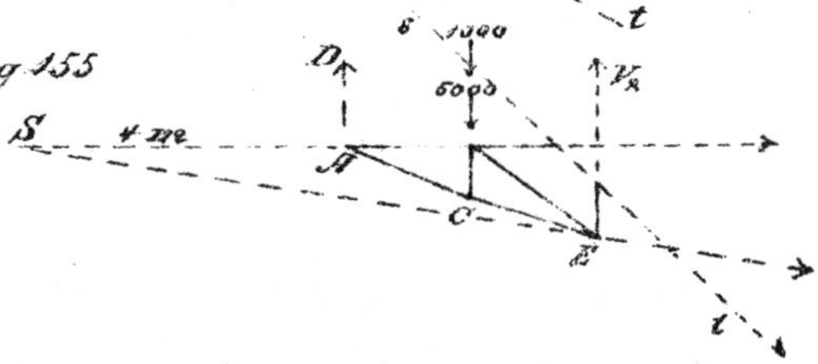

156
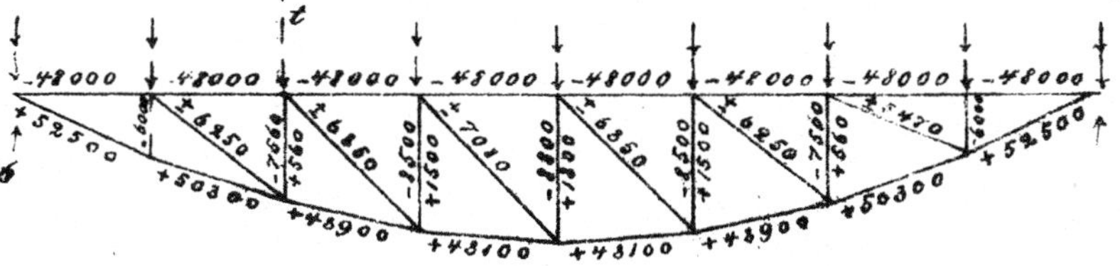

-157
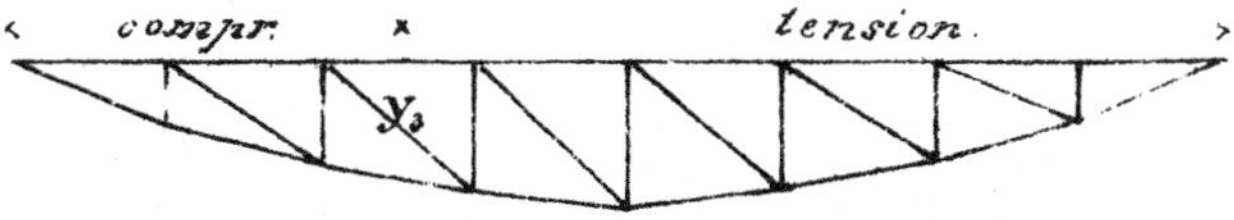

g.158
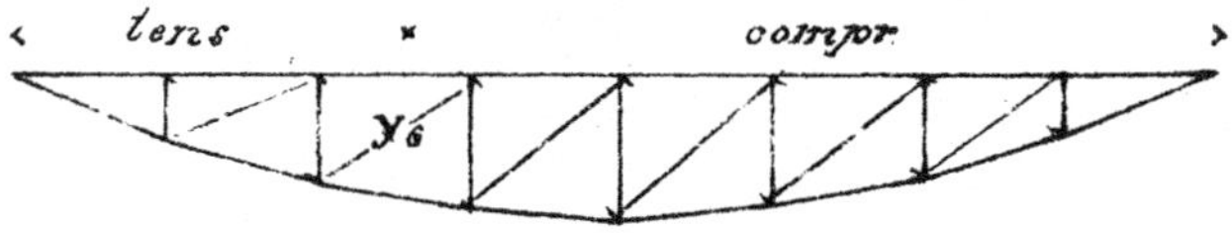

ig.159
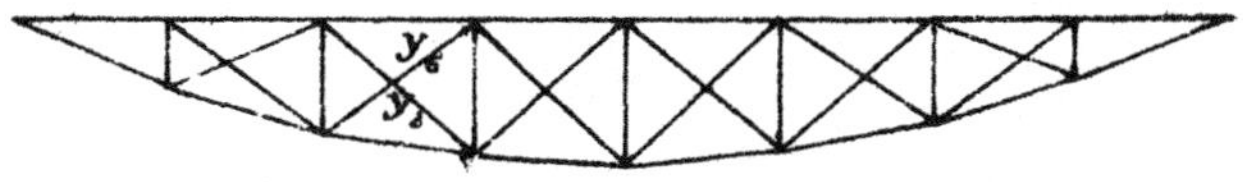

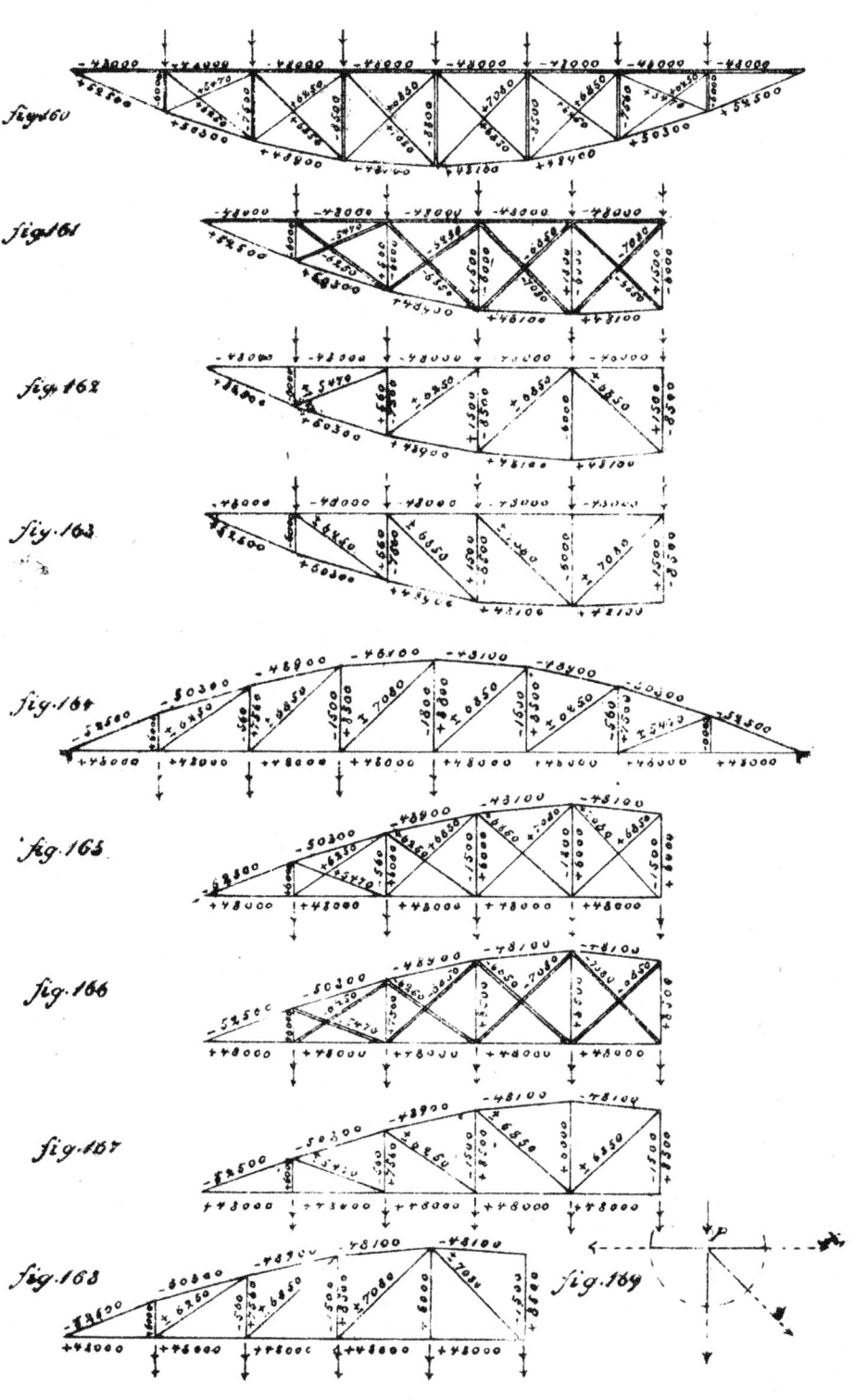

PARABOLIC GIRDER OF 48 FEET SPAN.

$$0 = -V_7 \cdot 2 - 1000 \cdot 2 - 5000 \cdot 2;$$
$$V_7 = -6000 \text{ kil.};$$
$$0 = -x_8 \cdot 0{,}875 - 1000 \left(\tfrac{1}{8} + \ldots \tfrac{7}{8}\right) 2 - 5000 \left(\tfrac{1}{8} + \ldots \tfrac{7}{8}\right) 2;$$
$$x_8 = -48000 \text{ kil.};$$
$$0 = z_8 \cdot 0{,}8 - 1000 \left(\tfrac{1}{8} + \ldots \tfrac{7}{8}\right) 2 - 5000 \left(\tfrac{1}{8} + \ldots \tfrac{7}{8}\right) 2;$$
$$z_8 = +52500 \text{ kil.}$$

156.] In the skeleton (Fig. 156) will be found the combined results.

157.] Comparing the equations with the skeleton, we find the most strain in a certain diagonal, say y_3, in the third panel, when all the apexes to the right are loaded, and the most compression when all the apexes to the left are loaded. (Fig. 157.)

158.] In the same panel, when the diagonal is reversed or replaced by y_6, the strain will be like y_6. (Fig. 158.)

159.] When both diagonals, y_3 and y_6, in panel 3, are existing and constructed like tie-rods, then each one separately will only be strained by a load producing tension. Meanwhile the other is inactive, and in this case only the positive strains of y come into consideration. So for y_3 and y_6 in panel 3 (Fig. 159),

Plate 26,
Fig. 160.] and in the same manner with the other diagonals, as in the skeleton. (Fig. 160.)

For the verticals only the greatest negative (—) strains come into consideration. Because the diagonals have tensile strain, there can be compression only in the verticals.

In a construction with vertical tie-rods and diagonal braces, for the braces only the greatest negative (—) strains, and for the verticals the positive (+) strains, come into consideration. The only compression in the verticals results from the direct load, varying between 1000 kil. and 1000 + 5000 kil., and is, therefore, the maximum compression in the verticals,

$$V = -6000 \text{ kil.}$$

161,
162,
163.] In this case the inability of diagonals for tensile strain is to be represented by double lines. Also for a girder with single diagonal, but symmetrical system, the compression of the vertical at the centre will be only — 6000; the other strains all resulting from the first calculation.

Here may follow a combination of different cases in Figs. 161, 162 and 163.

When in the first skeleton (Fig. 156) the symbols $+$ and $-$ are reversed, it represents the strains for a parabolic girder, with the horizontal flange on below; and the variations of this case can be made in the same manner as before. (See Figs. 164 to 168.)

164 to 168.

Remark.—Two peculiarities we observe by the calculation of parabolic girders. First, the strength in the horizontal chords or flanges is the largest with a full load, and is the same all over. Second, the strain in each diagonal is with a full load $= 0$.

This last fact presents itself from the first theorem, for $x = x_1$ in Fig. 169 is only possible when $y = 0$, otherwise the horizontal component of y would enlarge or diminish x or x_1, and this will be true also in case the width of panels should be different, when only the apexes are in a parabolic curve. This shows the necessity for the application of the rule to calculate the maximum and minimum strain as prescribed in the example.

169.]

[Plates 25 and 26—embracing Figs. 150 to 169.]

D. THE ARCHED TRUSS.

Plate 27, Fig. 170.

The following calculations are for the roof of the Central Depot at Birmingham:

Girder, 208 feet in length. (Fig. 170.)

13 panels, each 16 feet in horizontal length, and 24 feet in depth.

The distances of top intersections to the distances of bottom intersections from the horizontal line are as 40 to 16, or $= 2\frac{1}{2}$ to 1.

The distance of main rafters $= 24$ feet; weight and pressure of snow and wind $= 40$ lbs. per square foot of horizontal projection.

$$208 \times 24 \times 40 = 199680 \text{ lbs. (the weight of load)},$$

or for each panel $=$

$$\frac{199680}{13} = 15360 \text{ lbs., or } 7,5 \text{ tons.}$$

THE ARCHED TRUSS.

The weight of structure = 1,5 tons for each panel.

The pressure, D, on the abutment, will be

$$D = (1,5 + 7,5)\left(\tfrac{1}{13} + \tfrac{2}{13} + \tfrac{3}{13} + \ldots + \tfrac{11}{13} + \tfrac{12}{13}\right) = 9 \times \tfrac{78}{13} = 54 \text{ tons.}$$

171.] Therefore, per example for x_4, in Fig. 171, when the length of 16 feet is taken as unit, or $=1$,

$$0 = x_4 \cdot 1{,}205 + 54 \times 4 - (7{,}5 + 1{,}5)(1 + 2 + 3) \text{ (rot. round } M\text{)}:$$

$$x_4 = -134{,}4 \text{ tons;}$$

and for z_4,

$$0 = -z_4 \cdot 1{,}055 + 54 \times 3 - (7{,}5 + 1{,}5)(1 + 2) \text{ (rot. } r \cdot N\text{);}$$

$$z_4 = +128{,}0 \text{ tons.}$$

In the same manner,

$0 = x_1 \cdot 0{,}347 + 54 \times 1,$ or $x_1 = -155{,}6$ t.

$0 = -z_1 \cdot 0{,}41 + 54 \times 1,$ or $z_1 = +131{,}7$ t.

$0 = x_2 \cdot 0{,}672 + 54 \times 2 - 9 \times 1,$ or $x_2 = -147{,}3$ t.

$0 = -z_2 \cdot 0{,}415 + 54 \times 1,$ or $z_2 = +130{,}2$ t.

$0 = x_3 \cdot 0{,}963 + 54 \times 3 - 9 \cdot (1 + 2),$ or $x_3 = -140{,}2$ t.

$0 = -z_3 \cdot 0{,}767 + 54 \times 2 - 9 \times 1,$ or $z_3 = +129{,}1$ t.

$0 = x_5 \cdot 1{,}382 + 54 \times 5 - 9(1 + 2 + 3 + 4),$ or $x_5 = -130{,}2$ t.

$0 = -z_5 \cdot 1{,}272 + 54 \times 4 - 9(1 + 2 + 3),$ or $z_5 = +127{,}3$ t.

$0 = x_6 \cdot 1{,}481 + 54 \times 6 - 9(1 + 2 + 3 + 4 + 5),$ or $x_6 = -127{,}6$ t.

$0 = -z_6 \cdot 1{,}419 + 54 \times 5 - 9(1 + 2 + 3 + 4),$ or $z_6 = +126{,}9$ t.

$0 = x_7 \cdot 1{,}491 + 54 \times 7 - 9(1 + 2 + 3 + 4 + 5 + 6),$ or $x_7 = -126{,}7$ t.

$0 = -z_7 \cdot 1{,}491 + 54 \times 6 - 9(1 + 2 + 3 + 4 + 5),$ or $z_7 = +126{,}7$ t.

$0 = x_8 \cdot 1{,}41 + 54 \times 8 - 9(1 + 2 + \ldots 7),$ or $x_8 = -127{,}6$ t.

$0 = -z_8 \cdot 1{,}489 + 54 \times 7 - 9(1 + 2 + \ldots 6),$ or $z_8 = +126{,}9$ t.

$0 = x_9 \cdot 1{,}244 + 54 \times 9 - 9(1 + 2 + \ldots 8),$ or $x_9 = -130{,}2$ t.

$0 = -z_9 \cdot 1{,}414 + 54 \times 8 - 9(1 + 2 + \ldots 7),$ or $z_9 = +127{,}3$ t.

$0 = x_{10} \cdot 1{,}004 + 54 \times 10 - 9\,(1 + 2 + \ldots 9)$, or $x_{10} = -134{,}4$ t.

$0 = -z_{10} \cdot 1{,}265 + 54 \times 9 - 9\,(1 + 2 + \ldots 8)$, or $z_{10} = +128{,}0$ t.

$0 = x_{11} \cdot 0{,}706 + 54 \times 11 - 9\,(1 + 2 + \ldots 10)$, or $x_{11} = -140{,}2$ t.

$0 = -z_{11} \cdot 1{,}046 + 54 \times 10 - 9\,(1 + 2 + \ldots 9)$, or $z_{11} = +129{,}1$ t.

$0 = x_{12} \cdot 0{,}367 + 54 \times 12 - 9\,(1 + 2 + \ldots 11)$, or $x_{12} = -147{,}3$ t.

$0 = -z_{12} \cdot 0{,}76 + 54 \times 11 - 9\,(1 + 2 + \ldots 10)$, or $z_{12} = +130{,}2$ t.

$0 = x_{13} \cdot 0{,}347 + 54 \times 12 - 9\,(1 + 2 + \ldots 11)$, or $x_{13} = -155{,}6$ t.

$0 = -z_{13} \cdot 0{,}41 + 54 \times 12 - 9\,(1 + 2 + \ldots 11)$, or $z_{13} = +131{,}7$ t.

Remark.—The results noted in Fig. 176 show that the greatest strains in the symmetrical sections of flanges are the same, though the diagonals of one-half of the girder are reversed to the others, and it follows that for the definition of strain in flanges it will be the same if we take the point for rotation in the right or left apex.

This is only possible when the strain in the diagonal $= 0$, and therefore shows us that by a full load, as in parabolic girders, no strain in diagonals exists. Nevertheless, a partial load (from snow or wind or removing of sheeting) being unavoidable, the diagonal connections are a necessity.

Calculation of Strain y in the Diagonals.

172.] For y_4 (see Fig. 172), when the point of rotation, O, in the intersection of x_4 and z_4 and the length OA, found by construction $= 32$ feet, or, for easier calculation, 16 feet $=$ unit (1); therefore $OA = 2$, and the lever for $y_4 = PO = 4{,}68$.

$0 = y_4 \cdot 4{,}68 - D \cdot 2 + 1{,}5\,[(3 + 2) + (2 + 2) + (1 + 2)] + 7{,}5\,[(3 + 2) + (2 + 2) + (1 + 2)]$,

and $D = 1{,}5\,(\tfrac{1}{13} + \tfrac{2}{13} + \ldots \tfrac{12}{13}) + 7{,}5\,(\tfrac{1}{13} + \tfrac{2}{13} + \ldots \tfrac{12}{13})$,

substituted with its members of permanent and variable load on their respective places,

$0 = y_4 \cdot 4{,}68 - 1{,}5\,[(\tfrac{1}{13} + \tfrac{2}{13} + \ldots \tfrac{9}{13})\,2 - (3 + 2 + 1)\,(1 + \tfrac{2}{13})] - 7{,}5\,\tfrac{1}{13} + \tfrac{2}{13} + \ldots \tfrac{9}{13}) + 7{,}5\,(3 + 2 + 1)\,(1 + \tfrac{2}{13})$.

The solution of this equation shows the member for a permanent load $= 0$, and therefore our equation in its more simple form—

CALCULATION OF STRAIN y IN THE DIAGONALS. 89

$$0 = -y_4 \cdot 4{,}68 - 7{,}5 \left(\tfrac{1}{13} + \tfrac{2}{13} + \ldots \tfrac{9}{13}\right) 2 + 7{,}5 \left(3 + 2 + 1\right)\left(1 + \tfrac{2}{13}\right),$$

or, according to the rule formerly given,

I. $\quad 0 = -y_4 \cdot 4{,}68 - 7{,}5 \left(\tfrac{1}{13} + \tfrac{2}{13} + \ldots \tfrac{9}{13}\right) 2;$

II. $\quad 0 = -y_4 \cdot 4{,}68 + 7{,}5 \left(3 + 2 + 1\right)\left(1 + \tfrac{2}{13}\right),$

or $\quad y_4 = +11{,}1$ tons, and $y_4 = -11{,}1$ tons.

In the same way for the other diagonals and the length of lever from construction,

$$0 = y_2 \cdot 0{,}92 - 7{,}5 \left(\tfrac{1}{13} + \tfrac{2}{13} + \ldots \tfrac{11}{13}\right) \cdot 0{,}2 + 7{,}5 \left(1 + \tfrac{0{,}2}{13}\right);$$

$y_2 = +8{,}3,$ and $y_3 = -8{,}3$ tons;

$$0 = y_3 \cdot 2{,}52 - 7{,}5 \left(\tfrac{1}{13} + \ldots \tfrac{10}{13}\right) 0{,}75 + 7{,}5 \left(2 + 1\right)\left(1 + \tfrac{0{,}75}{13}\right);$$

$y_3 = +9{,}5,$ and $y_3 = -9{,}5$ tons;

$$0 = y_5 \cdot 8{,}3 - 7{,}5 \left(\tfrac{1}{13} + \ldots \tfrac{8}{13}\right) 5 + 7{,}5 \left(4 + 3 + 2 + 1\right)\left(1 + \tfrac{5}{13}\right);$$

$y_5 = +12{,}6,$ and $y_5 = -12{,}6$ tons;

$$0 = y_6 \cdot 17{,}6 - 7{,}5 \left(\tfrac{1}{13} + \ldots \tfrac{7}{13}\right) 15 + 7{,}5 \left(5 + 4 + 3 + 2 + 1\right)\left(1 + \tfrac{15}{13}\right);$$

$y_6 = +13{,}8,$ and $y_6 = -13{,}8$ tons.

The point of rotation, O, is for the diagonal of the middle panel in infinite distance. (See girders with horizontal top and bottom flanges.)

The sinus of the angle formed by y_7 and a horizontal line $= 0{,}831$, leading to the equation in its most simple form (as before explained in examples for girders with horizontal top and bottom flanges).

$$0 = y_7 \cdot 0{,}831 - 7{,}5 \left(\tfrac{1}{13} + \ldots \tfrac{6}{13}\right) + 7{,}5 \left(6 + \ldots 1\right) \tfrac{1}{13};$$

$y_7 = +14{,}6,$ and $y_7 = -14{,}6$ tons.

For the equations now following, the point of rotation will be on the opposite side; therefore the symbols of moments are reversed.

$$0 = -y_8 \cdot 16{,}1 + 7{,}5 \left(\tfrac{1}{13} + \ldots \tfrac{5}{13}\right) 28 - 7{,}5 \left(7 + \ldots + 1\right)\left(\tfrac{28}{13} - 1\right);$$

$y_8 = +15{,}0,$ and $y_8 = -15{,}0$ tons;

$$0 = -y_9 \cdot 7{,}1 + 7{,}5 \left(\tfrac{1}{13} + \ldots \tfrac{4}{13}\right) 18 - 7{,}5 \left(8 + \ldots + 1\right)\left(\tfrac{18}{13} - 1\right);$$

$y_9 = +14{,}6,$ and $y_9 = -14{,}6$ tons;

$0 = -y_{10} \cdot 3{,}68 + 7{,}5\,(\tfrac{1}{13}+\tfrac{2}{13}+\tfrac{3}{13})\,15 - 7{,}5\,(9+\ldots 1)\,(\tfrac{15}{13}-1);$

$y_{10} = +14{,}1,$ and $y_{10} = -14{,}1$ tons;

$0 = -y_{11} \cdot 1{,}82 + 7{,}5\,(\tfrac{1}{13}+\tfrac{2}{13}) \cdot 13{,}75 - 7{,}5\,(10+\ldots 1)\,(\tfrac{13{,}75}{13}-1);$

$y_{11} = +13{,}0,$ and $y_{11} = -13{,}0$ tons;

$0 = -y_{12} \cdot 0{,}65 + 7{,}5 \times \tfrac{1}{13} \times 13{,}2 - 7{,}5\,(11+\ldots 1)\,(\tfrac{13{,}2}{13}-1);$

$y_{12} = +11{,}6,$ and $y_{12} = -11{,}6$ tons.

Calculation of Strain in the Verticals V.

[173.] For V_1, when the point of rotation in the intersection of x_1 and z_1, which by construction $= 0{,}1$ to the right of A (Fig. 173),

$$0 = -V_1 \cdot 0{,}9 + D \cdot 0{,}1,$$

or $0 = -V_1 \cdot 0{,}9 + 1{,}5\,(\tfrac{1}{13}+\tfrac{2}{13}+\ldots \tfrac{12}{13})\,0{,}1 + 7{,}5\,(\tfrac{1}{13}+\tfrac{2}{13}+\ldots \tfrac{12}{13})\,0{,}1;$

$$V_1 = +6 \text{ tons.}$$

[174.] For V_2, the point of rotation in the intersection of x_2 and $z_2 = 0{,}06$ to the right of A. (Fig. 174.)

$0 = -V_2 \cdot 1{,}94 + D \cdot 0{,}06 + 1{,}5 \times 0{,}94 + 7{,}5 \times 0{,}94;$

$0 = -V_2 \cdot 1{,}94 + 1{,}5\,[(\tfrac{1}{13}+\ldots \tfrac{11}{13})\,0{,}06 + (1 - \tfrac{0{,}06}{13})]$

$\quad + 7{,}5\,(\tfrac{1}{13}+\ldots \tfrac{11}{13})\,0{,}06 + 7{,}5\,(1 - \tfrac{0{,}06}{13});$

$$V_2 = +6 \text{ tons.}$$

[175.] For the equations now following, the point of rotation, O, will appear to the left of $A = 0{,}214$ for the intersection of x_3 and z_4, and for V_3 (Fig. 175) we have

$0 = -V_3 \cdot 3{,}214 - 1{,}5\,[(\tfrac{1}{13}+\ldots \tfrac{10}{13})\,0{,}214 - (2+1)\,(1 + \tfrac{0{,}214}{13})]$

$\quad - 7{,}5\,(\tfrac{1}{13}+\ldots \tfrac{10}{13})\,0{,}214 + 7{,}5\,(2+1)\,(1 + \tfrac{0{,}214}{13});$

and omitting at one time the positive and at another time the negative members of the movable load, we find

$$V_3 \text{ (max.)} = +8{,}1 \text{ tons}$$
$$V_3 \text{ (min.)} = -1{,}1 \text{ ``}$$

and $V_3 = +6$ tons when no member is omitted, which will be the

CALCULATION OF STRAIN IN THE VERTICALS V. 91

same for the other verticals, or $V_4 = V_5 = V_6 \ldots = 6$ tons; *i. e.*, for a full load of the truss.

In the same way

$$0 = -V_4 \cdot 4{,}91 - 1{,}5 \left[(\tfrac{1}{13} + \ldots \tfrac{9}{13}) 0{,}91 - (3+2+1)(1 + \tfrac{0{,}91}{13}) \right]$$
$$- 7{,}5 \, (\tfrac{1}{13} + \ldots \tfrac{9}{13}) \, 0{,}91 + 7{,}5 \, (3+2+1)(1 + \tfrac{0{,}91}{13});$$
$$V_4 \,(\text{max.}) = + 10{,}8;$$
$$V_4 \,(\text{min.}) = - 3{,}8;$$

$$0 = -V_5 \cdot 7{,}5 - 1{,}5 \left[(\tfrac{1}{13} + \ldots \tfrac{8}{13}) 2{,}5 - (4+\ldots 1)(1 + \tfrac{2{,}5}{13}) \right]$$
$$- 7{,}5 \, (\tfrac{1}{13} + \ldots \tfrac{8}{13}) \, 2{,}5 + 7{,}5 \, (4+\ldots 1)(1 + \tfrac{2{,}5}{13});$$
$$V_5 = + 12{,}9;$$
$$V_5 = - 5{,}9;$$

$$0 = -V_6 \cdot 12{,}6 - 1{,}5 \left[(\tfrac{1}{13} + \ldots \tfrac{7}{13}) 6{,}6 - (5+\ldots 1)(1 + \tfrac{6{,}6}{13}) \right]$$
$$- 7{,}5 \, (\tfrac{1}{13} + \ldots \tfrac{7}{13}) \, 6{,}6 + 7{,}5 \, (5+\ldots 1)(1 + \tfrac{6{,}6}{13});$$
$$V_6 = + 14{,}5;$$
$$V_6 = - 7{,}5;$$

$$0 = -V_7 \cdot 31{,}5 - 1{,}5 \left[(\tfrac{1}{13} + \ldots \tfrac{6}{13}) 24{,}5 - (6+\ldots 1)(1 + \tfrac{24{,}5}{13}) \right]$$
$$- 7{,}5 \, (\tfrac{1}{13} + \ldots \tfrac{6}{13}) \, 24{,}5 + 7{,}5 \, (6+\ldots 1)(1 + \tfrac{24{,}5}{13});$$
$$V_7 = + 15{,}4;$$
$$V_7 = - 8{,}4.$$

In the equations now following, the point of rotation on the opposite side gives,

$$0 = V_8 \cdot 60 + 1{,}5 \left[(\tfrac{1}{13} + \ldots \tfrac{5}{13}) 68 - (7+\ldots 1)(\tfrac{68}{13} - 1) \right]$$
$$+ 7{,}5 \, (\tfrac{1}{13} + \ldots \tfrac{5}{13}) \, 68 - 7{,}5 \, (7+\ldots 1)(\tfrac{68}{13} - 1);$$
$$V_8 = + 15{,}8;$$
$$V_8 = - 8{,}8;$$

$$0 = V_9 \cdot 13{,}5 + 1{,}5 \left[(\tfrac{1}{13} + \ldots \tfrac{4}{13}) 22{,}5 - (8+\ldots 1)(\tfrac{22{,}5}{13} - 1) \right]$$
$$+ 7{,}5 \, (\tfrac{1}{13} + \ldots \tfrac{4}{13}) \, 2{,}25 - 7{,}5 \, (8+\ldots 1)(\tfrac{22{,}5}{13} - 1);$$
$$V_9 = + 15{,}6;$$
$$V_9 = - 8{,}6;$$

$$0 = V_{10} \cdot 6{,}43 + 1{,}5 \left[(\tfrac{1}{13} + \tfrac{2}{13} + \tfrac{3}{13}) \, 16{,}43 - (9+1)(\tfrac{16{,}43}{13} - 1) \right]$$
$$+ 7{,}5 \, (\tfrac{1}{13} + \tfrac{2}{13} + \tfrac{3}{13}) \, 16{,}43 - 7{,}5 \, (9 + \ldots 1) \, (\tfrac{16{,}43}{13} - 1);$$
$$V_{10} = + 14{,}8;$$
$$V_{10} = - 7{,}8;$$

$$0 = V_{11} \cdot 3{,}3 + 1{,}5 \left[(\tfrac{1}{13} + \tfrac{2}{13}) \, 14{,}3 - (10 + \ldots 1) \tfrac{14{,}3}{13} - 1 \right]$$
$$+ 7{,}5 \, (\tfrac{1}{13} + \tfrac{2}{13}) \, 14{,}3 - 7{,}5 \, (10 + \ldots 1) \, (\tfrac{14{,}3}{13} - 1);$$
$$V_{11} = + 13{,}5;$$
$$V_{11} = - 6{,}5;$$

$$0 = V_{12} \cdot 1{,}385 + 1{,}5 \left[\tfrac{1}{13} \times 13{,}385 - (11 + \ldots 1) \, (\tfrac{13{,}385}{13} - 1) \right]$$
$$+ 7{,}5 \times \tfrac{1}{13} \times 13{,}385 - 7{,}5 \, (11 + \ldots 1) \, (\tfrac{13{,}385}{13} - 1);$$
$$V_{12} = + 11{,}6;$$
$$V_{12} = - 4{,}6 \text{ tons.}$$

The strains, V, in the verticals have been calculated under the supposition that the whole permanent load (weight of structure) is charged to the upper apexes. In reality, such is not true; and in consideration that about one-third of this load should be transmitted to the lower apexes, we increase the strains in verticals (in this case tie-rods) for 0,5 tons each, which changes the above results to the following:

$$V_1 (\text{max.}) = + 6{,}5 \text{ tons};$$
$$V_2 (\text{max.}) = + 6{,}5 \text{ “}$$
$$V_3 \begin{cases} (\text{max.}) = + 8{,}6 \\ (\text{min.}) = - 0{,}6 \end{cases} V_3 = + 6{,}5;$$
$$V_4 \begin{cases} (\text{max.}) = + 11{,}3 \\ (\text{min.}) = - 3{,}3 \end{cases} V_4 = + 6{,}5;$$
$$V_5 \begin{cases} (\text{max.}) = + 13{,}4 \\ (\text{min.}) = - 5{,}4 \end{cases} V_5 = + 6{,}5;$$
$$V_6 \begin{cases} (\text{max.}) = + 15{,}0 \\ (\text{min.}) = - 7{,}0 \end{cases} V_6 = + 6{,}5;$$
$$V_7 \begin{cases} (\text{max.}) = + 15{,}9 \\ (\text{min.}) = - 7{,}9 \end{cases} V_7 = + 6{,}5;$$
$$V_8 \begin{cases} (\text{max.}) = + 16{,}3 \\ (\text{min.}) = - 8{,}3 \end{cases} V_8 = + 6{,}5;$$

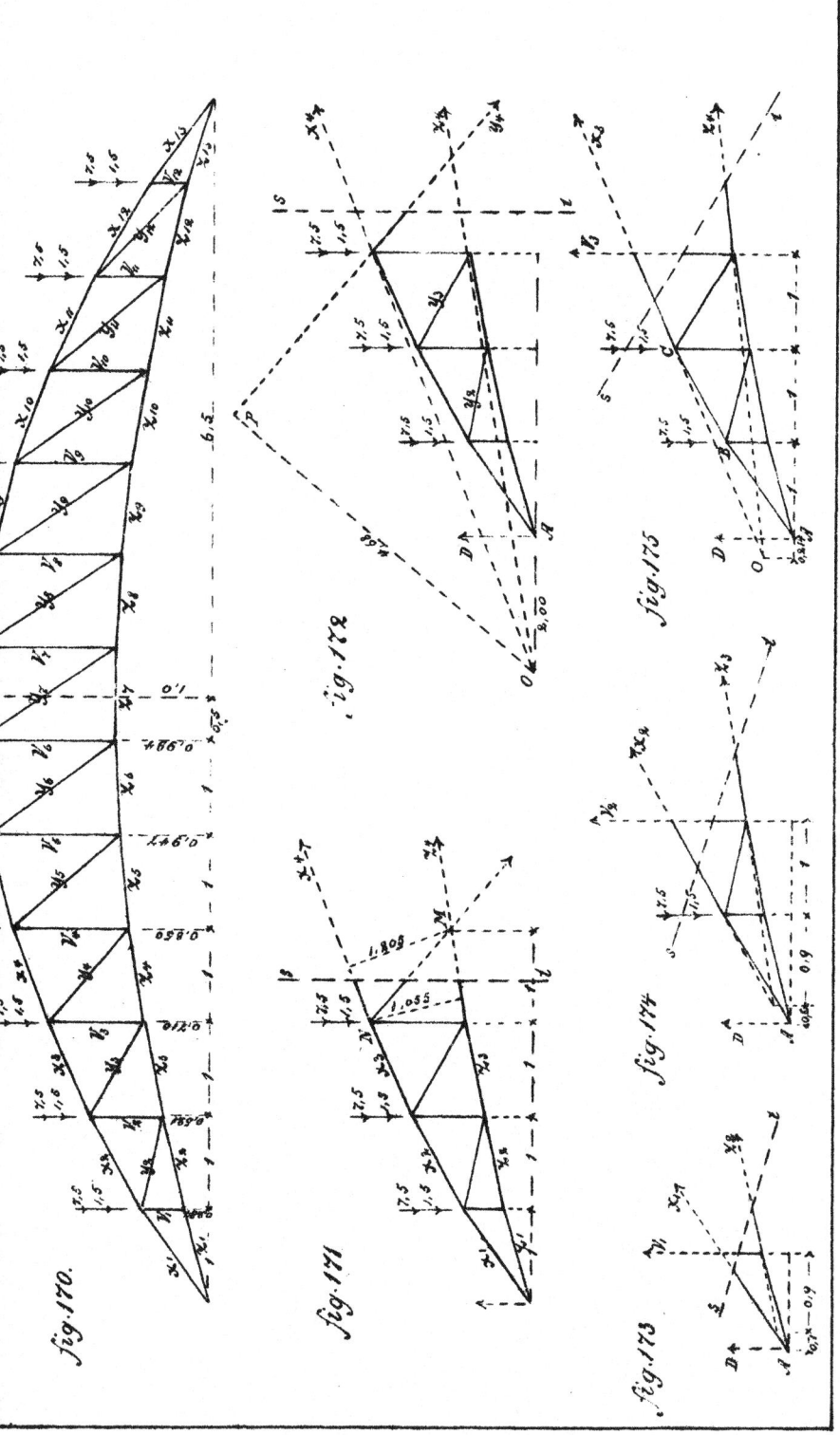

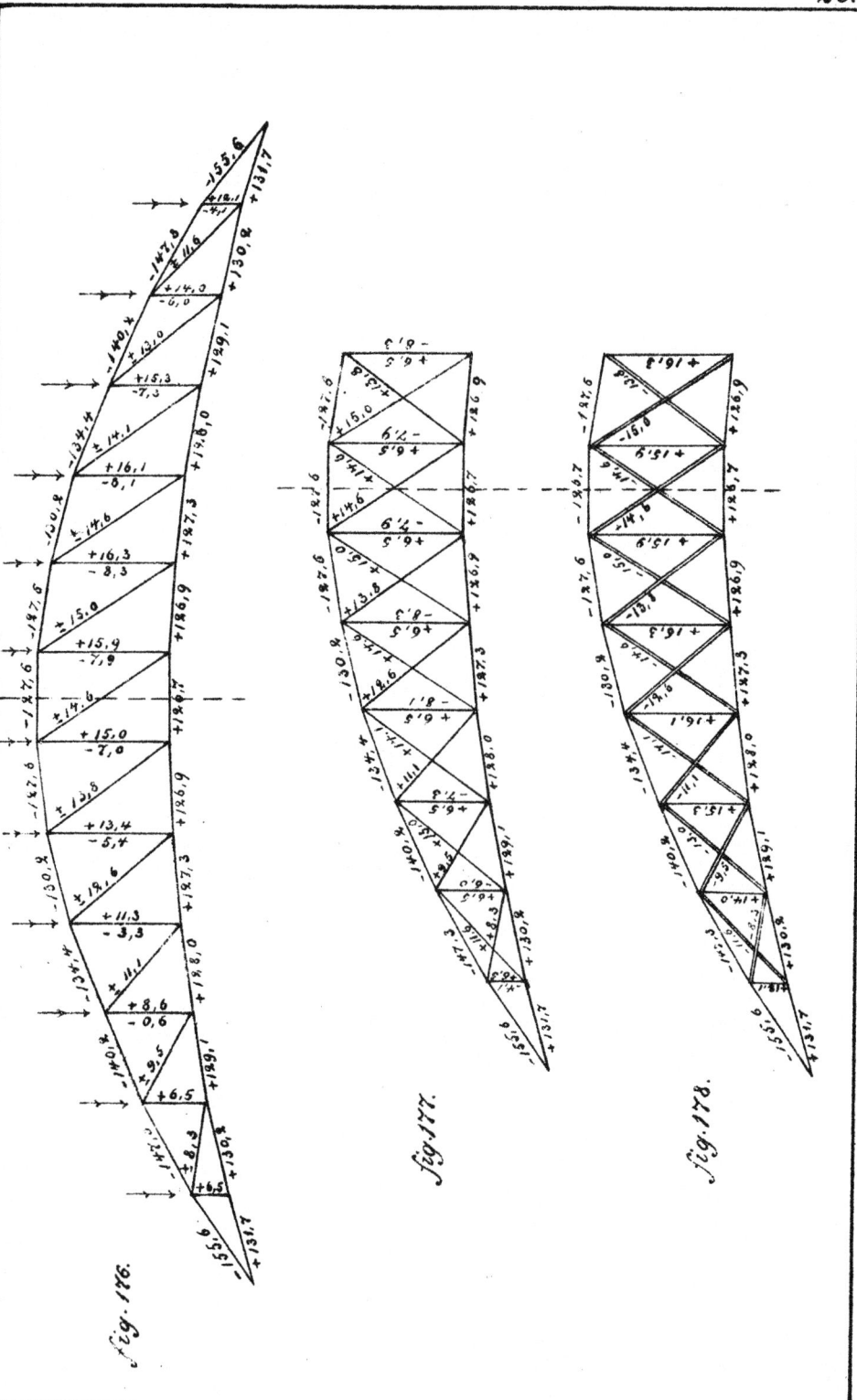

Fig. 176. Fig. 177. Fig. 178.

TRANSFORMATIONS. 93

$$V_9 \begin{cases} (\text{max.}) = +16,1 \\ (\text{min.}) = -8,1 \end{cases} V_9 = +6,5;$$

$$V_{10} \begin{cases} (\text{max.}) = +15,3 \\ (\text{min.}) = -7,3 \end{cases} V_{10} = +6,5;$$

$$V_{11} \begin{cases} (\text{max.}) = +14,0 \\ (\text{min.}) = -6,0 \end{cases} V_{11} = +6,5;$$

$$V_{12} \begin{cases} (\text{max.}) = +12,1 \\ (\text{min.}) = -4,1 \end{cases} V_{12} = +6,5.$$

The results are combined in Fig. 176, and show that the strains in arches are independent of the direction of diagonals, because to both sides of the centre line their strain is the same, though the direction of the diagonal is not symmetrical to the centre line; therefore, for the definition of strain in x or z, it will make no difference if we choose in certain panels the left or right apex for the point of rotation.

TRANSFORMATIONS.

Plate 28, Fig. 176.] From the results above we see that for a single diagonal system the diagonals are strained both for tension and compression. For a girder with a single diagonal, but symmetrical system, we pursue the same course as in the parabolic girder, and it needs no further explanation to form from the preceding figure a girder with symmetrical diagonals, sloping right downward for one and right upward for the other half of girder; or, reversed, right upward for one and right downward for the other half of girder.

177.] The transformation for a girder with crossed diagonals will be apparent from Skeleton 177, and it is only necessary to remark that, where the diagonals as tie-rods are constructed, for the verticals only the greatest compressive (—) strains come into consideration—observing from this that, per example, the minimum strain of V_4 will be replaced by the greater minimum strain of V_9 as its symmetrical opposite.

178.] When the diagonals (for instance, by timbers) are constructed like braces as in Skeleton 178, designed by double lines, for the verticals only the maximum or greatest (+) strains come into consideration. The verticals are tie-rods in this case, acting for tensile strain.

[Plates 27 and 28—embracing Figs. 170 to 178.]

E. THRUST CONSTRUCTION.

To form the equations of equilibrium, in the preceding calculations the reactive force of supports has formed an essential part, in place of which, by the thrust construction, the resulting force at the vertex comes into consideration. To define its intensity, a single weight, W, may be supposed to rest at E (Fig. 179) on an arch-shaped girder, fixed at the heels, A and B, and butted at F.

[Plate 29, Fig. 179.]

The weight, W, at a distance, x, from the right support, results in the force AW, intersecting the vertex F, and in the force WB toward the right support.

When R is the intensity in the direction AW, its components are H and V (downward) for the left section, and H and V (upward) for the right section (Fig. 180^a); and for the equilibrium we have

[180^a.]

left section, $0 = V.10 - H.4$ (rot. A);

right section, $0 = V.10 + H.4 - Wx$ (rot. B),

in which, by addition,

$$0 = V.20 - Wx, \quad \text{or } V = \frac{Wx}{20},$$

and by subtraction,

$$0 = H.8 - Wx, \quad \text{or } H = \frac{Wx}{8}.$$

When $x = 10$ feet (i. e., the weight, W, removed to the centre of the girder, Fig. 180^a), then

$$V = \frac{W.10}{20}, \quad \text{or } V = \frac{W}{2};$$

$$H = \frac{W.10}{8}, \quad \text{or } H = \tfrac{5}{4} W,$$

(being for a weight, $W = 100000$ lbs.);

$V = 50000$ lbs.,   and $H = 125000$ lbs.

Thus, having defined the forces at the vertex for a single weight, W, at the centre, for the diagonals we have the following equations of equilibrium, a cut, $s_i t_i$, being supposed to separate the members next to the left support.

29.

fig. 179

fig. 180^a

fig. 180^b

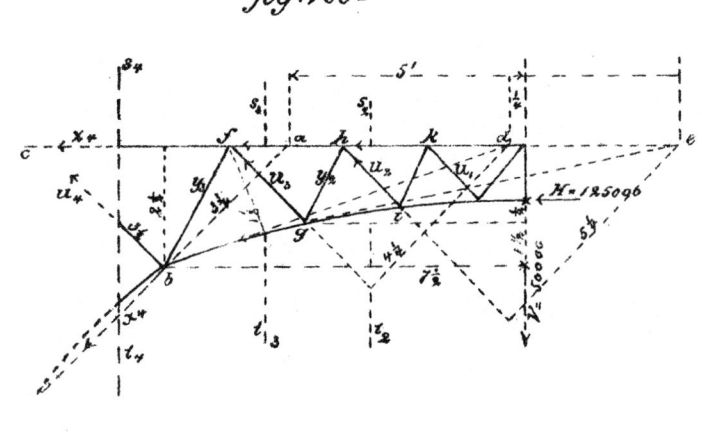

THRUST CONSTRUCTION.

180^b.] $0 = u_4 \cdot 3\frac{3}{4} + H \times 1 + V \times 5$ (rot. a, Fig. 180^b);

$$0 = u_4 \cdot 3\frac{3}{4} + 125000 + 250000;$$

$$u_4 = -100000.$$

$$0 = u_3 \cdot 4\frac{1}{4} + H \times 1 + V \times \tfrac{1}{4} \text{ (rot. } d);$$

$$0 = u_3 \cdot 4\frac{1}{4} + 125000 + 12500;$$

$$u_3 = -32353.$$

For u_2, the intersection, e, of the adjoining members, z of the upper and x of the lower string, is to the right of the centre; therefore, for the equilibrium,

$$0 = u_2 \cdot 5\frac{1}{4} + H \times 1 - V \times 3\frac{1}{2} \text{ (rot. } e);$$

$$0 = u_2 \cdot 5\frac{1}{4} + 125000 - 175000;$$

$$u_2 = +9524.$$

For the diagonals u_1 and y_0 we suppose the intersection to be in infinite distance (*i.e.*, z and x parallel); then H will have no leverage, and therefore will be without influence, and when the angle of y_0 with a horizontal line $= 45°$, sin $45° = 0{,}707$,

$$-\frac{V}{y_0} = \sin 45, \quad \text{or } y_0 = -\frac{V}{0{,}707} = -\frac{50000}{0{,}707} = -71428;$$

also, $\qquad u_1 = +71428.$

For y_2 we have

$$0 = -y_2 \times 5\tfrac{7}{8} - V \times 3 + H \times 1 \text{ (rot. } e);$$

$$y_2 = -4255;$$

also, $\qquad y_3 = +28947.$

The other diagonals, y, will be found in the same manner, and will be in numerical value the same as the diagonals u, in case their angle with the horizontal line is the same.

For the strains z in the upper string the rotation will be at the lower apexes; so for z_4,

$$0 = -z_4 \times 2\tfrac{1}{2} - H \times 1\tfrac{1}{2} + V \times 7\tfrac{1}{2} \text{ (rot. } b);$$

$$0 = -z_4 \times 2\tfrac{1}{2} - 187500 + 375000;$$

$$z_4 = +75000;$$

$$0 = -z_3 \times 1\tfrac{1}{2} - H \times \tfrac{1}{2} + V \times 4\tfrac{1}{2} \text{ (rot. } g\text{)};$$

$$z_3 = +108333;$$

$$0 = -z_2 \times 1\tfrac{1}{3} - H \times \tfrac{1}{3} + V \times 2\tfrac{5}{8} \text{ (rot. } i\text{)};$$

$$z_2 = 102777.$$

In the same way, but with the rotation in the upper apexes, we have for the forces x in the lower stringer,

$$0 = x_4' \times 3\tfrac{1}{2} + H \times 1 + V \times 10 \text{ (rot. } c\text{)};$$

$$x_4 = -178571;$$

$$0 = x_3 \times 1\tfrac{7}{8} + H \times 1 + V \times 6 \text{ (rot. } f\text{)};$$

$$x_3 = -226666;$$

$$0 = x_2 \times 1\tfrac{1}{4} + H + V \times 3\tfrac{3}{4} \text{ (rot. } h\text{)};$$

$$x_2 = -250000;$$

$$0 = x_1 \times 1\tfrac{1}{8} + H \times 1 + V \times 2 \text{ (rot. } k\text{)};$$

$$x_1 = -200000.$$

The results are given in the right section of Fig. 180a.

Plate 30, Fig. 181.] For a combined (permanent and rolling) load another example will explain the definition of strains:

Span = 72 feet, or 24 metres;   (Fig. 181.)

permanent load = 2 tons for each apex;

rolling load = 6 tons for each apex.

To ascertain the maximum strain of the single members we again first take into consideration what influence a single load, Q, upon the structure will have.

For a single weight, Q, to the right of the centre line, and the produced pressure, R, toward the left abutment, it will be observed that the reaction of the left support is in the line AS, the prolongation of which intersects in P with a vertical line in Q, the reaction of A_1 being also directed toward P.

182.] The pressure at the link in the vertex S we divide in its horizontal and vertical components, H and V, and when the moments are formed each for one-half of the structure in relation to their respective supports, we find from Fig. 182,

DEFINITION OF STRAIN x IN HORIZONTAL FLANGES.

$0 = V.12 + H.4 - Q.3$ for the right section (rot. A_1);
$0 = V.12 - H.4$ for the left section (rot. A).

These equations, when at one time added and at another subtracted, result in

$$V = \frac{Q}{8}, \quad \text{and } H = \tfrac{3}{8}Q.$$

As by this mode of observation we are enabled to ascertain the influence of a weight, Q, upon the whole system, for the definition of strain in a certain member of the structure we make a cut, st, and form for the considered section the equation of moments.

DEFINITION OF STRAIN x IN THE HORIZONTAL FLANGES.

For a point of rotation we take the foot, E, of the diagonal. (B, E, Fig. 182.)

Each weight to the left of the centre line produces a pressure in the vertex, S, the direction of which is from A_1 toward S, to keep the section in its position.

The components of this pressure (H and V) aim to turn to the left round A, similar to the strain x_1 itself, thereby making x_1 compressive.

Each weight to the right of the centre line produces for the left part a pressure in the vertex, the direction of which is through the point of rotation, E, and for this reason has no influence.

For the greatest compression, therefore, we consider one-half of the girder, containing the flange in question, charged with a full load. The other half can be either loaded or unloaded without influence, as already stated.

183.] Both halves being loaded, we have, from Fig. 183, for the pressure in the vertex,

$0 = V.12 + H.4 - 4 \times 12 - 8(9 + 6 + 3)(b)$ rot. A_1;
$0 = V.12 - H.4 + 4 \times 12 + 8(9 + 6 + 3)(a)$ rot. A;
$V = 0, \quad \text{and } H = 48.$

184.] From this for x_1 (rot. $r.E$, Fig. 184),

$0 = -x_1.3{,}5 - 48 \times 3 + 8(3 + 6) + 4 \times 9;$
$x_1 = -10{,}29$ tons;

THE THEORY OF STRAINS.

and in the same way,

$$0 = -x_2 \cdot 2{,}5 - 48 \times 2 + 8 \times 3 + 4 \times 6;$$
$$x_2 = -19{,}2 \text{ tons};$$
$$0 = -x_3 \cdot 1{,}5 - 48 \times 1 + 4 \times 3;$$
$$x_3 = -24 \text{ tons};$$
$$0 = -x_4 \cdot 0{,}5;$$
$$x_4 = 0.$$

DEFINITION OF STRAIN y IN THE DIAGONALS.

When for a section (Fig. 186) the strain in the diagonal, y_2, is to be calculated, the first thing is to define the strain in the vertex.

185.] For y_2, maximum, the apexes 3 and 4 ought to be loaded. The others are indifferent, and we have for the strain in the vertex (Fig. 185),

$$0 = -V \cdot 12 + H \cdot 4 - 1 \times 12 - 2(9 + 6 + 3) \text{ (rot. } A_1\text{)};$$
$$0 = -V \cdot 12 - H \cdot 4 + 1 \times 12 + 2(9 + 6 + 3) + 6(9 + 6)$$
$$\text{(rot. } A\text{)};$$
$$V = 3{,}75, \quad \text{and } H = 23{,}25,$$

which gives for Fig. 186 the equation of equilibrium.

$$0 = y_2 \cdot 6{,}72 + 23{,}25 \times 0{,}5 + 3{,}75 \times 1{,}5 - 1 \times 1{,}5 - 8(4{,}5 + 7{,}5 \text{ (rot. } F\text{)};$$
$$y_2 \text{ (max.)} = +11{,}94 \text{ tons}.$$

186.] For y_2, (min.), the apexes 3 and 4 ought to be unloaded, the second loaded. The others again are indifferent, and may be unloaded.

187.] For the strain in the vertex is from the equations formed from Fig. 187,

$$0 = -V \cdot 12 + H \cdot 4 - 1 \times 12 - 2(9 + 6 + 3) \text{ (rot. } r \cdot A_1\text{)};$$
$$0 = -V \cdot 12 - H \cdot 4 + 1 \times 12 + 2(9 + 6 + 3) + 6 \times 3 \text{ (rot.} r \cdot A\text{)};$$
$$V_0 = 0{,}75, \quad \text{and } H = 14{,}25;$$

Plate 31, Fig. 188.] And thus we find for the moments upon the section (Fig. 188),

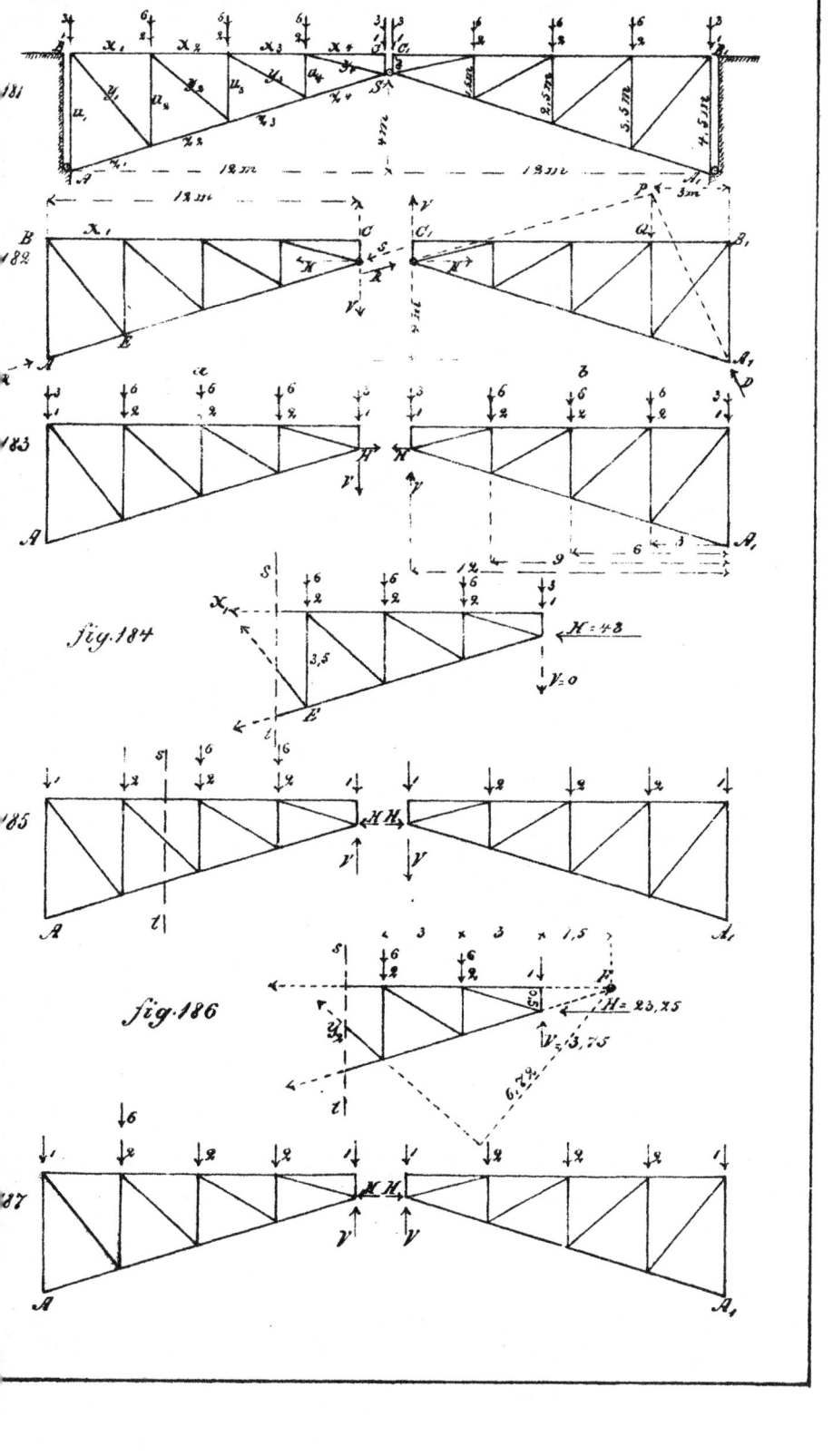

DEFINITION OF STRAIN y IN THE DIAGONALS.

$$0 = y_2 \cdot 6{,}72 + 0{,}75 \times 1{,}5 + 14{,}25 \times 0{,}5 - 1 \times 1{,}5 - 2\,(4{,}5 + 7{,}5);$$
$$y_2\,(\text{min.}) = +\,2{,}75 \text{ tons.}$$

In the same manner we find for y_1 (max.) the following equations:
With a full load, $V = 0$, and $H = 48$;
therefore, $0 = y_1 \cdot 10{,}25 + 48 \times 0{,}5 - 4 \times 1{,}5 - 8\,(4{,}5 + 7{,}5 + 10{,}5);$
$$y_1\,(\text{max.}) = +\,15{,}8 \text{ tons.}$$

y_1 (min.) does not exist, because in this diagonal no compression can be produced.

For y_3 (max.) only the fourth apex should be loaded.
$$V = 2{,}25, \quad \text{and } H = 18{,}75;$$
$$0 = y_3 \cdot 3{,}35 + 2{,}25 \times 1{,}5 + 18{,}75 \times 0{,}5 - 1 \times 1{,}5 - 8 \times 4{,}5;$$
$$y_3\,(\text{max.}) = +\,7{,}39 \text{ tons.}$$

For y_3 (min.), when only the second and third apexes are loaded,
$$V = 2{,}25, \quad \text{and } H = 18{,}75;$$
$$0 = y_3 \cdot 3{,}35 + 2{,}25 \times 1{,}5 + 18{,}75 \times 0{,}5 - 1 \times 1{,}5 - 2 \times 4{,}5;$$
$$y_3\,(\text{min.}) = -\,0{,}67 \text{ tons.}$$

For y_4, a compressive strain will not exist, and we have only y_4 (min.) to calculate, for which Apexes 2, 3 and 4 are loaded
$$V = 4{,}5, \quad \text{and } H = 25{,}5;$$
$$0 = y_4 \cdot 0{,}738 + 4{,}5 \times 1{,}5 + 25{,}5 \times 0{,}5 - 1 \times 1{,}5;$$
$$y_4\,(\text{min.}) = -\,24{,}4 \text{ tons.}$$

CALCULATION OF THE TENSILE STRAINS z IN THE LOWER FLANGES.

[189.] For z_3 we find, after short contemplation, that st, in Fig. 189, is the separating line, in which a weight, q, produces no strain in z_3. Every load to the right of this line produces compression, and every load to the left produces tension, making z_3 positive; therefore we have for z_3 (max.) the strain in the vertex from Fig. 189,

100   THE THEORY OF STRAINS.

$$0 = -V.12 + H.4 - 1 \times 2 - 2(9+6+3) \text{ (rot. } r.A_1);$$

$$0 = -V.12 - H.4 + 1 \times 12 + 2(9+6+3) + 6(6+3)$$
$$\text{(rot. } r.A);$$

$$V = 2{,}25, \quad \text{and } H = 18{,}75;$$

190.] and from Fig. 190, for the equations of equilibrium,

$$0 = z_3.2{,}37 - 2{,}25 \times 6 + 18{,}75 \times 0{,}5 + 1 \times 6 + 2 \times 3 \text{ (rot. } I);$$

$$z_3 \text{ (max.)} = -3{,}32 \text{ tons.}$$

191.] For z_3 (min.), from Fig. 191,

$$0 = V.12 + H.4 - 1 \times 12 - 2(9+6+3) - 3 \times 12 - 6(9+6+3) \text{ (rot. } r.A_1);$$

$$0 = V.12 - H.4 + 1 \times 12 + 2(9+6+3) + 3 \times 12 + 6 \times 9$$
$$\text{(rot. } r.A);$$

$$V = 2{,}25, \quad \text{and } H = 41{,}25;$$

192.] and from this,

$$0 = z_3.2{,}37 + 2{,}25 \times 6 + 41{,}25 \times 0{,}5 + 4 \times 6 + 8 \times 3 \text{ (rot. } r.I, \text{ Fig. 192)};$$

$$z_3 \text{ (min.)} = -34{,}6 \text{ tons.}$$

In the same manner for z_1, for which the separating line in the first apex and the minimum strain by a full load,

$$V = 0, \quad \text{and } H = 48;$$

$$0 = z_1.4{,}27 + 48 \times 0{,}5 + 4 \times 12 + 8(9+6+3);$$

$$z_1 \text{ (min.)} = -50{,}6 \text{ tons};$$

and for z_2, separating line between Apexes 2 and 3,

$$V = 0{,}75, \quad \text{and } H = 14{,}25;$$

$$0 = z_2.3{,}32 - 0{,}75 \times 9 + 14{,}25 \times 0{,}5 + 1 \times 9 + 2(6+3);$$

$$z_2 \text{ (max.)} = -8{,}25 \text{ tons};$$

and for the minimum, where

$$V = 0{,}75, \quad \text{and } H = 45{,}75;$$

$$0 = z_2.3{,}32 + 0{,}75 \times 9 + 45{,}75 \times 0{,}5 + 4 \times 9 + 8(6+3);$$

$$z_2 \text{ (min.)} = -41{,}45 \text{ tons.}$$

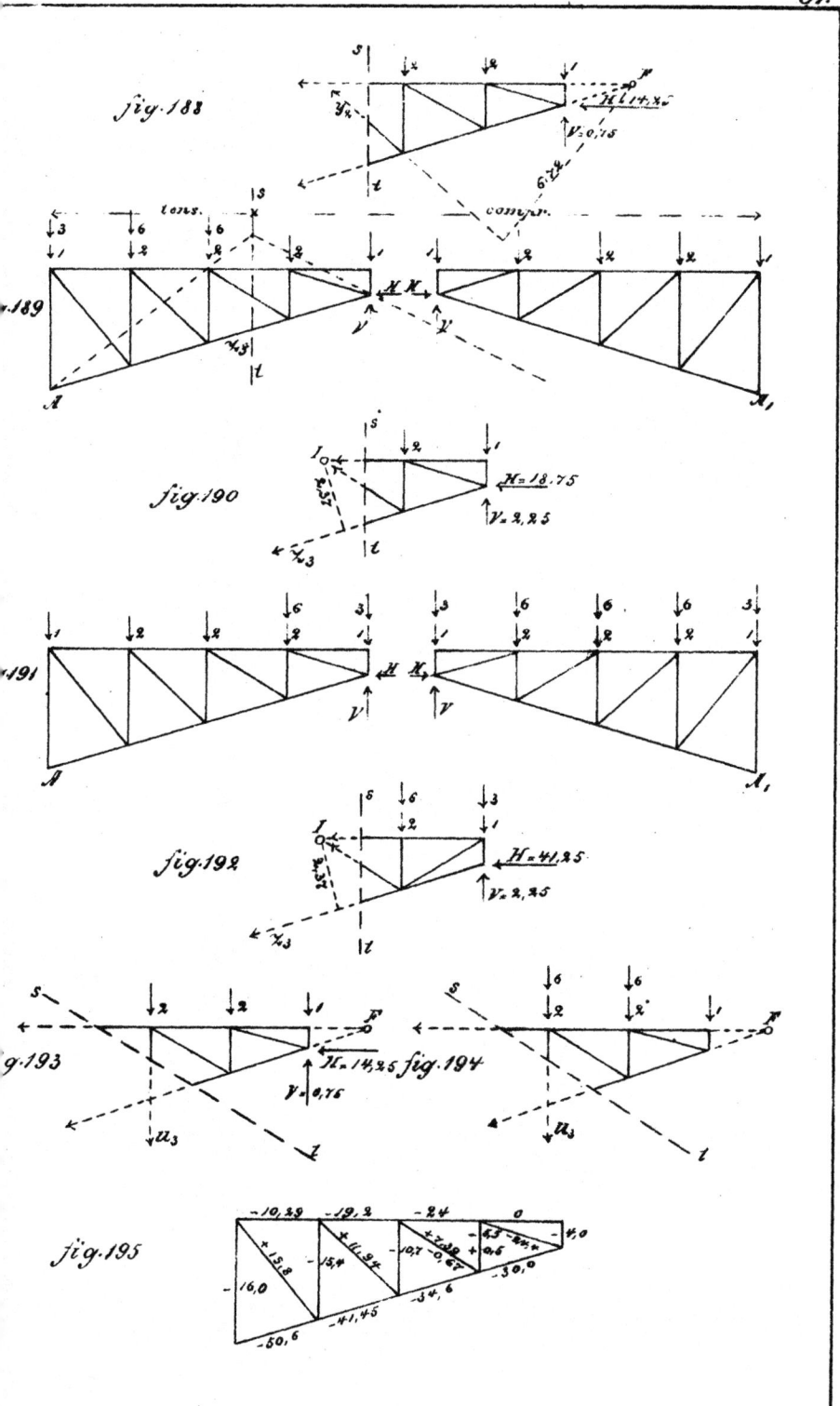

For z_4, separating the line between Apexes 4 and 5,
$$V = 4{,}5, \quad \text{and } H = 25{,}5;$$
$$0 = z_4 \cdot 1{,}423 - 4{,}5 \times 3 + 25{,}5 \times 0{,}5 + 1 \times 3;$$
$$z_4 \text{ (max.)} = -1{,}58 \text{ tons.}$$

For the minimum,
$$V = 4{,}5, \quad \text{and } H = 34{,}5;$$
$$0 = z_4 \cdot 1{,}423 + 4{,}5 \times 3 + 34{,}5 \times 0{,}5 + 4 \times 3;$$
$$z_4 \text{ (min.)} = -30{,}0 \text{ tons.}$$

Calculation of the Verticals u.

For u_3, per example, we have from Fig. 187,
$$V = 0{,}75, \quad \text{and } H = 14{,}25;$$

193.] and the equation of equilibrium from Fig. 193,
$$0 = -u_3 \cdot 7{,}5 + 0{,}75 \times 1{,}5 + 14{,}25 \times 0{,}5 - 1 \times 1{,}5 - 2\,(4{,}5 + 7{,}5)\,(\text{rot. } r \cdot F);$$
$$u_3 \text{ (max.)} = -2{,}3 \text{ tons;}$$

For the minimum from Fig. 185,
$$V = 3{,}75, \quad \text{and } H = 23{,}25;$$

194.] and from Fig. 194,
$$0 = -u_3 \cdot 7{,}5 + 3{,}75 \times 1{,}5 + 23{,}25 \times 0{,}5 - 1 \times 1{,}5 - 8\,(4{,}5 + 7{,}5)\,(\text{rot } r \cdot F);$$
$$u_3 \text{ (min.)} = -10{,}7 \text{ tons.}$$

In the same way we find for u_1, where $V = 0$, and $H = 48$,
$$u_1 \text{ (min.)} = -16{,}0 \text{ tons.}$$

For u_2, $\quad V = 0, \quad \text{and } H = 48;$
$$u_2 \text{ (min.)} = -15{,}4 \text{ tons;}$$

and for u_4, where $V = 2{,}25$, and $H = 18{,}75$;
$$0 = -u_4 \cdot 4{,}5 + 2{,}25 \times 1{,}5 + 18{,}75 \times 0{,}5 - 1 \times 1{,}5 - 2 \cdot 4{,}5;$$
$$u_4 \text{ (max.)} = +0{,}5 \text{ tons.}$$

THE THEORY OF STRAINS.

For the minimum,

$$V = 2{,}25, \quad \text{and } H = 18{,}75;$$

$$0 = -u_4 \cdot 4{,}5 + 2{,}25 \times 1{,}5 + 18{,}75 \times 0{,}5 - 1 \times 1{,}5 - 8 \times 4{,}5;$$

$$u_4 \text{ (min.)} = -5{,}5 \text{ tons};$$

$$u_5 = -4 \text{ tons}.$$

195.] The results are combined in Fig. 195.

II. CALCULATION OF A TRUSS SUSTAINING A DOME.

Plate 32, Figs. 196–7. For the construction of a dome (Figs. 196-7), the distribution of the load at the apexes should be first considered. The ribs not being parallel, but intersecting at the vertex, therefore the variable load increases toward the base, AB, in the same relation as the sections of the horizontal circles drawn through the apexes.

These sections are proportional to their radii. When, therefore, their length is measured, and at a certain apex the load is defined, the proportion of the radius of this point compared with any other radius will give the weight or load at such apex. The weight of the rib itself will be the only constant load. Every other weight, as sheeting, snow and wind-pressure, should be calculated as a variable load—for instance, when the sheeting is displaced at one side for repairs.

This problem may be still further explained by the following example: On a dome of 100 yards span, the outlines may form a semi-globe whose radius = 51 yards. Its area being 16338 square yards, each of the eight ribs will sustain the weight of an area = 2042 square yards. The load, including the weight of sheeting, snow and wind-pressure, estimated at 470 lbs. per square yard, gives 480 tons (at 2000 lbs.) for each rib.

The weight of a rib whose outside and inside circles (chords) are 2 yards apart may be estimated = 60 tons, this being the permanent load, which when equally distributed to the panels, 15 in number, will give for each apex a permanent load of 4 tons.

For the proportion of the variable load, the distances of the

CALCULATION OF A TRUSS SUSTAINING A DOME. 103

apexes from the vertical centre line require to be measured, resulting in

0	5,3	10,6	15,8	20,7	25,5	30	34,1	37,9	41,3	44,2	46,6	48,5	49,9	50,7	51
0	1	2	3	4	5	6	7	8	9	10	11	12	13	14	15

Proportional to these figures is the variable load; therefore, when the whole sum (being 512) is divided into the whole load = 480 tons, and the result multiplied by those figures, then the variable load for each apex will be

5	9,9	14,8	19,4	23,9	28,1	32	35,5	38,7	41,4	43,7	45,5	46,8	47,6
1	2	3	4	5	6	7	8	9	10	11	12	13	14

This being defined, for the further calculation we suppose the ribs on their supports secured against the horizontal thrust by means of a horizontal wrought-iron band (ring); then the supports will sustain only a vertical pressure equal to the weight of the structure.

Each pair of opposite ribs thus fixed at the heels, and resting at the top against a globe or universal joint (providing expansion and contraction), will show conformity to the preceding example. In the calculation, therefore, we can follow the same principles.

So we find again by an unloaded and also by a completely loaded state the vertical pressure at the vertex $= 0$.

The horizontal force will be defined in forming the equation for all the moments of the loaded apexes in regard to the point A of support, their levers being

50	44,7	39,4	34,2	29,3	24,5	20	15,9	12,1	8,7	5,8	3,4	1,5	0,1	— 0,7
0	1	2	3	4	5	6	7	8	9	10	11	12	13	14

For an unloaded state of ribs it will be

$$H \cdot 50 = 4 \left(\tfrac{50}{2} + 44{,}7 + 39{,}4 + \ldots + 1{,}5 + 0{,}1 - 0{,}7\right) = 1056;$$

$$H = 21{,}12;$$

but for a loaded state,

$$H \cdot 50 = 4 \left(\tfrac{50}{2} + 47{,}7 + 39{,}4 + \ldots + 1{,}5 + 0{,}1 - 0{,}7\right);$$
$$+ 5 \times 44{,}7 + 9{,}9 \times 39{,}4 + \ldots + 45{,}5 \times 1{,}5 + 46{,}8 \times 0{,}1) - 47{,}6 \times 0{,}7.$$

104 THE THEORY OF STRAINS.

These figures show the moments of the movable load in regard to the point A, and for use in the following the value of each may be stated here:

223,5	390	506,2	568,4	585,6	562	598,8	429,6	336,7	240,1	148,6	68,3	4,7	—33,3
1	2	3	4	5	6	7	8	9	10	11	12	13	14

From this we find for H in the preceding equation,

$$H \times 50 = 1056 + 223{,}5 + 390 + \ldots + 68{,}3 + 4{,}7 - 33{,}3 = 5595;$$
$$H = 111{,}9.$$

Calculation of Strains x of the Outside Arch.

198.] To explain the calculation, we choose the section of the arch between the Apexes 5 and 6, M to be the point of rotation. (Fig. 198.)

The vertical line at E, distinguishing the influence of the load upon tensile and compressive strain, can be constructed in making a line from the opposite support through S, and another line from A through the point of rotation, M. The distance of this line from the vertical centre line is 13 yards, being between the Apexes 2 and 3.

The tension, x, will be a maximum when the points 3, 4, 5 ... 14 are in an unloaded state, and the others in a loaded state; then for the pressure at the vertex for the formation of moments of both opposite ribs,

$$H . 50 = 5595 - V \times 50 \text{ (for the rib to the right)};$$

$$H . 50 = 5595 + V . 50 - 506 - 568 - 586 - \ldots - 4{,}7 + 33{,}3$$
(for the rib to the left);

$$H = 72{,}7; \quad V = 39{,}2.$$

Plate 33, Fig. 199.] From this, for x (max.), from Fig. 199,

$$0 = -x . 2 - 72{,}7 \times 8{,}9 + 39{,}2 \times 26{,}7$$
$$+ 4 \left(\tfrac{26{,}7}{2} + 21{,}4 + 16{,}1 + 10{,}9 + 6 + 1{,}2\right);$$
$$+ 5 \times 21{,}4 + 9{,}9 \times 16{,}1 \text{ (rot. } M\text{)};$$

$$x \text{ (max.)} = + 470{,}9 \text{ tons.}$$

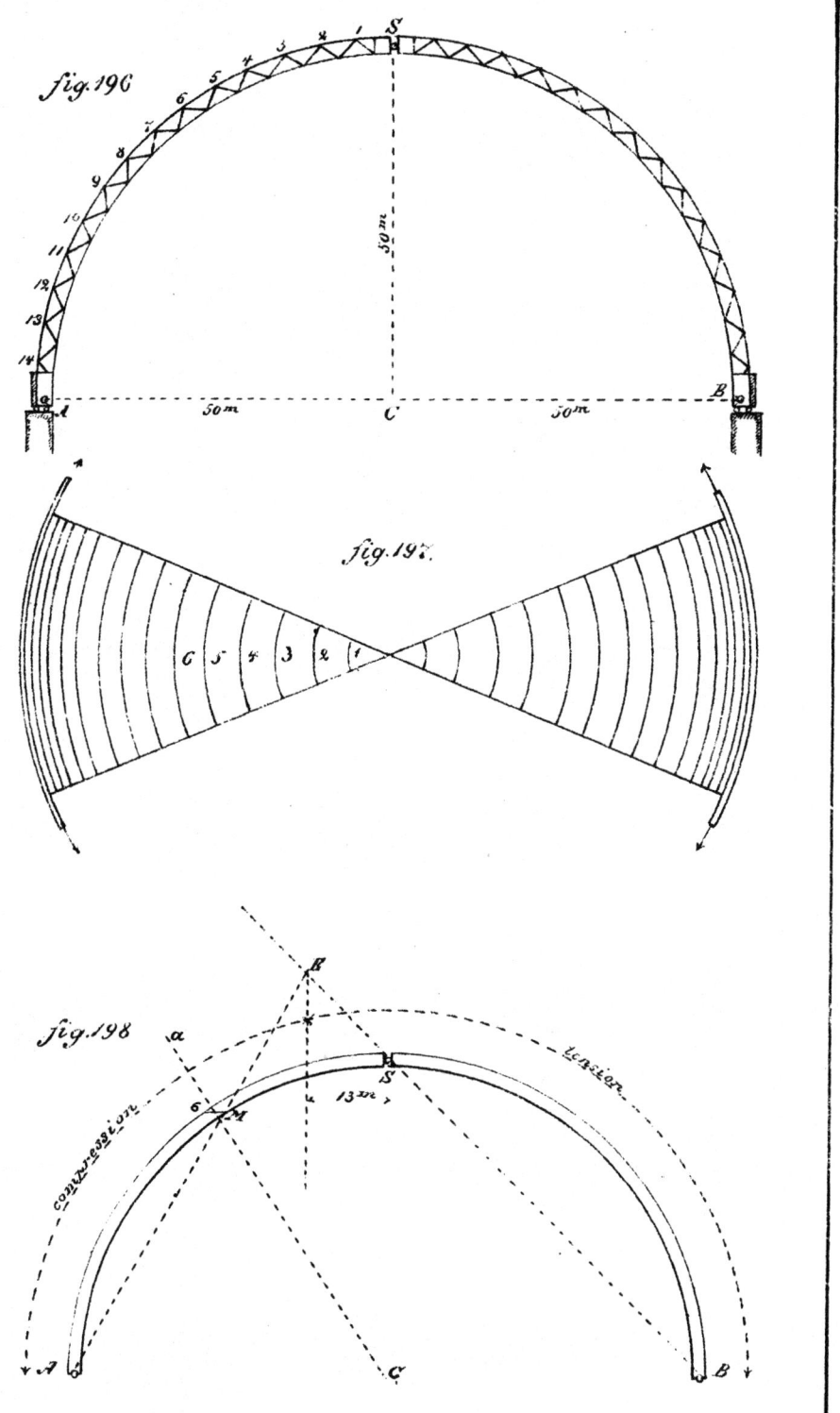

CALCULATION OF STRAINS z OF THE INSIDE ARCH.

For x (min.) only the Apexes 3, 4, 5 ... 14 are supposed to be loaded; then the components of the resulting strain at the vertex of the ribs will be found in forming the equations for each of the two sides, adding for the left side to the permanent load the values of the variable load from Apexes 3 to 14.

$$0 = H \times 50 - V \times 50 - 1056;$$

$$0 = -H \times 50 - V.50 + 1056 + 506 + 568 + 586 + \ldots + 4{,}7 - 33{,}3;$$

$$H = 60{,}3, \quad \text{and } V = 39{,}2.$$

200.] Then for x (min.), from Fig. 200,

$$0 = -x \cdot 2 - 60{,}3 \times 8{,}9 - 39{,}2 \times 26{,}7 + 4 \left(\tfrac{26{,}7}{2} + 21{,}4 + 16{,}1 + 10{,}9 + 6 + 1{,}2\right)$$

$$+ 14{,}8 \times 10{,}9 + 19{,}4 \times 6 + 23{,}9 \times 1{,}2;$$

$$x \text{ (min.)} = -500{,}6 \text{ tons.}$$

CALCULATION OF STRAINS z OF THE INSIDE ARCH.

The same panel may serve for calculation, being the section opposite Apex 6.

For the equation of equilibrium of this section, the point of rotation will be in 6. To find the vertical line, distinguishing the action of the load upon tensile or compressive strain, the direction from A through 6 and from B through S gives the point of intersection, F (Fig. 201), being 17,3 yards from the vertical centre line between Apexes 3 and 4.

201.]

For z (max.), only the points 4, 5 ... 14 should be loaded; then, for the components at the vertex,

$$0 = H.50 - V.50 - 1056;$$

$$0 = H.50 - V.50 + 1056 + 568 + 586 + \ldots + 4{,}7 - 33{,}3;$$

$$H = 55{,}3, \quad \text{and } V = 34{,}2.$$

202.] Now, from Fig. 202,

$$0 = z \cdot 2 - 55{,}3 \times 8{,}74 - 34{,}2 \times 30;$$

$$+ 4 \left(\tfrac{30}{2} + 24{,}7 + 19{,}4 + 14{,}2 + 9{,}3 + 4{,}5\right)$$

THE THEORY OF STRAINS.

$$+ 19{,}4 \times 9{,}3 + 23{,}9 \times 4{,}5;$$

$$z \text{ (max.)} = + 436{,}5 \text{ tons};$$

and further, for the components at the vertex, for z (min.), the Apexes 4, 5 ... 14 are to be unloaded, all the others to be loaded; and for the negative value of the moments for Apexes 4 and 5, added to the sum of moments of the left rib, when entirely loaded,

$$0 = H.50 + V.50 - 5595;$$

$$0 = -H.50 + V.50 + 5595 - 568 - 586 - \ldots 4{,}7 + 33{,}3;$$

$$H = 77{,}7, \quad \text{and } V = 34{,}2.$$

203.] Now, according to Fig. 203,

$$0 = z.2 - 77{,}7 \times 8{,}74 + 34{,}2 \times 30$$
$$+ 4 \left(\tfrac{30}{2} + 24{,}7 + 19{,}4 + 14{,}2 + 9{,}3 + 4{,}5\right)$$
$$+ 5 \times 24{,}7 + 9{,}9 \times 19{,}4 + 14{,}8 \times 14{,}2;$$

$$z \text{ (min.)} = - 610{,}5 \text{ tons}.$$

CALCULATION OF THE DIAGONALS y.

The diagonal between 9 and 10, intersecting with the outside arch at Apex 10, may serve for explanation.

Plate 34, Fig. 204.] In the cut st (Fig. 204), separating the diagonal and the arches, the point of intersection of the latter will be again in infinite distance (see calculation of trusses with parallel top and bottom flanges) in the tangent of a circle half way between the outside and inside arches.

This tangent forms an angle of $58\tfrac{1}{2}$ degrees with the vertical line at the centre, or with the horizontal line CA.

The forces parallel to the tangent have no influence upon y, their direction going in infinite distance through the intersection of the inside and outside arches.

Therefore, all the forces acting upon the section Sst should be separated in forces right-angled and parallel to the tangent, the parallel forces to be omitted.

The vertical separating line of the weights acting upon compression or tension will be found in drawing a line through A (Fig. 204), parallel to the tangent, and through BS, intersecting at J. A

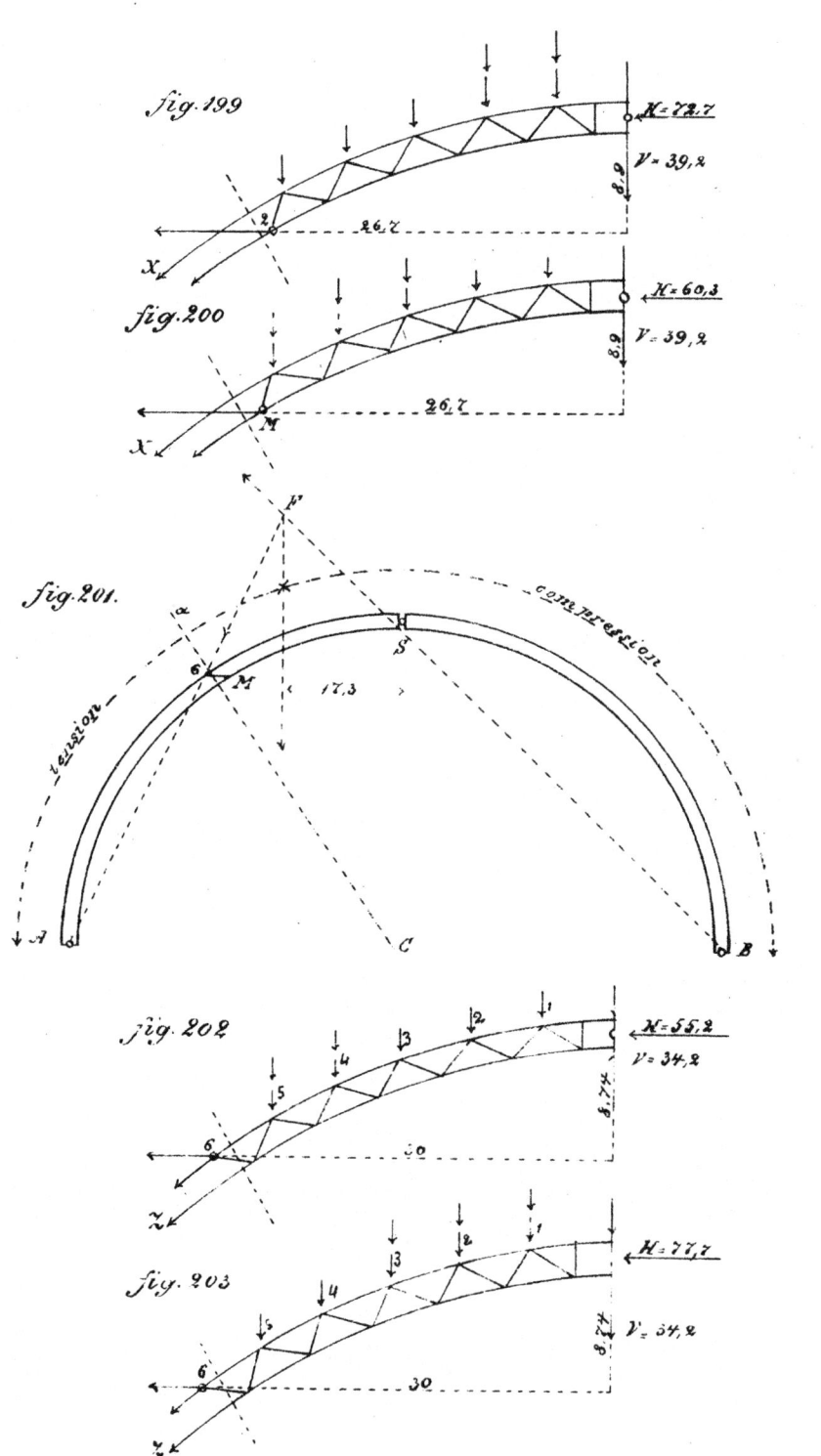

CALCULATION OF THE DIAGONALS y.

weight suspended in the vertical direction through J creates with its pressure at the vertex a resulting strain, being without influence upon the diagonal, y.

Every load to the right of the vertical line in J creates compression, and every load to the left to the separating line, st, produces tension. From this point down to the support, A, compression is produced.

The distance, J, from the vertex being 12 yards (*i. e.*, between the second and third apexes), the force, y, will be a maximum when the apexes 3, 4, 5, 6, 7, 8 and 9 are loaded.

For the forces at the vertex,

$$0 = H.50 - V.50 - 1056;$$
$$0 = -H.50 - V.50 + 1056 + 506 + 568 + 586 + 562 + 509 + 430 + 337;$$
$$H = 56{,}1 \text{ tons,} \quad \text{and } V = 35 \text{ tons.}$$

205.] From Fig. 205, for the equilibrium, all the forces acting in the direction N being 0,

$$0 = N + 56{,}1 \times \cos 31\tfrac{1}{2}° + 35 \times \sin 31\tfrac{1}{2}° - 4 \times 9{,}5 \times \sin 31\tfrac{1}{2}°$$
$$- (14{,}8 + 19{,}4 + 23{,}9 + 28{,}1 + 32 + 35{,}5 + 38{,}7) \sin 31\tfrac{1}{2}°$$

the solution being $N \text{ (max.)} = 54{,}3$,

which gives for y, forming with the force N an angle of 52° 35′,

$$y \text{ (max.)} = \frac{54{,}3}{\cos 52° 35'} = + 89{,}3 \text{ tons.}$$

y (min.) will be defined when, with the exception of Apexes 3, 4, 5, 6, 7, 8 and 9, all the others are loaded.

Then, for the pressure at the vertex,

$$0 = H.50 + V.50 - 5595;$$
$$0 = -H.50 + V.50 + 5595 - 506 - 568 - 586 - 562$$
$$- 509 - 430 - 337;$$
$$H = 77, \quad \text{and } V = 35;$$

206.] and from Fig. 206, for N (min.),

$$0 = N + 77 \cos 31\tfrac{1}{2}° - 35 \sin 31\tfrac{1}{2}° - 4 \times 9{,}5 \times \sin 31\tfrac{1}{2}°$$
$$- (5 + 9{,}9) \sin 31\tfrac{1}{2}°;$$

$$N \text{ (min.)} = -19{,}7;$$

therefore, for y, $\quad y = \dfrac{-19{,}7}{\cos 52° 35'} = -32{,}5 \text{ tons.}$

This may be sufficient to show the calculation of the single members, and we still want to show only the calculation of the strain, S, in the horizontal ring or band at the heels of the ribs.

207.] As in the case above described there are only a limited number of ribs, forming at their base a polygon (Fig. 207), which will also be the form of the ring, then

$$2 \sin 22\tfrac{1}{2}° = H;$$

$$S = \frac{111{,}9}{2 \cdot 0{,}3827} = 146{,}1 \text{ tons.}$$

208.] But when numerous ribs form the dome, so that the horizontal thrust toward the ring (as in Fig. 208) is equally distributed, and p the horizontal pressure per unit of length, then

$$p \times 2r\varphi = 2 S\varphi, \qquad \text{or } S = p \cdot r.$$

So for our example,

$$p = \frac{H}{r \cdot \dfrac{\pi}{4}} = \frac{111{,}9}{51 \times 0{,}785} = 2{,}794;$$

and therefore $\quad S = 2{,}794 \times 51 = 142{,}5 \text{ tons.}$

[Plates 29, 30, 31, 32, 33 and 34—embracing Figs. 179 to 208.]

THE END.

34

CATALOGUE

OF

MILITARY, NAVAL,

AND

SCIENTIFIC BOOKS

PUBLISHED BY

D. Van Nostrand,

23 *MURRAY STREET*
AND
27 *WARREN STREET,*
Publisher, Importer, and Bookseller.

NEW YORK.
1872.

MILITARY BOOKS.

MILITARY AND POLITICAL LIFE OF THE EMPEROR NAPOLEON. By BARON JOMINI, General-in-Chief and Aid-de-Camp to the Emperor of Russia. Translated from the French, with notes, by H. W. HALLECK, LL. D., Major-General U. S. Army. 4 vols., royal 8vo. With an Atlas of 60 Maps and Plans. Cloth, $25; Half-Calf or Morocco, $35; Half-Russia, $37.50.

"The Atlas attached to this version of JOMINI's *Napoleon* adds very materially to its value. It contains *sixty* Maps, illustrative of Napoleon's extraordinary military career, beginning with the immortal Italian campaigns of 1796, and closing with the decisive Campaign of Flanders, in 1815, the last map showing the battle of Wavre. These maps take the reader to Italy, Egypt, Palestine, Germany, Moravia, Russia, Spain, Portugal, and Flanders; and their number and variety, and the vast and various theatres of action which they indicate, testify to the immense extent of Napoleon's operations, and to the gigantic character of his power. They are admirably prepared, being as remarkable for the beauty of their execution as for their strict fidelity as illustrations of some of the greatest deeds in the annals of human warfare. They are worthy of the work to which they belong, which has been most excellently presented typographically, and deserving of the place which it has taken in Mr. Van Nostrand's noble and extensive library of military publications."—*Boston Daily Evening Traveller.*

"It is needless to say anything in praise of JOMINI as a writer on the science of war.

"General HALLECK has laid the professional soldier and the student of military history under equal obligations by the service he has done to the cause of military literature in the preparation of this work for the press. His rare qualifications for the task thus undertaken will be acknowledged by all.

'The notes with which the text is illustrated by General HALLECK are not among the least of the merits of the publication, which, in this respect, has a value not possessed by the original work."—*National Intelligencer.*

"The narrative is so brief and clear, and the style so simple and perspicuous, that it will be found as interesting to unprofessional readers as it is valuable to military officers and students."
—*New York Times.*

*** This is the only English translation of this important strategical life of the great Napoleon.

THE POLITICAL AND MILITARY HISTORY OF THE CAMPAIGN OF WATERLOO. Translated from the French of General BARON DE JOMINI. By Col. S. V. BENÉT, U. S. Ordnance. 1 vol., 12mo, cloth. Third edition. $1.25.

Military Books. 3

TREATISE ON GRAND MILITARY OPERATIONS. Illustrated by a Critical and Military History of the Wars of Frederick the Great. With a summary of the most important principles of the Art of War. By BARON DE JOMINI. Illustrated by Maps and Plans. Translated from the French by Col. S. B. HOLABIRD, A. D. C., U. S. Army. In 2 vols., 8vo, and Atlas. Cloth, $15; Half-Calf or Half-Morocco, $21; Half-Russia, $22.50.

"It is universally agreed that no art or science is more difficult than that of war; yet by an unaccountable contradiction of the human mind, those who embrace this profession take little or no pains to study it. They seem to think that the knowledge of a few insignificant and useless trifles constitute a great officer. This art, like all others, is founded on certain and fixed principles, which are by their nature invariable; *the application of them* only can be varied."

In this work these principles will be found very fully developed and illustrated by immediate application to the most interesting campaigns of a great master. The theoretical and mechanical part of war may be acquired by any one who has the application to study, powers of reflection, and a sound, clear common sense.

Frederick the Great has the credit of having done much for tactics. He introduced the close column by division and deployments therefrom. He brought his army to a higher degree of skill than any other in manœuvring before the enemy to menace his wings or threaten his flanks.

SCOTT'S MILITARY DICTIONARY. Comprising Technical Definitions; Information on Raising and Keeping Troops; Actual service, including makeshifts and improved *materiel*, and Law, Government, Regulation, and Administration relating to Land Forces. By Colonel H. L. SCOTT, Inspector-General U. S. A. 1 vol., large 8vo, fully illustrated. Half-Morocco, $6; Half-Russia, $8; Full-Morocco, $10.

"It is a complete Encyclopædia of Military Science, and fully explains everything discovered in the art of war up to the present time."—*Philadelphia Evening Bulletin.*

"It should be made a text-book for the study of every volunteer."—*Harper's Magazine.*

CAVALRY; ITS HISTORY, MANAGEMENT, AND USES IN WAR. By J. ROEMER, LL.D., late an Officer of Cavalry in the Service of the Netherlands. Elegantly illustrated, with one hundred and twenty-seven fine wood-engravings. In one large octavo volume, beautifully printed on tinted paper. Cloth, $6; Half-calf, $7.50.

SUMMARY OF CONTENTS.—Cavalry in European Armies; Proportion of Cavalry to Infantry; What kind of Cavalry desirable; Cavalry indispensable in War; Strategy and Tactics; Organization of an Army; Route Marches; Rifled Fire-Arms; The Charge; The Attack; Cavalry versus Cavalry; Cavalry versus Infantry; Cavalry versus Artillery; Field Service; Different Objects of Cavalry; Historical Sketches of Cavalry among the early Greeks, the Romans, the Middle Ages; Different kinds of Modern Cavalry; Soldiers and Officers; Various systems of Training of Cavalry Horses; Remounting; Shoeing; Veterinary Surgeons, Saddlery; etc., etc.

WHAT GENERAL M'CLELLAN SAYS OF IT.

"I am exceedingly pleased with it, and regard it as a very valuable addition to our military literature. It will certainly be regarded as a standard work, and I know of none so valuable to our cavalry officers. Its usefulness, however, is not confined to officers of cavalry alone, but it contains a great deal of general information valuable to the officers of the other arms of service, especially those of the Staff."

D. Van Nostrand's Publications.

NOLAN'S SYSTEM FOR TRAINING CAVALRY HORSES By Kenner Garrard, Captain Fifth Cavalry, Bvt. Brig.-Gen. U. S. A. 1 vol., 12mo, cloth. 24 lithographed plates. $2.

COOKE'S CAVALRY TACTICS; or, Regulations for the Instruction, Formations, and Movements of the Cavalry of the Army and Volunteers of the United States. 100 illustrations, 12mo. Cloth, $1.

PATTEN'S CAVALRY DRILL. Containing Instructions on Foot; Instruction on Horseback; Basis of Instruction; School of the Squadron, and Sabre Exercise. 93 Engravings. 12mo, paper. 50 cents.

ELEMENTS OF MILITARY ART AND HISTORY. By Edward de la Barre Duparcq, Chef de Bataillon of Engineers in the Army of France, and Professor of the Military Art in the Imperial School of St. Cyr. Translated by Brigadier-General Geo. W. Cullum, U. S. A., Chief of the Staff of Major-General H. W. Halleck, General-in-Chief U. S. Army. 1 vol., 8vo, cloth. $5.

"I read the original a few years since, and considered it the very best work I had seen upon the subject. General Cullum's ability and familiarity with the technical language of French military writers, are a sufficient guarantee of the correctness of his translation
"H. W. HALLECK, Major-General U. S. A."

"I have read the book with great interest, and trust that it will have a large circulation. It cannot fail to do good by spreading that very knowledge, the want of which among our new, inexperienced, and untaught soldiers, has cost us so many lives, and so much toil and treasure.
"M. C. MEIGS, Quartermaster-General U. S. A."

THE CIVIL AND MILITARY ENGINEERS OF AMERICA. By Gen'l Charles B. Stuart, Author of "Naval Dry Docks of the United States," &c., &c. Embellished with several finely executed portraits on steel of eminent engineers, and illustrated by engravings of some of the most important and original works constructed in America. 8vo. Cloth. $5.

WEST POINT SCRAP BOOK. Being a Collection of Legends, Stories, Songs, &c. By Lieut. O. E. Wood, U. S. A. Profusely illustrated. Beautifully printed on tinted paper. 8vo. Cloth. $5.

THE PRINCIPLES OF STRATEGY AND GRAND TACTICS. Translated from the French of General G. H. Dufour. By William P. Craighill, Captain of Engineers U. S. Army, and Assistant Professor of Engineering, U. S. Military Academy, West Point. From the last French edition. Illustrated. In 1 vol., 12mo, cloth. $3.

"General Dufour is a distinguished civil and military engineer and a practical soldier, and in Europe one of the recognized authorities on military matters. He holds the office of Chief of the General Staff of the Army of Switzerland."—*Evening Post.*

"This work upon the principles of strategy, the application of which we have sorely stood in need of in all our campaigns, comes from an acknowledged authority. It was General Dufour who successfully arrayed the Federal Army of Switzerland against secession, and 'subdued' the rebellious Cantons."—*Boston Journal.*

Military Books. 5

ARMY OFFICERS' POCKET COMPANION. Principally designed for Staff Officers in the Field. Partly translated from the French of M. DE ROUVRE, Lieutenant-Colonel of the French Staff Corps, with Additions from standard American, French, and English authorities. By WM. P. CRAIGHILL, First-Lieutenant U. S. Corps of Engineers, Assistant Professor of Engineering at the U. S. Military Academy, West Point. 1 vol., 18mo, full roan. $2.

" I have carefully examined Captain Craighill's Pocket Companion. I find it one of the very best works of the kind I have ever seen. Any army or volunteer officer who will make himself acquainted with the contents of this little book will seldom be ignorant of his duties in camp or field. "H. W. HALLECK, Major-General U. S. A."

" I have carefully examined the 'Manual for Staff Officers in the Field.' It is a most invaluable work, admirable in arrangement, perspicuously written, abounding in most useful matters, and such a book as should be the constant pocket-companion of every army officer, Regular and Volunteer. "G. W. CULLUM, Brigadier-General U. S. A.,
"Chief of General Halleck's Staff, Chief Engineer Department Mississippi."

MAXIMS AND INSTRUCTIONS ON THE ART OF WAR. A Practical Military Guide for the use of Soldiers of all Arms and of all Countries. Translated from the French by Captain LENDY, Director of the Practical Military College, late of the French Staff, etc., etc. 1 vol., 18mo, cloth. 75 cents.

HISTORY OF WEST POINT, and its Military Importance during the American Revolution ; and the Origin and Progress of the United States Military Academy. By Bvt.-Maj. EDWARD C. BOYNTON, A. M., Adjutant of the Military Academy. Second Edition, with numerous Maps and Engravings. 1 vol., octavo. Cloth, $3.50.

" Aside from its value as an historical record, the volume under notice is an entertaining guide-book to the Military Academy and its surroundings. We have full details of Cadet life from the day of entrance to that of graduation, together with descriptions of the buildings, grounds, and monuments. To the multitude of those who have enjoyed at West Point the combined attractions, this book will give, in its descriptive and illustrated portion, especial pleasure."—*New York Evening Post.*

" The second part of the book gives the history of the Military Academy from its foundation in 1802, a description of the academic buildings, and the appearance to-day of this always beautiful spot, with the manner of appointment of the cadets, course of study, pay, time of service, and much other information yearly becoming of greater value, for West Point has not yet reached its palmiest days."—*Daily Advertiser.*

WEST POINT LIFE. A poem read before the Dialectic Society of the United States Military Academy. Illustrated with twenty-two full-page Pen and Ink Sketches. By a CADET. To which is added, the song, " Benny Havens, Oh !" Oblong 8vo., cloth, bevelled boards, $2.50.

GUIDE TO WEST POINT AND THE U. S. MILITARY ACADEMY. With Maps and Engravings. 18mo., cloth, $1.

BENTON'S ORDNANCE AND GUNNERY. A Course of Instruction in Ordnance and Gunnery; compiled for the use of the Cadets of the United States Military Academy, by Col. J. G. BENTON, Major Ordnance Department, late Instructor of Ordnance and Gunnery, Military Academy, West Point. Third Edition, revised and enlarged. 1 vol., 8vo, cloth, cuts, $5.

"A GREAT MILITARY WORK.—We have before us a bound volume of nearly six hundred pages, which is a complete and exhaustive 'Course of Instruction in Ordnance and Gunnery,' as its title states, and goes into every department of the science, including gunpowder, projectiles, cannon, carriages, machines, and implements, small-arms, pyrotechny, science of gunnery, loading, pointing, and discharging firearms, different kinds of fires, effects of projectiles and employment of artillery. These severally form chapter heads, and give thorough information on the subjects on which they treat. The most valuable and interesting information on all the above topics, including the history, manufacture, and use of small-arms, is here concentrated in compact and convenient form, making a work of rare merit and standard excellence. The work is abundantly and clearly illustrated."—*Boston Traveller.*

ELECTRO-BALLISTIC MACHINES, AND THE SCHULTZ CHRONOSCOPE. By Lt.-Col. S. V. BENÉT. 1 vol., 4to, illustrated, cloth, $3.

A TREATISE ON ORDNANCE AND ARMOR. Embracing Descriptions, Discussions, and Professional Opinions concerning the Material, Fabrication, Requirements, Capabilities, and Endurance of European and American Guns for Naval, Sea-Coast, and Iron-Clad Warfare, and their Rifling, Projectiles, and Breech-Loading; also, Results of Experiments against Armor, from Official Records. With an Appendix, referring to Gun-Cotton, Hooped Guns, etc., etc. By ALEXANDER L. HOLLEY, B. P. With 493 Illustrations. 1 vol. 8vo, 948 pages. Half roan, $10. Half Russia, $12.

"The special feature of this comprehensive volume is its ample record of facts relating to the subjects of which it treats, that have not before been distinctly presented to the attention of the public. It contains a more complete account than, as far as we are aware, can be found elsewhere, of the construction and effects of modern standard ordnance, including the improvements of Armstrong, Whitworth, Blakeley, Parrott, Brooks, Rodman, and Dahlgren; the wrought-iron and steel guns; and the latest system of rifling projectiles and breech-loading.

THE ARTILLERIST'S MANUAL. Compiled from various Sources, and adapted to the Service of the United States. Profusely illustrated with woodcuts and engravings on stone. Second edition, revised and corrected, with valuable additions. By Gen. JOHN GIBBON, U. S. Army. 1 vol., 8vo, half roan, $6.

This book is now considered the standard authority for that particular branch of the Service in the United States Army. The War Department, at Washington, has exhibited its thorough appreciation of the merits of this volume, the want of which has been hitherto much felt in the service, by subscribing for 700 copies.

"It is with great pleasure that we welcome the appearance of a new work on this subject, entitled 'The Artillerist's Manual,' by Capt. John Gibbon, a highly scientific and meritorious officer of artillery in our regular service. The work, an octavo volume of 500 pages, in large, clear type, appears to be well adapted to supply just what has been heretofore needed to fill the gap between the simple manual and the more abstruse demonstrations of the science of gunnery. The whole work is profusely illustrated with woodcuts and engravings on stone, tending to give a more complete and exact idea of the various matters described in the text. The book may well be considered as a valuable and important addition to the military science of the country."—*New York Herald.*

Military Books. 7

HAND-BOOK OF ARTILLERY. For the Service of the United States Army and Militia. Ninth edition, revised and greatly enlarged. By Col. JOSEPH ROBERTS, U. S. A. 1 vol., 18mo, cloth, $1.25.

The following is an extract from a report made by the committee appointed at a meeting of the staff of the Artillery School at Fort Monroe, Va., to whom the commanding officer of the School had referred this work:

* * * "In the opinion of your Committee, the arrangement of the subjects and the selection of the several questions and answers have been judicious. The work is one which may be advantageously used for reference by the officers, and is admirably adapted to the instruction of non-commissioned officers and privates of artillery.

"Your Committee do, therefore, recommend that it be substituted as a text-book."

(Signed,)   I. VOGDES, *Capt. 1st Artillery.*
(Signed,)   E. O. C. ORD, *Capt. 3d Artillery.*
(Signed,)   J. A. HASKIN, *Bvt. Maj. and Capt. 1st Artillery.*

INSTRUCTIONS FOR FIELD ARTILLERY. Prepared by a Board of Artillery Officers. To which is added the "Evolutions of Batteries," translated from the French, by Brig.-Gen. R. ANDERSON, U. S. A. 1 vol., 12mo, 122 plates. Cloth, $3.

"WAR DEPARTMENT,
"WASHINGTON, D. C., March 1, 1863.

"This system of Instruction for Field Artillery, prepared under direction of the War Department, having been approved by the President, is adopted for the instruction of troops when acting as field artillery.

"Accordingly, instruction in the same will be given after the method pointed out therein; and all additions to or departures from the exercise and manœuvres laid down in the system, are positively forbidden.

"EDWIN M. STANTON,
"Secretary of War."

PATTEN'S ARTILLERY DRILL. 1 vol., 12mo, paper, 50 cents.

HEAVY ARTILLERY TACTICS.—1863. Instruction for Heavy Artillery; prepared by a Board of Officers, for the use of the Army of the United States. With service of a gun mounted on an iron carriage. In 1 vol., 12mo, with numerous illustrations. Cloth, $2.50.

"WAR DEPARTMENT,
"WASHINGTON, D. C., Oct. 20, 1862.

"This system of Heavy Artillery Tactics, prepared under direction of the War Department, having been approved by the President, is adopted for the instruction of troops when acting as heavy artillery.

"EDWIN M. STANTON,
"Secretary of War."

EVOLUTIONS OF FIELD BATTERIES OF ARTILLERY. Translated from the French, and arranged for the Army and Militia of the United States. By Gen. ROBERT ANDERSON, U. S. A. Published by order of the War Department. 1 vol., cloth, 32 plates. $1.

GILLMORE'S FORT SUMTER. Official Report of Operations against the Defences of Charleston Harbor, 1863. Comprising the descent upon Morris Island, the demolition of Fort Sumter, and the siege and reduction of Forts Wagner and Gregg. By Maj.-Gen. Q. A. GILLMORE, U. S. Volunteers, and Major U. S. Corps of Engineers. With 76 lithographic plates, views, maps, etc. 1 vol., 8vo. Cloth, $10; Half-Russia, $12.

" General Gillmore has enjoyed and improved some very unusual opportunities for adding to the literature of military science, and for making a permanent record of his own professional achievements. It has fallen to his lot to conduct some of the most striking operations of the war, and to make trial of interesting experiments in engineering and artillery which were both calculated to throw light upon some of the great points of current discussion in military art, and also to fix the attention of spectators in no ordinary degree.

"His report of the siege of Fort Pulaski thus almost took the form of a popular scientific treatise; and we now have his report of his operations against Forts Wagner and Sumter, given to the public in a volume which promises to be even more attractive at bottom, both to the scientific and the general reader, than its predecessor.

"The volume is illustrated by seventy-six plates and views, which are admirably executed, and by a few excellent maps; and indeed the whole style of publication is such as to reflect the highest credit upon the publishers."—*Boston Daily Advertiser.*

SUPPLEMENTARY REPORT to the Engineer and Artillery Operations against the Defences of Charleston Harbor in 1863. By Major-General Q. A. GILLMORE, U. S. Volunteers, and Major U. S. Corps of Engineers. With Seven Lithographed Maps and Views. 1 vol., 8vo. Cloth. $5.

SIEGE AND REDUCTION OF FORT PULASKI, GEORGIA. Papers on Practical Engineering. No. 8. Official Report to the U. S. Engineer Department of the Siege and Reduction of Fort Pulaski, Ga., February, March, and April, 1862. By Brig.-Gen. Q. A. GILLMORE, U. S. A. Illustrated by maps and views. 1 vol., 8vo, cloth. $2.50.

PRACTICAL TREATISE ON LIMES, HYDRAULIC CEMENTS, AND MORTARS. Papers on Practical Engineering, U. S. Engineer Department, No. 9, containing Reports of numerous experiments conducted in New York City, during the years 1858 to 1861 inclusive. By Major-General Q. A. GILLMORE, U. S. Volunteers, and Major U. S. Corps of Engineers. With numerous illustrations. One volume, octavo. Cloth. $4.

SYSTEMS OF MILITARY BRIDGES, in Use by the United States Army; those adopted by the Great European Powers; and such as are employed in British India. With Directions for the Preservation, Destruction, and Re-establishment of Bridges. By Maj.-Gen. GEORGE W. CULLUM, Lieut.-Col. Corps of Engineers, United States Army. 1 vol. octavo. With numerous illustrations. Cloth. $3.50.

MILITARY BRIDGES: For the Passage of Infantry, Artillery, and Baggage-Trains; with suggestions of many new expedients and constructions for crossing streams and chasms; designed to utilize the resources ordinarily at command and reduce the amount and cost of army transportation. Including also designs for Trestle and Truss-Bridges for Military Railroads, adapted especially to the wants of the Service of the United States. By HERMAN HAUPT, Brig.-Gen. in charge of the construction and operation of the U. S. Military Railways, Author of "General Theory of Bridge Construction, &c." Illustrated by sixty-nine lithographic engravings. Octavo, cloth. $6.50.

"This elaborate and carefully prepared, though thoroughly practical and simple work, is peculiarly adapted to the military service of the United States. Mr. Haupt has added very much to the ordinary facilities for crossing streams and chasms, by the instructions afforded in this work."—*Boston Courier.*

BENÉT'S MILITARY LAW. A Treatise on Military Law and the Practice of Courts-Martial. By Col. S. V. BENÉT, Ordnance Department, U. S. A., late Assistant Professor of Ethics, Law, &c., Military Academy, West Point. 1 vol., 8vo, sixth edition, revised and enlarged. Law sheep. $4.50.

"Captain Benét presents the army with a complete compilation of the precedents and decisions of rare value which have accumulated since the creation of the office of Judge-Advocate, thoroughly digested and judiciously arranged, with an index of the most minute accuracy. Military Law and Courts-Martial are treated from the composition of the latter to the Finding and Sentence, with the Revision and Execution of the same, all set forth in a clear, exhaustive style that is a cardinal excellence in every work of legal reference. That portion of the work devoted to Evidence is especially good. In fact, the whole performance entitles the author to the thanks of the entire army, not a leading officer of which should fail to supply himself at once with so serviceable a guide to the intricacies of legal military government."—*N. Y. Times.*

JUDGE-ADVOCATE GENERAL'S OFFICE, }
October 13, 1862.

* * * So far as I have been enabled to examine this volume, it seems to me carefully and accurately prepared, and I am satisfied that you have rendered an acceptable service to the army and the country by its publication at this moment. In consequence of the gigantic proportions so suddenly assumed by the military operations of the Government, there have been necessarily called into the field, from civil life, a vast number of officers, unacquainted, from their previous studies and pursuits, both with the principles of military law and with the course of judicial proceedings under it. To all such, this treatise will prove an easily accessible storehouse of knowledge, which it is equally the duty of the soldier in command to acquire, as it is to draw his sword against the common enemy. The military spirit of our people now being thoroughly aroused, added to a growing conviction that in future we may have to depend quite as much upon the bayonet as upon the ballot-box for the preservation of our institutions, cannot fail to secure to this work an extended and earnest appreciation. In bringing the results of legislation and of decisions upon the questions down to so recent a period, the author has added greatly to the interest and usefulness of the volume. Very respectfully,

Your obedient servant, J. HOLT.

HALLECK'S INTERNATIONAL LAW; or, Rules Regulating the Intercourse of States in Peace and War. By Maj.-Gen. H. W. HALLECK, Commanding the Army. 1 vol., 8vo. Law sheep. $6.

REPORT OF THE ENGINEER AND ARTILLERY OPERA-
TIONS OF THE ARMY OF THE POTOMAC, from its Or-
ganization to the Close of the Peninsular Campaign. By Maj.-Gen.
J. G. BARNARD, and other Engineer Officers, and Maj.-Gen. W. F.
BARRY, Chief of Artillery. Illustrated by numerous Maps, Plans,
&c. Octavo. Cloth. $4.

"The title of this work sufficiently indicates its importance and value as a contribution to the history of the great rebellion. Gen. Barnard's report is a narrative of the engineer operations of the Army of the Potomac from the time of its organization to the date it was withdrawn from the James River. Thus a record is given of an important part in the great work which the nation found before it when it was first confronted with the necessity of war, and perhaps on no other point in the annals of the rebellion will future generations look with a deeper or more admiring interest."—*Buffalo Courier*.

THE "C. S. A.," AND THE BATTLE OF BULL RUN. (A
Letter to an English friend), by Major J. G. BARNARD, Colonel
of Engineers, U. S. A., Major-General and Chief Engineer, Army
of the Potomac. With five maps. 1 vol., 8vo. Cloth. $2.

THE PENINSULAR CAMPAIGN AND ITS ANTECEDENTS,
as developed by the Report of Major-General GEO. B. MCCLELLAN,
and other published Documents. By J. G. BARNARD, Colonel of
Engineers and Brevet Major-General Volunteers, and Chief Engineer in the Army of the Potomac from its organization to the close
of the Peninsular Campaign. 1 vol., 12mo. Paper. 30 cents.

NOTES ON SEA-COAST DEFENCE: Consisting of Sea-Coast
Fortification; the Fifteen-Inch Gun; and Casemate Embrasure.
By Major-General J. G. BARNARD, Col. of Corps of Engineers,
U. S. A. 1 vol., 8vo. Cloth. Plates. $2.

MANUAL FOR ENGINEER TROOPS: Consisting of—Part I.
Ponton Drill; II. Practical Operations of a Siege; III. School
of the Sap; IV. Military Mining; V. Construction of Batteries.
By General J. C. DUANE, Corps of Engineers, U. S. Army. 1 vol.,
12mo. Half morocco. With plates. $2.50.

"I have carefully examined Capt. J. C. Duane's 'Manual for Engineer Troops,' and do not hesitate to pronounce it the very best work on the subject of which it treats.
"H. W. HALLECK, Major-General U. S. A."

"A work of this kind has been much needed in our military literature. For the Army's sake, I hope the book will have a wide circulation among its officers.
"G. B. McCLELLAN, Major-General U. S. A."

A TREATISE ON MILITARY SURVEYING. Theoretical and
Practical, including a description of Surveying Instruments. By
G. H. MENDELL, Major of Engineers. 1 vol., 12mo. With nu-
merous illustrations. Cloth. $2.

"The author is a Captain of Engineers, and has for his chief authorities Salneuve, Lalobre, and Simms. He has presented the subject in a simple form, and has liberally illustrated it with diagrams, that it may be readily comprehended by every one who is liable to be called upon to furnish a military sketch of a portion of country."—*N. Y. Evening Post*.

Military Books. 11

ABBOT (H. L.) Siege Artillery in the Campaign against Richmond, with Notes on the 15-inch Gun, including an Algebraic Analysis of the Trajectory of a Shot in its ricochet upon smooth Water. Illustrated with detailed drawings of the U. S. and Confederate rifled projectiles. By HENRY L. ABBOT, Major of Engineers, and Brevet Major-General U. S. Volunteers, commanding Siege Artillery, Armies before Richmond. Paper No. 14, Professional Papers, Corps of Engineers. 1 vol., 8vo. Cloth. $3.50.

AUTHORIZED U. S. INFANTRY TACTICS. For the Instruction, Exercise, and Manœuvres of the Soldier, a Company, Line of Skirmishers, Battalion, Brigade, or Corps d'Armée. By Brig.-Gen. SILAS CASEY, U. S. A. 3 vols., 24mo. Vol. I.—School of the Soldier; School of the Company; Instruction for Skirmishers. Vol. II.—School of the Battalion. Vol. III. Evolutions of a Brigade; Evolutions of a Corps d'Armée. Cloth, lithographed plates. $2.50.

MORRIS'S INFANTRY TACTICS. Comprising the School of the Soldier, School of the Company, Instruction for Skirmishers, School of the Battalion, Evolutions of the Brigade, and Directions for Manœuvring the Division and the Corps d'Armée. By Brig.-Gen. WILLIAM H. MORRIS, U. S. Vols., and late U. S. Second Infantry. 2 vols., 24mo. Cloth. $2.

U. S. TACTICS FOR COLORED TROOPS. U. S. Infantry Tactics, for the Instruction, Exercise, and Manœuvres of the Soldier, a Company, Line of Skirmishers, and Battalion, for the use of the COLORED TROOPS of the United States Infantry. Prepared under the direction of the War Department. 1 vol., 24mo. Plates. Cloth. $1.50.

"WAR DEPARTMENT, WASHINGTON, March 9, 1868.
"This system of United States Infantry Tactics, prepared under the direction of the War Department, for the use of the colored troops of the United States Infantry, having been approved by the President, is adopted for the instruction of such troops.
"EDWIN M. STANTON, Secretary of War."

FIELD TACTICS FOR INFANTRY. Comprising the Battalion movements, and Brigade evolutions, useful in the Field, on the March, and in the presence of the Enemy. The tabular form is used to distinguish the commands of the General, and the commands of the Colonel. By Brig.-Gen. WM. H. MORRIS, U. S. Vols., late Second U. S. Infantry. 18mo. Illustrated. 75 cents.

LIGHT INFANTRY COMPANY AND SKIRMISH DRILL. The Company Drill of the Infantry of the Line, together with the Skirmish Drill of the Company and Battalion, after the method of General LE LOUTEREL. Bayonet Fencing; with a Supplement on the Handling and Service of Light Infantry. By J. MONROE, Col. 22d Regiment, N. G., N. Y. S. M., formerly Captain U. S. Infantry. 1 vol., 32mo. 75 cents.

SCHOOL OF THE GUIDES. Designed for the use of the Militia of the United States. Flexible cloth. 60 cents.

STANDING ORDERS OF THE SEVENTH REGIMENT, NATIONAL GUARD. For the Regulation and Government of the Regiment in the Field or in Quarters. By A. DURYEA, Colonel. New Edition. Flexible cloth. 50 cents.

HETH'S SYSTEM OF TARGET PRACTICE: For the use of Troops when armed with the Musket, Rifle-Musket, Rifle, or Carbine. Prepared, principally from the French, by Captain HENRY HETH, 10th Infantry, U. S. A. 18mo. Cloth. 75 cents.

SWORD-PLAY. The Militiaman's Manual and Sword-Play without a Master.—Rapier and Broad-Sword Exercises, copiously Explained and Illustrated; Small-Arm Light Infantry Drill of the United States Army; Infantry Manual of Percussion Muskets; Company Drill of the United States Cavalry. By Major M. W. BERRIMAN, engaged for the last thirty years in the practical instruction of Military Students. Fourth edition. 1 vol., 12mo. Red cloth. $1.

PATTEN'S INFANTRY TACTICS. Containing Nomenclature of the Musket; School of the Soldier; Manual of Arms for the Rifle Musket; Instructions for Recruits, without regard to Arms; School of the Company; Skirmishers, or Light Infantry and Rifle Company Movements; the Bayonet Exercise; the Small-Sword Exercise; Manual of the Sword or Sabre. 12mo. 92 Engravings. Paper. 50 cents.

PATTEN'S INFANTRY TACTICS. Contains Nomenclature of the Musket; School of the Company; Skirmishers, or Light Infantry and Rifle Company Movements; School of the Battalion; Bayonet Exercise; Small-Sword Exercise; Manual of the Sword or Sabre. 12mo. 100 Engravings. Paper. Revised edition. 75 cents.

NEW BAYONET EXERCISE. A New Manual of the Bayonet, for the Army and Militia of the United States. By General J. C. KELTON, U. S. A. With Forty beautifully-engraved Plates. Fifth edition, revised. Red cloth. $2.

This Manual was prepared for the use of the Corps of Cadets, and has been introduced at the Military Academy with satisfactory results. It is simply the theory of the attack and defence of the sword applied to the bayonet, on the authority of men skilled in the use of arms.

The Manual contains practical lessons in Fencing, and prescribes the defence against Cavalry, and the manner of conducting a contest with a swordsman.

"This work merits a favorable reception at the hands of all military men. It contains all the instruction necessary to enable an officer to drill his men in the use of this weapon. The introduction of the Sabre Bayonet in our army renders a knowledge of the exercise more imperative."—*New York Times.*

RHYMED TACTICS, BY "GOV." 1 vol., 18mo. Paper. With portraits. 25 cents.

HINTS TO COMPANY OFFICERS ON THEIR MILITARY DUTIES. By Gen. C. C. ANDREWS, Third Regt. Minnesota Vols. 1 vol., 18mo. Cloth. 60 cents.

"This is a hand-book of good practical advice, which officers of all ranks may study with advantage."—*Philadelphia Press.*

Military Books. 13

AUSTRIAN INFANTRY TACTICS. Evolutions of the Line as practised by the Austrian Infantry, and adopted in 1853. Translated by Captain C. M. WILCOX, Seventh Regiment U. S. Infantry. 1 vol., 12mo. Three large plates. Cloth. $1.

VIELE'S HAND-BOOK. Hand-Book for Active Service, containing Practical Instructions in Campaign Duties. For the use of Volunteers. By Brig.-Gen. EGBERT L. VIELE, U. S. A. 12mo. Cloth. $1.

THE BATTLE-FIELDS OF VIRGINIA. Chancellorsville, embracing the Operations of the Army of Northern Virginia. From the First Battle of Fredericksburg to the Death of Lt.-Gen. S. J. Jackson. By JED. HOTCHKISS and WILLIAM ALLAN. 1 vol., 8vo. Cloth. Illustrated with Maps and Portrait of Stonewall Jackson. $5.

"Though written from a Confederate stand-point this is a valuable accession to the military history of the country. It embraces the operations of the rebel army of Northern Virginia from the first battle of Fredericksburg to the death of Stonewall Jackson."—*Washington Star*.

CAMPAIGN OF MOBILE, including the Co-operation of General Wilson's Cavalry in Alabama. By Brevet Maj-Gen. C. C. ANDREWS. With Maps and Illustrations. 8vo. Cloth. $3.50.

"This is an elaborate account of a memorable campaign conducted by General Canby with great skill, and resulting in a great success. That success, owing to the fact that it occurred at the time the rebellion collapsed in Virginia, has not occupied in the public mind the place due to its intrinsic importance and the generalship which made it possible. To military readers, however, the campaign must be of more than ordinary interest."—*Boston Transcript*.

RIFLES AND RIFLE PRACTICE. An Elementary Treatise on the Theory of Rifle Firing; explaining the Causes of Inaccuracy of Fire and the manner of correcting it, with descriptions of the Infantry Rifles of Europe and the United States, their Balls and Cartridges. By Captain C. M. WILCOX, U. S. A. New edition, with engravings and cuts. Green cloth. $2.

"Although eminently a scientific work, special care seems to have been taken to avoid the use of technical terms, and to make the whole subject comprehensible to the practical inquirer. It was designed chiefly for the use of Volunteers and the Militia; but the War Department has evinced its approval of its merits by ordering from the publisher one thousand copies for the use of the United States Army."—*Louisville Journal*.

RIFLED ORDNANCE: A Practical Treatise on the Application of the Principle of the Rifle to Guns and Mortars of every calibre. To which is added a new theory of the initial action and force of Fired Gunpowder. By LYNALL THOMAS, F. R. S. L. Fifth edition, revised. One volume, octavo, illustrated. Cloth. $2.

"An important contribution to a branch of military science, which is just now a subject of warm discussion in America as well as England. Mr. Thomas's conclusions are based on a large number of careful experiments, and are entitled to careful consideration. In regard to the famous Armstrong guns, while considering their inventor as entitled to the honor of suggesting the only successful method of constructing wrought-iron guns, he disagrees with him in nearly all that relates to the projection of the shot, and holds that the Armstrong must still be an experimental gun—particularly objectionable as breech-loaders. Its asserted overcoming of the scientific and mechanical difficulties of other guns, is based wholly on its revival of breech-loading—a method generally considered obsolete and objectionable."

THREE YEARS IN THE SIXTH CORPS. A concise narrative of events in the Army of the Potomac from 1861 to the Close of the Rebellion, April, 1865. By GEO. T. STEVENS, Surgeon of the 77th Regt. New York Volunteers. Illustrated with 17 engravings and 6 steel portraits. New and revised edition. 8vo. Cloth. $3.

"This story of 'Three Years in the Sixth Corps' is a valuable contribution to the history of the great struggle, and we are glad to see that its success necessitates this second edition. The work is graphically written, and brings vividly before the mind of the reader the varied scenes which came before the writer's eye. Not only will it be found interesting to the members of the old Sixth, but to every American reader. Fine portraits on steel of six of the leading Generals connected with the corps, and a number of wood-cuts, accompany this edition."—*Mail.*

THE VOLUNTEER QUARTERMASTER. Containing a Collection and Codification of the Laws, Regulations, Rules, and Practices governing the Quartermaster's Department of the United States Army, and in force March 4, 1865. By Captain ROELIFF BRINKERHOFF, Assistant Quartermaster U. S. Volunteers, and Post Quartermaster at Washington. 1 vol., 12mo. Cloth. $2.50.

MANUAL FOR QUARTERMASTERS AND COMMISSARIES. Containing Instructions in the Preparation of Vouchers, Abstracts, Returns, &c., embracing all the recent changes in the Army Regulations, together with instructions respecting Taxation of Salaries, &c. By Captain R. F. HUNTER, late of the U. S. Army. 12mo. Cloth. $1.25. Flexible morocco. $1.50.

THE WAR IN THE UNITED STATES. A Report to the Swiss Military Department. Preceded by a Discourse to the Federal Military Society assembled at Berne, Aug. 18, 1862. By FERDINAND LECOMTE, Lieut.-Col. Swiss Confederation. Author of "Relation Historique et Critique de la Campagne d'Italie en 1859," "L'Italie en 1860," and "Le Général Jomini, sa Vie, et ses Ecrits," &c., &c. Translated from the French by a Staff Officer. 1 vol., 12mo. Cloth. $1.

TODLEBEN'S (GENERAL) HISTORY OF THE DEFENCE OF SEBASTOPOL. By WILLIAM HOWARD RUSSELL, LL.D., of the London Times. 1 vol., 12mo. Cloth. $2.

GUNNERY IN 1858. A Treatise on Rifles, Cannon, and Sporting Arms. By WM. GREENER, R. C. E. 1 vol., 8vo. Cloth. $4. Full calf. $6.00.

MANUAL OF SIGNALS, for the use of Signal Officers in the Field, and for Military and Naval Students, Military Schools, &c. A new edition, enlarged and illustrated. By Brig.-Gen. ALBERT Y. MYER, Chief Signal Officer of the Army, Colonel of the Signal Corps during the War of the Rebellion. A new edition, enlarged, and illustrated with 42 Plates. 12mo. Roan. $5.

MANUAL OF INSTRUCTIONS FOR MILITARY SURGEONS, in the Examination of Recruits and Discharge of Soldiers. With an Appendix containing the Official Regulations of the Provost-Marshal-General's Bureau, and those for the formation of the Invalid Corps, &c., &c. Prepared at the request of the United States Sanitary Commission. By JOHN ORDRONAUX, M. D., Professor of Medical Jurisprudence in Columbia College, New York. 12mo. Half morocco. $1.50.

HINTS ON THE PRESERVATION OF HEALTH IN ARMIES. For the use of Volunteer Officers and Soldiers. By JOHN ORDRONAUX, M. D. New edition, 18mo. Cloth. 75 cents.

SIEGE OF BOMARSUND (1854). Journals of Operations of the Artillery and Engineers. Published by permission of the Minister of War. Illustrated by Maps and Plans. Translated from the French by an Army Officer. 12mo. Cloth. $1.

PATTEN'S ARMY MANUAL. Containing Instructions for Officers in the Preparation of Rolls, Returns, and Accounts required of Regimental and Company Commanders, and pertaining to the Subsistence and Quartermaster's Departments, &c., &c. 1 vol., 8vo. Cloth. $2.

A TREATISE ON THE CAMP AND MARCH. With which is connected the Construction of Field-Works and Military Bridges; with an Appendix of Artillery Ranges, &c. For the use of Volunteers and Militia in the United States. By Captain HENRY D. GRAFTON, U. S. A. 1 vol., 12mo. Cloth. 75 cents.

THE AUTOMATON REGIMENT; OR, INFANTRY SOLDIERS' PRACTICAL INSTRUCTOR. For all Regimental Movements in the Field. By G. DOUGLAS BREWERTON, U. S. Army. Neatly put up in boxes, price $1. When sent by mail, $1.40.

The "Automaton Regiment" is a simple combination of blocks and counters, so arranged and designated by a carefully considered contrast of colors, that it supplies the student with a perfect miniature regiment, in which the position in the battalion, of each company, and of every officer and man in each division, company, platoon, and section, is clearly indicated. It supplies the studious soldier with the means whereby he can consult his " tactics," and at the same time join practice to theory by manœuvring a mimic regiment.

THE AUTOMATON COMPANY; OR, INFANTRY SOLDIERS' PRACTICAL INSTRUCTOR. For all Company Movements in the Field. By G. DOUGLAS BREWERTON, U. S. A. Price, in boxes, $1.25. When sent by mail, $1.95.

THE AUTOMATON BATTERY; OR, ARTILLERISTS' PRACTICAL INSTRUCTOR. For all Mounted Artillery Manœuvres in the Field. By G. DOUGLAS BREWERTON, U. S. A. Price, in boxes, $1. When sent by mail, $1.40.

SERGEANT'S ROLL BOOK, FOR THE COMPANY, DETAIL, AND SQUAD. Pocket-book fo m. $1.25.

MILITARY MEASURES OF THE UNITED STATES CONGRESS, 1861–65. By Hon HENRY WILSON. 8vo. Paper. 50 cents.

LIEBER ON GUERRILLA PARTIES. Guerrilla Parties considered with reference to the Laws and Usages of War. Written at the request of Major-General HENRY W. HALLECK, General-in-Chief of the Army of the United States. By FRANCIS LIEBER. 12mo. Paper. 25 cents.

UNION FOUNDATIONS. A Study of American Nationality, as a Fact of Science. By Captain E. B. HUNT, Corps of Engineers, U. S. A. 1 vol., 8vo. 30 cents.

TEXAS, AND ITS LATE MILITARY OCCUPATION AND EVACUATION. By Captain EDWIN D. PHILLIPS, 1st Infantry, U. S. A. 8vo. Paper. 25 cents.

INSTRUCTIONS FOR THE GOVERNMENT OF ARMIES OF THE U. S. IN THE FIELD. Prepared by FRANCIS LIEBER, LL.D., and revised by a Board of Officers, and approved by the War Department, in General Order No. 100. 12mo. Price 25 cents, paper covers.

PICKETT'S MEN. A Fragment of War History. By Col. WALTER HARRISON. With portrait of Gen'l Pickett. 12mo. Cloth. $2.

"This contribution to a Southern History of the War will do good service, in so far as it relates to the operations of a particular command. As a record of the splendid gallantry of Pickett's men, from its first organization to the battle of Gettysburg, with brief biographies of its chief officers, it will be found, not only interesting, but of considerable historical value."—*Balt. Am.*

PORTRAIT GALLERY OF THE WAR, CIVIL, MILITARY, AND NAVAL. A Biographical Record. Edited by FRANK MOORE. Illustrated with sixty fine portraits on steel. 1 vol., 8vo. Cloth, $6; cloth, full gilt, $7.50.

NOTES ON HORSES FOR CAVALRY SERVICE, embodying the Quality, Purchase, Care, and Diseases most frequently encountered, with lessons for bitting the Horse, and bending the neck. By Bvt. Major A. K. ARNOLD, Capt. 5th Cavalry, Assistant Instructor of Cavalry Tactics, U. S. Mil. Academy. 18mo. Illustrated. Clo. 75cts.

REPORT TO THE GOVERNMENT OF THE UNITED STATES ON THE MUNITIONS OF WAR exhibited at the Paris Universal Exhibition, 1867. By CHARLES B. NORTON, U. S. V., and W. J. VALENTINE, Esq., U. S. Commissioners. With 80 Illustrations. 1 vol., 8vo. Cloth. Published at $5.00; now reduced to $3.50.

Military Books.   17

LIPPITT. A Treatise on the Tactical Use of the Three Arms; Infantry, Artillery, and Cavalry. By FRANCIS J. LIPPITT, Ex-Colonel Second Infantry, California Volunteers, &c., &c. 12mo. Cloth. $1.25.

"The formation, the manner of use, and the general handling are very practically presented, and we are glad to see that, while many of the illustrative examples are taken from the Napoleonic wars, our own war has not been neglected. We recommend this book for use as a simple, accurate, and brief manual in military institutions, and for instruction in militia organizations."- *United States Service Magazine.*

LIPPITT. A Treatise on Intrenchments. By FRANCIS J. LIPPITT, Ex-Colonel Second Infantry, California Volunteers, &c., &c. Illustrated by 41 engravings. 12mo. Cloth. $1.50.

"It is a brief but comprehensive statement of all that needs to be known upon the subject by any except professional engineers. All the principles of the art of field fortification are clearly explained, with copious illustrations, drawn from military history, especially from the operations of our late war, the whole made plain by diagrams."—*Army and Navy Journal.*

LIPPITT. The Special Operations of War: comprising the Forcing and Defence of Defiles; the Forcing and Defence of Rivers, and the Passage of Rivers in Retreat; the Attack and Defence of Open Towns and Villages; the Conduct of Detachments for Special Purposes, and Notes on Practical Operations in Sieges. By FRANCIS J. LIPPITT, Ex-Colonel Second California Infantry, &c., &c. With illustrative cuts. 12mo. Cloth. $1.25.

"In the illustration of the principles set forth by the writer, he makes frequent and important use of the movements in the late war of the Rebellion, as well as of operations in the wars of Napoleon, and other European campaigns. The work thus assumes, in some sense, the character of a historical commentary on celebrated military actions, and becomes of interest to the general reader, as well as to the student of the art of war."—*New York Tribune.*

LIPPITT. Field Service in War: comprising Marches, Camps, and Cantonments, Outposts, Convoys, Reconnaissances, Foraging, and Notes on Logistics. By FRANCIS J. LIPPITT, Ex-Colonel Second California Infantry, &c., &c. 1 vol., 12mo. Cloth. $1.25.

HEAD. A New System of Fortifications. By GEORGE E. HEAD, A. M., Capt. 29th Infantry, and Bvt. Major U. S. Army. 4to. Illustrated. Paper $1.00.

SERVICE MANUAL for the Instruction of newly appointed Commissioned Officers, and the Rank and File of the Army, as compiled from Army Regulations, The Articles of War, and the Customs of Service. By HENRY D. WALLEN, Bvt. Brigadier-General U. S. Army. 12mo. Clo. $1.50.

In my estimation, Gen. Wallen's Service Manual is a book of great value. It contains not only extracts from the regulations, but also includes, in a concise form, the customs of service at well-regulated Posts, as well as in Regiments,—*the unwritten law*, which takes so long to learn, and which is so soon forgotten or overlooked. I consider it a very useful compendium for Junior Officers, and a good book for the instruction of Non-Commissioned Officers in their duties. I have prescribed that it be taught in my regiment and at the Post where I command.
J. VOGDES,
Colonel 1st Artillery, Bvt.-Brig. Genl. U. S. A.,
Fort Hamilton, New York Harbor.

REBELLION RECORD. A Diary of American Events. 1860-1864. Edited by FRANK MOORE. Complete in 12 Volumes. Illustrated with 158 finely engraved steel portraits of distinguished Generals and Prominent Men, together with numerous Maps and Plans. The work can now be supplied complete in 12 volumes at the following prices, viz. : Green cloth, $60.00 ; library sheep, $72.00 ; half calf, antique, $78.00 ; half morocco, $78.00 ; half Russia, $84.00.

This work is a compendium of information, made up of special correspondence, officia. reports, and gleanings from the newspapers of both sections of the United States and of Europe. Of these latter, over five huɫdred are used in its preparation.

The REBELLION RECORD has now become so firmly established as the standard authcrity of the war that individuals in all departments of the Army, Navy, and Government are constantly referring to it, for narratives of important events, and official reports unpublished elsewhere.

In addition to this, most of the speeches, narratives, &c., elsewhere published, have been revised by their authors, specially for the RECORD.

The editor has aimed at completeness, accuracy, and impartiality. Completeness has been secured by the fullest possible sources of information. Accuracy has been attained by deferring publication of all matter long enough after events for the accounts of them to be sifted. Impartiality has been a special object. Every authority from the Southern side has been sought for without regard to labor or expense, and all statements and documents have been inserted as originally found, without editorial comment of any kind.

The REBELLION RECORD is already the main source of history of the war. Most of the histories of the war yet published have been, in a great measure, compiled from the REBELLION RECORD. This is proved by the fact that documents cited in those works are *quoted in the phraseology of the copies revised by their authors specially for the Record, and published nowhere else*

This work is of special value to statesmen, inasmuch as the course and policy of all prominent men are fully traced in it.

It is indispensable to lawyers. A large and increasing amount of litigation is arising on subjects connected with the war, and the REBELLION RECORD is the only complete repository of evidence and authority. All important Laws and leading Decisions arising out of the war are reported in it ; and it has already been received as authentic evidence in trial for Piracy and Treason in the United States Courts of Philadelphia, New York, Boston, and San Francisco.

The Philadelphia *Press*, of October 26, 1861, thus speaks of it :

"During the trial, which terminated yesterday, for piracy, of one of the crew of the Jeff Davis, a great deal of evidence was offered by the counsel for defence taken from FRANK MOORE'S REBELLION RECORD, and received by Judges Grier and Cadwallader, who presided. This is a remarkable compliment to the work in question ; but not higher than it merits, from the fulness and fairness of its various information respecting the rebellion. It is the first time in legal and literary history that a book not yet completed has been so stamped with authenticity as to be admitted as evidence in a court of law, and on a trial for a capital offence."

" We presume that there can be no question that there never was so complete a body of *mémoires pour servir* published as this, and at least that it is destined to be the resort of all those who wish to study, from a political, social, or military point of view, the events of the years 1860-65. That no libraries fit to be called such, whether public or private, can dispense with it is certain. The portraits of prominent officers and politicians which have generally accompanied each monthly part, have been of a high order of excellence, and add materially to the value and attractiveness of the RECORD."—*The Nation.*

NAVAL BOOKS.

A TREATISE ON ORDNANCE AND NAVAL GUNNERY. Compiled and arranged as a Text-Book for the U. S. Naval Academy, by Commander EDWARD SIMPSON, U. S. N. Fourth edition, revised and enlarged. 1 vol., 8vo. Plates and cuts. Cloth. $5.

"As the compiler has charge of the instruction in Naval Gunnery at the Naval Academy, his work, in the compilation of which he has consulted a large number of eminent authorities, is probably well suited for the purpose designed by it—namely, the circulation of information which many officers, owing to constant service afloat, may not have been able to collect. In simple and plain language it gives instruction as to cannon, gun-carriages, gunpowder, projectiles, fuses, locks and primers; the theory of pointing guns, rifles, the practice of gunnery, and a great variety of other similar matters, interesting to fighting men on sea and land."—*Washington Daily Globe.*

GUNNERY CATECHISM. As applied to the service of Naval Ordnance. Adapted to the latest Official Regulations, and approved by the Bureau of Ordnance, Navy Department. By J. D. BRANDT, formerly of the U. S. Navy. Revised edition. 1 vol., 18mo. Cloth. $1.50.

"BUREAU OF ORDNANCE—NAVY DEPARTMENT,
Washington City, July 30, 1864.

"MR. J. D. BRANDT,—

"SIR:—Your 'CATECHISM OF GUNNERY,' as applied to the service of Naval Ordnance,' having been submitted to the examination of ordnance officers, and favorably recommended by them, is approved by this Bureau. I am, Sir, your obedient servant,

"H. A. WISE, Chief of Bureau."

ORDNANCE INSTRUCTIONS FOR THE UNITED STATES NAVY. Part I. Relating to the Preparation of Vessels of War for Battle, and to the Duties of Officers and others when at Quarters. Part II. The Equipment and Manœuvre of Boats, and Exercise of Howitzers. Part III. Ordnance and Ordnance Stores. Published by order of the Navy Department. 1 vol., 8vo. Cloth. With plates. $5.

THE NAVAL HOWITZER ASHORE. By FOXHALL A. PARKER, Captain U. S. Navy. 1 vol., 8vo. With plates. Cloth. $4.00. Approved by the Navy Department.

THE NAVAL HOWITZER AFLOAT. By FOXHALL A. PARKER, Captain U. S. Navy. 1 vol., 8vo. With plates. Cloth. $4.00. Approved by the Navy Department.

GUNNERY INSTRUCTIONS. Simplified for the Volunteer Officers of the U. S. Navy, with hints to Executive and other Officers. By Lieutenant EDWARD BARRETT, U. S. N., Instructor of Gunnery, Navy Yard, Brooklyn. 1 vol., 12mo. Cloth. $1.25.

'It is a thorough work, treating plainly on its subject, and contains also some valuable hints to executive officers. No officer in the volunteer navy should be without a copy."—*Boston Evening Traveller.*

CALCULATED TABLES OF RANGES FOR NAVY AND ARMY GUNS. With a Method of finding the Distance of an Object at Sea. By Lieutenant W. P. BUCKNER, U. S. N. 1 vol., 8vo. Cloth. $1.50.

NAVAL LIGHT ARTILLERY. Instructions for Naval Light Artillery, afloat and ashore, prepared and arranged for the U. S. Naval Academy, by Lieutenant W. H. PARKER, U. S. N. Third edition, revised by Lieut. S. B. LUCE, U. S. N., Assistant Instructor of Gunnery and Tactics at the United States Naval Academy. 1 vol., 8vo. Cloth. With 22 plates. $3.

ELEMENTARY INSTRUCTION IN NAVAL ORDNANCE AND GUNNERY. By JAMES H. WARD, Commander U. S. Navy, Author of "Naval Tactics," and "Steam for the Million." New Edition, revised and enlarged. 8vo. Cloth. $2.

"It conveys an amount of information in the same space to be found nowhere else, and given with a clearness which renders it useful as well to the general as the professional inquirer."—*N. Y. Evening Post.*

MANUAL OF NAVAL TACTICS; Together with a Brief Critical Analysis of the principal Modern Naval Battles. By JAMES H. WARD, Commander U. S. N. With an Appendix, being an extract from Sir Howard Douglas's "Naval Warfare with Steam." 1 vol., 8vo. Cloth. $3.

NAVIGATION AND NAUTICAL ASTRONOMY. Prepared for the use of the U. S. Naval Academy. By Prof. J. H. C. COFFIN, Fourth edition, enlarged. 1 vol., 12mo. Cloth. $3.50.

SQUADRON TACTICS UNDER STEAM. By FOXHALL A. PARKER, Captain U. S. Navy. Published by authority of the Navy Department. 1 vol., 8vo. With numerous plates. Cloth. $5.

JEFFERS. Treatise on Nautical Surveying. By Capt. W. N. JEFFERS, U. S. N. Illustrated. 8vo. Cloth. $5.

OSBON'S HAND-BOOK OF THE UNITED STATES NAVY. Being a compilation of all the principal events in the history of every vessel of the United States Navy, from April, 1861, to May, 1864. Compiled and arranged by B. S. OSBON. 1 vol., 12mo. Cloth. $2.50.

HISTORY OF THE UNITED STATES NAVAL ACADEMY. With Biographical Sketches, and the names of all the Superintendents, Professors, and Graduates; to which is added a Record of some of the earliest votes by Congress, of Thanks, Medals, and Swords to Naval Officers. By EDWARD CHAUNCEY MARSHALL, A. M. 1 vol., 12mo. Cloth. Plates. $1.

NAVAL DUTIES AND DISCIPLINE: With the Policy and Principles of Naval Organization. By F. A. ROE, late Commander U. S. Navy. 1 vol., 12mo. Cloth. $1.50.

"The author's design was undoubtedly to furnish young officers some general instruction drawn from long experience, to aid in the better discharge of their official duties, and, at the same time, to furnish other people with a book which is not technical, and yet thoroughly professional. It throws light upon the Navy—its organization, its achievements, its interior life. Everything is stated as tersely as possible, and this is one of the advantages of the book, considering that the experience and professional knowledge of twenty-five years' service, are crowded somewhere into its pages."—*Army and Navy Journal.*

MANUAL OF THE BOAT EXERCISE at the U. S. Naval Academy, designed for the practical instruction of the Senior Class in Naval Tactics. 18mo. Flexible Cloth. 75c.

MANUAL OF INTERNAL RULES AND REGULATIONS FOR MEN-OF-WAR. By Commodore U. P. LEVY, U. S. N., late Flag-Officer commanding U. S. Naval Force in the Mediterranean, &c. Flexible blue cloth. Third edition, revised and enlarged. 50 cents.

"Among the professional publications for which we are indebted to the war, we willingly give a prominent place to this useful little Manual of Rules and Regulations to be observed on board of ships of war. Its authorship is a sufficient guarantee for its accuracy and practical value; and as a guide to young officers in providing for the discipline, police, and sanitary government of the vessels under their command, we know of nothing superior."—*N. Y. Herald.*

TOTTEN'S NAVAL TEXT-BOOK. Naval Text-Book and Dictionary, compiled for the use of the Midshipmen of the U. S. Navy. By Commander B. J. TOTTEN, U. S. N. Second and revised edition. 1 vol., 12mo. $3.

"This work is prepared for the Midshipmen of the United States Navy. It is a complete manual of instructions as to the duties which pertain to their office, and appears to have been prepared with great care, avoiding errors and inaccuracies which had crept into a former edition of the work, and embracing valuable additional matter. It is a book which should be in the hands of every midshipman, and officers of high rank in the navy would often find it a useful companion."—*Boston Journal.*

LUCE'S SEAMANSHIP: Compiled from various authorities, and Illustrated with numerous Original and Selected Designs. For the use of the United States Naval Academy. By S. B. LUCE, Lieutenant-Commander U. S. N. In two parts. Fourth edition, revised and improved. 1 vol., crown octavo. Half Roan. $7.50.

LESSONS AND PRACTICAL NOTES ON STEAM. The Steam-Engine, Propellers, &c., &c., for Young Marine Engineers, Students, and others. By the late W. R. KING, U. S. N. Revised by Chief-Engineer J. W. KING, U. S. Navy. Twelfth edition, enlarged. 8vo. Cloth. $2.

STEAM FOR THE MILLION. A Popular Treatise on Steam and its Application to the Useful Arts, especially to Navigation. By J. H. WARD, Commander U. S. Navy. New and revised edition. 1 vol., 8vo. Cloth. $1.

THE STEAM-ENGINE INDICATOR, and the Improved Manometer Steam and Vacuum Gauges: Their Utility and Application. By PAUL STILLMAN. New edition. 1 vol., 12mo. Flexible cloth. $1.

SCREW PROPULSION. Notes on Screw Propulsion, its Rise and History. By Capt. W. H. WALKER, U. S. Navy. 1 vol., 8vo. Cloth. 75 cents.

POOK'S METHOD OF COMPARING THE LINES AND DRAUGHTING VESSELS PROPELLED BY SAIL OR STEAM, including a Chapter on Laying off on the Mould-Loft Floor. By SAMUEL M. POOK, Naval Constructor. 1 vol., 8vo, with illustrations. Cloth. $5.

HARWOOD'S LAW AND PRACTICE OF UNITED STATES NAVAL COURTS-MARTIAL. By A. A. HARWOOD, U. S. N. Adopted as a Text-Book at the U. S. Naval Academy. 8vo. **Law** binding. $4.

FLEET TACTICS UNDER STEAM. By FOXHALL A. PARKER, Captain U. S. Navy. 18mo. Cloth. Illustrated. $2.50.

NAUTICAL ROUTINE AND STOWAGE. With Short Rules in Navigation. By JOHN MCLEOD MURPHY and WM. N. JEFFERS, Jr., U. S. N. 1 vol., 8vo. Blue cloth. $2.50.

STUART'S NAVAL DRY DOCKS OF THE UNITED STATES. By Gen'l C. B. STUART. Illustrated with twenty-four fine engravings on steel. 4th edition. 4to. Cloth. $6.

TREATISE ON THE MARINE BOILERS OF THE UNITED STATES. By H. H. BARTOL. Illustrated. 8vo. Cloth. $1.50.

DEAD RECKONING; Or, Day's Work. By EDWARD BARRETT, U. S. Navy. 8vo. Flexible cloth. $1.25.

SUBMARINE WARFARE, DEFENSIVE AND OFFENSIVE. Comprising a full and complete History of the invention of the Torpedo, its employment in War, and results of its use. Descriptions of the various forms of Torpedoes, Submarine Batteries and Torpedo Boats actually used in War. Methods of ignition by Machinery, Contact Fuzes, and Electricity, and a full account of experiments made to determine the Explosive Force of Gunpowder under Water. Also a discussion of the offensive Torpedo system, its effect upon Iron-Clad Ship systems, and influence upon Future Naval Wars. By Lieut.-Commander JOHN S. BARNES, U. S. N. With illustrations. 1 vol., 8vo. Clo. $5.00.

Scientific Books.

1 **FRANCIS' (J. B.) Hydraulic Experiments.** Lowell Hydraulic Experiments—being a Selection from Experiments on Hydraulic Motors, on the Flow of Water over Weirs, and in Open Canals of Uniform Rectangular Section, made at Lowell, Mass. By J. B. FRANCIS, Civil Engineer. Second edition, revised and enlarged, including many New Experiments on Gauging Water in Open Canals, and on the Flow through Submerged Orifices and Diverging Tubes. With 23 copperplates, beautifully engraved, and about 100 new pages of text. 1 vol., 4to. Cloth. $15.

Most of the practical rules given in the books on hydraulics have been determined from experiments made in other countries, with insufficient apparatus, and on such a minute scale, that in applying them to the large operations arising in practice in this country, the engineer cannot but doubt their reliable applicability. The parties controlling the great water-power furnished by the Merrimack River at Lowell, Massachusetts, felt this so keenly, that they have deemed it necessary, at great expense, to determine anew some of the most important rules for gauging the flow of large streams of water, and for this purpose have caused to be made, with great care, several series of experiments on a large scale, a selection from which are minutely detailed in this volume.

The work is divided into two parts—PART I., on hydraulic motors, includes ninety-two experiments on an improved Fourneyron Turbine Water-Wheel, of about two hundred horse-power, with rules and tables for the construction of similar motors:—Thirteen experiments on a model of a centre-vent water-wheel of the most simple design, and thirty-nine experiments on a centre-vent water-wheel of about two hundred and thirty horse-power.

PART II. includes seventy-four experiments made for the purpose of determining the form of the formula for computing the flow of water over weirs; nine experiments on the effect of backwater on the flow over weirs; eighty-eight experiments made for the purpose of determining the formula for computing the flow over weirs of regular or standard forms, with several tables of comparisons of the new formula with the results obtained by former experimenters; five experiments on the flow over a dam in which the crest was of the same form as that built by the Essex Company across the Merrimack River at Lawrence, Massachusetts; twenty-one experiments on the effect of observing the depths of water on a weir at different distances from the weir; an extensive series of experiments made for the purpose of determining rules for gauging streams of water in open canals, with tables for facilitating the same; and one hundred and one experiments on the discharge of water through submerged orifices and diverging tubes, the whole being fully illustrated by twenty-three double plates engraved on copper.

In 1855 the proprietors of the Locks and Canals on Merrimack River, at whose expense most of the experiments were made, being willing that the public should share the benefits of the scientific operations promoted by them, consented to the publication of the first edition of this work, which contained a selection of the most important hydraulic experiments made at Lowell up to that time. In this second edition the principal hydraulic experiments made there, subsequent to 1855, have been added, including the important series above mentioned, for determining rules for the gauging the flow of water in open canals, and the interesting series on the flow through a submerged Venturi's tube, in which a larger flow was obtained than any we find recorded.

FRANCIS (J. B.) On the Strength of Cast-Iron Pillars, with Tables for the use of Engineers, Architects, and Builders. By JAMES B. FRANCIS, Civil Engineer. 1 vol., 8vo. Cloth. $2.

HOLLEY'S RAILWAY PRACTICE. American and European Railway Practice, in the Economical Generation of Steam, including the materials and construction of Coal-burning Boilers, Combustion, the Variable Blast, Vaporization, Circulation, Superheating, Supplying and Heating Feed-water, &c., and the adaptation of Wood and Coke-burning Engines to Coal-burning; and in Permanent Way, including Road-bed, Sleepers, Rails, Joint Fastenings, Street Railways, &c., &c. By ALEXANDER L. HOLLEY, B. P. With 77 lithographed plates. 1 vol., folio. Cloth. $12.

"This is an elaborate treatise by one of our ablest civil engineers, on the construction and use of locomotives, with a few chapters on the building of Railroads. * * * All these subjects are treated by the author, who is a first-class railroad engineer, in both an intelligent and intelligible manner. The facts and ideas are well arranged, and presented in a clear and simple style, accompanied by beautiful engravings, and we presume the work will be regarded as indispensable by all who are interested in a knowledge of the construction of railroads and rolling stock, or the working of locomotives."—*Scientific American.*

HENRICI (OLAUS). Skeleton Structures, especially in their Application to the Building of Steel and Iron Bridges. By OLAUS HENRICI. With folding plates and diagrams. 1 vol., 8vo. Cloth. $3.

WHILDEN (J. K.) On the Strength of Materials used in Engineering Construction. By J. K. WHILDEN. 1 vol., 12mo. Cloth. $2.

"We find in this work tables of the tensile strength of timber, metals, stones, wire, rope, hempen cable, strength of thin cylinders of cast-iron; modulus of elasticity, strength of thick cylinders, as cannon, &c., effects of reheating, &c., resistance of timber, metals, and stone to crushing; experiments on brick-work; strength of pillars; collapse of tube; experiments on punching and shearing; the transverse strength of materials; beams of uniform strength; table of coefficients of timber, stone, and iron; relative strength of weight in cast-iron, transverse strength of alloys; experiments on wrought and cast-iron beams: lattice girders, trussed cast-iron girders; deflection of beams; torsional strength and torsional elasticity."—*American Artisan.*

CAMPIN (F.) On the Construction of Iron Roofs. A Theoretical and Practical Treatise. By FRANCIS CAMPIN. With wood-cuts and plates of Roofs lately executed. Large 8vo. Cloth. $3.

BROOKLYN WATER-WORKS AND SEWERS. Containing a Descriptive Account of the Construction of the Works, and also Reports on the Brooklyn, Hartford, Belleville, and Cambridge Pumping Engines. Prepared and printed by order of the Board of Water Commissioners. With illustrations. 1 vol., folio. Cloth. $15.

ROEBLING (J. A.) Long and Short Span Railway Bridges. By JOHN A. ROEBLING, C. E. Illustrated with large copperplate engravings of plans and views. Imperial folio, cloth. $25.

CLARKE (T. C.) Description of the Iron Railway Bridge across the Mississippi River at Quincy, Illinois. By THOMAS CURTIS CLARKE, Chief Engineer. Illustrated with numerous lithographed plans. 1 vol., 4to. Cloth. $7.50.

WILLIAMSON (R. S.) On the Use of the Barometer on Surveys and Reconnaissances. Part I. Meteorology in its Connection with Hypsometry. Part II. Barometric Hypsometry. By R. S. WILLIAMSON, Bvt. Lieut.-Col. U. S. A., Major Corps of Engineers. With Illustrative Tables and Engravings. Paper No. 15, Professional Papers, Corps of Engineers. 1 vol., 4to. Cloth. $15.

"SAN FRANCISCO, CAL., Feb. 27, 1867.
"Gen. A. A. HUMPHREYS, Chief of Engineers, U. S. Army:

"GENERAL—I have the honor to submit to you, in the following pages, the results of my investigations in meteorology and hypsometry, made with the view of ascertaining how far the barometer can be used as a reliable instrument for determining altitudes on extended lines of survey and reconnaissances. These investigations have occupied the leisure permitted me from my professional duties during the last ten years, and I hope the results will be deemed of sufficient value to have a place assigned them among the printed professional papers of the United States Corps of Engineers. Very respectfully, your obedient servant,
"R. S. WILLIAMSON,
"Bvt. Lt.-Col. U. S. A., Major Corps of U. S. Engineers."

TUNNER (P.) A Treatise on Roll-Turning for the Manufacture of Iron. By PETER TUNNER. Translated and adapted. By JOHN B. PEARSE, of the Pennsylvania Steel Works. With numerous engravings and wood-cuts. 1 vol., 8vo., with 1 vol. folio of plates. Cloth. $10

SHAFFNER (T. P.) Telegraph Manual. A Complete History and Description of the Semaphoric, Electric, and Magnetic Telegraphs of Europe, Asia, and Africa, with 625 illustrations. By TAL. P. SHAFFNER, of Kentucky. New edition. 1 vol., 8vo. Cloth. 850 pp. $6.50.

MINIFIE (WM.) Mechanical Drawing. A Text-Book of Geometrical Drawing for the use of Mechanics and Schools, in which the Definitions and Rules of Geometry are familiarly explained; the Practical Problems are arranged, from the most simple to the more complex, and in their description technicalities are avoided as much as possible. With illustrations for Drawing Plans, Sections, and Elevations of Buildings and Machinery; an Introduction to Isometrical Drawing, and an Essay on Linear Perspective and Shadows. Illustrated with over 200 diagrams engraved on steel. By WM. MINIFIE, Architect. Seventh edition. With an Appendix on the Theory and Application of Colors. 1 vol., 8vo. Cloth. $4.

* It is the best work on Drawing that we have ever seen, and is especially a text-book of Geometrical Drawing for the use of Mechanics and Schools. No young Mechanic, such as a Machinist, Engineer, Cabinet-Maker, Millwright, or Carpenter should be without it."—*Scientific American.*

"One of the most comprehensive works of the kind ever published, and cannot but possess great value to builders. The style is at once elegant and substantial."—*Pennsylvania Inquirer.*

"Whatever is said is rendered perfectly intelligible by remarkably well-executed diagrams on steel, leaving nothing for mere vague supposition; and the addition of an introduction to isometrical drawing, linear perspective, and the projection of shadows, winding up with a useful index to technical terms."—*Glasgow Mechanics' Journal.*

☞ The British Government has authorized the use of this book in their schools of art at Somerset House, London, and throughout the kingdom.

MINIFIE (WM.) Geometrical Drawing. Abridged from the octavo edition, for the use of Schools. Illustrated with 48 steel plates. New edition, enlarged. 1 vol., 12mo, cloth. $2.

"It is well adapted as a text-book of drawing to be used in our High Schools and Academies where this useful branch of the fine arts has been hitherto too much neglected."—*Boston Journal.*

PEIRCE'S SYSTEM OF ANALYTIC MECHANICS. Physical and Celestial Mechanics, by BENJAMIN PEIRCE, Perkins Professor of Astronomy and Mathematics in Harvard University, and Consulting Astronomer of the American Ephemeris and Nautical Almanac. Developed in four systems of Analytic Mechanics, Celestial Mechanics, Potential Physics, and Analytic Morphology. 1 vol., 4to. Cloth. $10.

GILLMORE. Practical Treatise on Limes, Hydraulic Cements, and Mortars. Papers on Practical Engineering, U. S. Engineer Department, No. 9, containing Reports of numerous experiments conducted in New York City, during the years 1858 to 1861, inclusive. By Q. A. GILLMORE, Brig.-General U. S. Volunteers, and Major U. S. Corps of Engineers. With numerous illustrations. One volume, octavo. Cloth. $4.

ROGERS (H. D.) Geology of Pennsylvania. A complete Scientific Treatise on the Coal Formations. By HENRY D. ROGERS, Geologist. 3 vols., 4to., plates and maps. Boards. $30.00.

BURGH (N. P.) Modern Marine Engineering, applied to Paddle and Screw Propulsion. Consisting of 36 colored plates, 259 Practical Woodcut Illustrations, and 403 pages of Descriptive Matter, the whole being an exposition of the present practice of the following firms: Messrs. J. Penn & Sons; Messrs. Maudslay, Sons, & Field; Messrs. James Watt & Co.; Messrs. J. & G. Rennie; Messrs. R. Napier & Sons; Messrs. J. & W. Dudgeon; Messrs. Ravenhill & Hodgson; Messrs. Humphreys & Tenant; Mr. J. T. Spencer, and Messrs. Forrester & Co. By N. P. BURGH, Engineer. In one thick vol., 4to. Cloth. $25.00. Half morocco. $30.00.

KING. Lessons and Practical Notes on Steam, the Steam-Engine, Propellers, &c., &c., for Young Marine Engineers, Students, and others. By the late W. R. KING, U. S. N. Revised by Chief-Engineer J. W. KING, U. S. Navy. Twelfth edition, enlarged. 8vo. Cloth. $2.

WARD. Steam for the Million. A Popular Treatise on Steam and its Application to the Useful Arts, especially to Navigation. By J. H. WARD, Commander U. S. Navy. New and revised edition. 1 vol., 8vo. Cloth. $1.

WALKER. Screw Propulsion. Notes on Screw Propulsion, its Rise and History. By Capt. W. H. WALKER, U. S. Navy. 1 vol., 8vo. Cloth. 75 cents.

THE STEAM-ENGINE INDICATOR, and the Improved Manometer Steam and Vacuum Gauges: Their Utility and Application. By PAUL STILLMAN. New edition. 1 vol., 12mo. Flexible cloth. $1.

ISHERWOOD. Engineering Precedents for Steam Machinery. Arranged in the most practical and useful manner for Engineers. By B. F. ISHERWOOD, Civil Engineer U. S. Navy. With illustrations. Two volumes in one. 8vo. Cloth. $2.50.

POOK'S METHOD OF COMPARING THE LINES AND DRAUGHTING VESSELS PROPELLED BY SAIL OR STEAM, including a Chapter on Laying off on the Mould-Loft Floor. By SAMUEL M. POOK, Naval Constructor. 1 vol., 8vo. With illustrations. Cloth. $5.

SWEET (S. H.) Special Report on Coal; showing its Distribution, Classification and Cost delivered over different routes to various points in the State of New York, and the principal cities on the Atlantic Coast. By S. H. SWEET. With maps. 1 vol., 8vo. Cloth. $3.

ALEXANDER (J. H.) Universal Dictionary of Weights and Measures, Ancient and Modern, reduced to the standards of the United States of America. By J. H. ALEXANDER. New edition. 1 vol., 8vo. Cloth. $3.50.

"As a standard work of reference this book should be in every library; it is one which we have long wanted, and it will save us much trouble and research."—*Scientific American.*

CRAIG (B. F.) Weights and Measures. An Account of the Decimal System, with Tables of Conversion for Commercial and Scientific Uses. By B. F. CRAIG, M. D. 1 vol., square 32mo. Limp cloth. 50 cents.

"The most lucid, accurate, and useful of all the hand-books on this subject that we have yet seen. It gives forty-seven tables of comparison between the English and French denominations of length, area, capacity, weight, and the centigrade and Fahrenheit thermometers, with clear instructions how to use them; and to this practical portion, which helps to make the transition as easy as possible, is prefixed a scientific explanation of the errors in the metric system, and how they may be corrected in the laboratory."—*Nation.*

BAUERMAN. Treatise on the Metallurgy of Iron, containing outlines of the History of Iron manufacture, methods of Assay, and analysis of Iron Ores, processes of manufacture of iron and Steel, etc., etc. By H. BAUERMAN. First American edition. Revised and enlarged, with an appendix on the Martin Process for making Steel, from the report of Abram S. Hewitt. Illustrated with numerous wood engravings. 12mo. Cloth. $2.50.

"This is an important addition to the stock of technical works published in this country. It embodies the latest facts, discoveries, and processes connected with the manufacture of iron and steel, and should be in the hands of every person interested in the subject, as well as in all technical and scientific libraries."—*Scientific American.*

HARRISON. Mechanic's Tool Book, with practical rules and suggestions, for the use of Machinists, Iron Workers, and others. By W. B. HARRISON, associate editor of the "American Artisan." Illustrated with 44 engravings. 12mo. Cloth. $2.50.

"This work is specially adapted to meet the wants of Machinists and workers in iron generally. It is made up of the work-day experience of an intelligent and ingenious mechanic, who had the faculty of adapting tools to various purposes. The practicability of his plans and suggestions are made apparent even to the unpractised eye by a series of well-executed wood engravings."—*Philadelphia Inquirer.*

D. Van Nostrand's Publications.

PLYMPTON. The Blow-Pipe: A System of Instruction in its practical use, being a graduated course of Analysis for the use of students, and all those engaged in the Examination of Metallic Combinations. Second edition, with an appendix and a copious index. By GEORGE W. PLYMPTON, of the Polytechnic Institute, Brooklyn. 12mo. Cloth. $2.

"This manual probably has no superior in the English language as a text-book for beginners, or as a guide to the student working without a teacher. To the latter many illustrations of the utensils and apparatus required in using the blow-pipe, as well as the fully illustrated description of the blow-pipe flame, will be especially serviceable."—*New York Teacher.*

NUGENT. Treatise on Optics: or, Light and Sight, theoretically and practically treated; with the application to Fine Art and Industrial Pursuits. By E. NUGENT. With one hundred and three illustrations. 12mo. Cloth. $2.

"This book is of a practical rather than a theoretical kind, and is designed to afford accurate and complete information to all interested in applications of the science."—*Round Table.*

SILVERSMITH (Julius). A Practical Hand-Book for Miners, Metallurgists, and Assayers, comprising the most recent improvements in the disintegration, amalgamation, smelting, and parting of the Precious Ores, with a Comprehensive Digest of the Mining Laws. Greatly augmented, revised, and corrected. By JULIUS SILVERSMITH. Fourth edition. Profusely illustrated. 1 vol., 12mo. Cloth. $3.

LARRABEE'S CIPHER AND SECRET LETTER AND TELEGRAPHIC CODE. By C. S. LARRABEE. 18mo. Cloth. $1.

BRÜNNOW. Spherical Astronomy. By F. BRÜNNOW, Ph. Dr. Translated by the Author from the Second German edition. 1 vol., 8vo. Cloth. $6.50.

CHAUVENET (Prof. Wm.) New method of Correcting Lunar Distances, and Improved Method of Finding the Error and Rate of a Chronometer, by equal altitudes. By WM. CHAUVENET, LL.D. 1 vol., 8vo. Cloth. $2.

POPE. Modern Practice of the Electric Telegraph. A Handbook for Electricians and Operators. By FRANK L. POPE. Fourth edition. Revised and enlarged, and fully illustrated. 8vo. Cloth. $2.

GAS WORKS OF LONDON. By ZERAH COLBURN. 12mo. Boards. 60 cents.

HEWSON. Principles and Practice of Embanking Lands from River Floods, as applied to the Levees of the Mississippi. By WILLIAM HEWSON, Civil Engineer. 1 vol., 8vo. Cloth. $2.

"This is a valuable treatise on the principles and practice of embanking lands from river floods, as applied to Levees of the Mississippi, by a highly intelligent and experienced engineer. The author says it is a first attempt to reduce to order and to rule the design, execution, and measurement of the Levees of the Mississippi. It is a most useful and needed contribution to scientific literature."—*Philadelphia Evening Journal.*

Scientific Books.

WEISBACH'S MECHANICS. New and revised edition. A Manual of the Mechanics of Engineering, and of the Construction of Machines. By JULIUS WEISBACH, PH. D. Translated from the fourth augmented and improved German edition, by ECKLEY B. COXE, A. M., Mining Engineer. Vol. I.—Theoretical Mechanics. 1 vol. 8vo, 1,100 pages, and 902 wood-cut illustrations, printed from electrotype copies of those of the best German edition. $10.

ABSTRACT OF CONTENTS.—Introduction to the Calculus—The General Principles of Mechanics—Phoronomics, or the Purely Mathematical Theory of Motion—Mechanics, or the General Physical Theory of Motion—Statics of Rigid Bodies—The Application of Statics to Elasticity and Strength—Dynamics of Rigid Bodies—Statics of Fluids—Dynamics of Fluids—The Theory of Oscillation, etc.

"The present edition is an entirely new work, greatly extended and very much improved. It forms a text-book which must find its way into the hands, not only of every student, but of every engineer who desires to refresh his memory or acquire clear ideas on doubtful points."—*The Technologist.*

HUNT (R. M.) Designs for the Gateways of the Southern Entrances to the Central Park. By RICHARD M. HUNT. With a description of the designs. 1 vol., 4to. Illustrated. Cloth. $5.

SILVER DISTRICTS OF NEVADA. 8vo., with map. Paper. 35 cents.

McCORMICK (R. C.) Arizona: Its Resources and Prospects. By Hon. R. C. McCORMICK. With map. 8vo. Paper. 25 cents.

SIMM'S LEVELLING. A Treatise on the Principles and Practice of Levelling, showing its application to purposes of Railway Engineering and the Construction of Roads, &c. By FREDERICK W. SIMMS, C. E. From the fifth London edition, revised and corrected, with the addition of Mr. Law's Practical Examples for Setting Out Railway Curves. Illustrated with three lithographic plates and numerous wood-cuts. 8vo. Cloth. $2.50.

SAELTZER. Treatise on Acoustics in Connection with Ventilation. With a new theory, based on an important discovery, of facilitating clear and intelligible sound in any building. By Alexander Saeltzer. 12mo. In press.

BURT. Key to the Solar Compass, and Surveyor's Companion; comprising all the Rules necessary for use in the field. By W. A. BURT, U. S. Deputy Surveyor. Second edition. Pocket-book form, tuck, $2.50.

GILLMORE. Coignet Béton and other Artificial Stone. By Q. A. GILLMORE. 9 Plates, Views, &c. 8vo, cloth, $2.50.

AUCHINCLOSS. Application of the Slide Valve and Link Motion to Stationary, Portable, Locomotive, and Marine Engines, with new and simple methods for proportioning the parts. By WILLIAM S. AUCHINCLOSS, Civil and Mechanical Engineer. Designed as a handbook for Mechanical Engineers, Master Mechanics, Draughtsmen, and Students of Steam Engineering. All dimensions of the valve are found with the greatest ease by means of a PRINTED SCALE, and proportions of the link determined *without* the assistance of a model. Illustrated by 37 woodcuts and 21 lithographic plates, together with a copperplate engraving of the Travel Scale. 1 vol. 8vo. Cloth. $3.

HUMBER'S STRAINS IN GIRDERS. A Handy Book for the Calculation of Strains in Girders and Similar Structures, and their Strength, consisting of Formulæ and Corresponding Diagrams, with numerous details for practical application. By WILLIAM HUMBER. 1 vol. 18mo. Fully illustrated. Cloth. $2.50.

GLYNN ON THE POWER OF WATER, as applied to drive Flour Mills, and to give motion to Turbines and other Hydrostatic Engines. By JOSEPH GLYNN, F. R. S. Third edition, revised and enlarged, with numerous illustrations. 12mo. Cloth. $1.25.

THE KANSAS CITY BRIDGE, with an Account of the Regimen of the Missouri River, and a description of the Methods used for Founding in that River. By O. CHANUTE, Chief Engineer, and GEORGE MORISON, Assistant Engineer. Illustrated with five lithographic views and 12 plates of plans. 4to. Cloth. $6.

TREATISE ON ORE DEPOSITS. By BERNHARD VON COTTA, Professor of Geology in the Royal School of Mines, Freidberg, Saxony. Translated from the second German edition, by FREDERICK PRIME, Jr., Mining Engineer, and revised by the author, with numerous illustrations. 1 vol. 8vo. Cloth, $4.

A TREATISE ON THE RICHARDS STEAM-ENGINE INDICATOR, with directions for its use. By CHARLES T. PORTER. Revised, with notes and large additions as developed by American Practice, with an Appendix containing useful formulæ and rules for Engineers. By F. W. BACON, M. E., member of the American Society of Civil Engineers. 12mo. Illustrated. Cloth. $1.

THE ART OF GRAINING. How Acquired and How Produced. By Charles Pickert and Abraham Metcalf. 8vo. Beautifully Illustrated. Tinted paper. In press.

INVESTIGATIONS OF FORMULAS, for the Strength of the Iron Parts of Steam Machinery. By J. D. VAN BUREN, Jr., C. E. 1 vol. 8vo. Illustrated. Cloth. $2.

Scientific Books.

THE MECHANIC'S AND STUDENT'S GUIDE in the Designing and Construction of General Machine Gearing, as Eccentrics, Screws, Toothed Wheels, etc., and the Drawing of Rectilineal and Curved Surfaces; with Practical Rules and Details. Edited by FRANCIS HERBERT JOYNSON. Illustrated with 18 folded plates. 8vo. Cloth. $2.00.

"The aim of this work is to be a guide to mechanics in the designing and construction of general machine-gearing. This design it well fulfils, being plainly and sensibly written, and profusely illustrated."—*Sunday Times.*

FREE-HAND DRAWING: a Guide to Ornamental, Figure, and Landscape Drawing. By an Art Student. 18mo. Cloth. 75 cents.

THE EARTH'S CRUST: a Handy Outline of Geology. By DAVID PAGE. Fourth edition. 18mo. Cloth. 75 cents.

"Such a work as this was much wanted—a work giving in clear and intelligible outline the leading facts of the science, without amplification or irksome details. It is admirable in arrangement, and clear and easy, and, at the same time, forcible in style. It will lead, we hope, to the introduction of Geology into many schools that have neither time nor room for the study of large treatises."—*The Museum.*

HISTORY AND PROGRESS OF THE ELECTRIC TELEGRAPH, with Descriptions of some of the Apparatus. By ROBERT SABINE, C. E. Second edition, with additions. 12mo. Cloth. $1.75.

IRON TRUSS BRIDGES FOR RAILROADS. The Method of Calculating Strains in Trusses, with a careful comparison of the most prominent Trusses, in reference to economy in combination, etc., etc. By Brevet Colonel WILLIAM E. MERRILL, U. S. A., Major Corps of Engineers. With illustrations. 4to. Cloth. $5.00.

USEFUL INFORMATION FOR RAILWAY MEN. Compiled by W. G. HAMILTON, Engineer. Fourth edition, revised and enlarged. 570 pages. Pocket form. Morocco, gilt. $2.00.

REPORT ON MACHINERY AND PROCESSES OF THE INDUSTRIAL ARTS AND APPARATUS, OF THE EXACT SCIENCES. By F. A. P. BARNARD, LL. D.—Paris Universal Exposition, 1867. 1 vol., 8vo. Cloth. $5.00.

THE METALS USED IN CONSTRUCTION: Iron, Steel, Bessemer Metal, etc., etc. By FRANCIS HERBERT JOYNSON. Illustrated. 12mo. Cloth. 75 cents.

"In the interests of practical science, we are bound to notice this work; and to those who wish further information, we should say, buy it; and the outlay, we honestly believe, will be considered well spent."—*Scientific Review.*

DICTIONARY OF MANUFACTURES, MINING, MACHINERY, AND THE INDUSTRIAL ARTS. By GEORGE DODD. 12mo Cloth. $2.00.

SUBMARINE BLASTING in Boston Harbor, Massachusetts—Removal of Tower and Corwin Rocks. By JOHN G. FOSTER, U. S. A. Illustrated with 7 plates. 4to. Cloth. $3.50.

KIRKWOOD. Report on the Filtration of River Waters, for the supply of Cities, as practised in Europe, made to the Board of Water Commissioners of the City of St. Louis. By JAMES P. KIRKWOOD. Illustrated by 30 double-plate engravings. 4to. Cloth. $15.00.

LECTURE NOTES ON PHYSICS. By ALFRED M. MAYER, Ph. D., Professor of Physics in the Lehigh University. 1 vol. 8vo. Cloth. $2.

THE PLANE TABLE, and its Uses in Topographical Surveying. From the Papers of the U. S. Coast Survey. 8vo. Cloth. $2.

DIEDRICHS. Theory of Strains; a Compendium for the Calculation and Construction of Bridges, Roofs, and Cranes, with the Application of Trigonometrical Notes. By John Diedrichs. Illustrated by numerous Plates and Diagrams. 8vo, cloth. $5.00.

WILLIAMSON. Practical Tables in Meteorology and Hypsometry, in connection with the use of the Barometer. By Col. R. S. Williamson, U. S. A. 1 vol. 4to, flexible cloth. $2.50.

CULLEY. A Hand-Book of Practical Telegraphy. By R. S. CULLEY. Engineer to the Electric and International Telegraph Company, Fourth edition, revised and enlarged. 8vo. Illustrated. Cloth. $5.

RANDALL'S QUARTZ OPERATOR'S HAND-BOOK. By P. M. RANDALL. New edition, revised and enlarged. Fully illustrated. 12mo. Cloth. $2.00.

GOUGE. New System of Ventilation, which has been thoroughly tested under the patronage of many distinguished persons. By HENRY A. GOUGE. Third edition, enlarged. With many illustrations. 8vo. Cloth. $2.

PLATTNER'S BLOW-PIPE ANALYSIS. A Complete Guide to Qualitative and Quantitative Examinations with the Blow-Pipe. Revised and enlarged by Prof. RICHTER, Freiberg. Translated from the latest German edition by HENRY B. CORNWALL, A. M., E. M. 8vo.

GRÜNER. The Manufacture of Steel. By M. L. Grüner. Translated from the French by Lenox Smith, A.M., E.M. With an Appendix on the Bessemer Process in the United States, by the Translator. Illustrated. 8vo. In press.

Printed in Dunstable, United Kingdom